Picturing Cornwall

An exploration of the history of Cornwall's portrayal on screen, from the earliest days of the moving image to the recent BBC TV adaptation of Winston Graham's Poldark books

Picturing Cornwall illuminates the construction of Cornwall in films and television programmes, looking at amateur film, newsreels and contemporary film practice as well as drama. It argues that Cornwall's screen identity has been dominated by the romantic coastal edge, leaving the regional interior absent from representation. In turn, the emphasis on the coast in Cornwall's screen history has had a significant and ongoing economic impact on the area.

Breathtakingly comprehensive and vivid in the telling, Rachel Moseley provides a detailed critical analysis of Cornwall's film and television history. Scholarly yet eminently readable, it takes us on a remarkable exploration of the myriad ways in which Cornwall has been imagined and depicted through the moving image.

Rachel Moseley teaches in the Department of Film and Television Studies, University of Warwick, UK.

Picturing Cornwall
*Landscape, Region
and the Moving Image*

Rachel Moseley

UNIVERSITY
of
EXETER
PRESS

First published in 2018 by
University of Exeter Press
Reed Hall, Streatham Drive
Exeter, Devon, EX4 4QR
www.exeterpress.co.uk

© 2018 Rachel Moseley

The right of Rachel Moseley to be identified as author of this work has been asserted by her in accordance with the Copyright, Designs and Patents Act 1988.

British Library Cataloguing in Publication Data
A catalogue record for this book is available from the British Library.

ISBNs
Hardback 978 0 85989 358 9
Paperback 978 0 85989 077 9

Cover image: Excellent PZ513 by John Turner
© John Turner

Typeset in Caslon by
BBR Design, Sheffield

To everyone who loves Cornwall but,
especially, to Johnny and Ned

Contents

List of Figures — viii
Preface — x

Introduction: A Journey into Cornwall — 1
1 Landscape, Region and the Moving Image — 11
2 The Outsider and the View: Travel, Tourism and Film — 27
3 Screen Fictions — 75
4 The 'Real' Cornwall — 132
5 A Different View — 183

Notes — 207
Filmography — 214
Television Programmes — 220
Bibliography — 222
Index — 236

Figures

Figure 1	A century of family holidays in Cornwall	35
Figure 2	Ancient, foreign Cornwall in *Cornwall—The Western Land* (Strand Film Company for GWR, 1938)	50
Figure 3	The Cornish 'clay' landscape as view in *China Clay* (British Pathé, 1964)	57
Figure 4	'Foreign' Cornwall in *Scilly Isles* (British Pathé, 1963)	65
Figure 5	Ancient Cornwall: the vignetted view in *Eve Helps the Flower Harvest* (British Pathé, 1932)	67
Figure 6	Wartime woman at the edge of Cornwall in *Sailor's Return* (British Pathé, 1946)	83
Figure 7	Woman as landscape: *Summer in February* (Menaul, 2013)	98
Figure 8	Intermedial Cornwall: *Summer in February* (Menaul, 2013)	99
Figure 9	Woman artist as art in *Summer in February* (Menaul, 2013)	100
Figure 10	Florence at the edge in *Summer in February* (Menaul, 2013)	101
Figure 11	Tourist Cornwall in *Poldark* (BBC, 2015)	108
Figure 12	Bodmin Moor as Wild West in *Jamaica Inn* (BBC, 2014)	114
Figure 13	The troubling modern woman at the Cornish edge in *A Seaside Parish* (BBC, 2004)	165
Figure 14	Spiritual reflection at the edge in *A Seaside Parish* (BBC, 2004)	166
Figure 15	*The Fisherman's Apprentice* (BBC, 2012)	171
Figure 16	*Cornwall with Caroline Quentin* (ITV, 2012)	181
Figure 17	Unfamiliar moorscape in *Brown Willy* (Harvey, 2016). By permission of the Malabar Film Unit.	195

Figure 18	Skin and rock in *Brown Willy* (Harvey, 2016). By permission of the Malabar Film Unit.	197
Figure 19	*The Essential Cornishman* (Jenkin, 2016; Super 8 black-and-white reversal film). By kind permission of Mark Jenkin.	198
Figure 20	The graphic qualities of the Cornish landscape in *Enough to Fill Up an Eggcup* (Jenkin, 2016; 16mm black-and-white negative). By kind permission of Mark Jenkin.	201

Preface

I can't resist comparing the writing of this book to a journey, given its focus. It's been a long and slightly bumpy one, and I owe lots of thanks to lots of people; I'm sorry if I've forgotten anyone. First of all, thank you to all the people who helped with the research for this book, including colleagues at the BFI National Archive, at the South West Film and Television Archive, the Royal Cornwall Museum, Truro (Sarah Lloyd Durrant, Sue Coney) and at STEAM—Museum of the Great Western Railway, especially Elaine Arthurs, who saved me a great deal of time via photocopying. Thanks are particularly due to Lawrence Napper (I'm pretty sure he would have done it even without the hevva cake!), Simon and Brett Harvey, and Mark Jenkin, who were all generous, both with their time in talking to me about their work, and in allowing the use of images for the book. Martin Pumphrey donated his late mother's collection of books about Cornwall to me, and I am so grateful for and touched by that gesture.

The Humanities Research Fund at the University of Warwick provided essential funds to support the illustration of this book—thank you Liese Perrin and Katie Klaassen for unwavering support of all kinds. My colleagues in the Department of Film and Television Studies at Warwick have also been generous in so many ways, from supporting periods of research leave, to reading drafts and sharing ideas (thank you Jon Burrows, so much). In particular, Karl Schoonover, as ever, offered incisive, insightful comments at a critical juncture, and I am more grateful for that than you can imagine. The students I have worked with have been formative for *Picturing Cornwall* in many ways, from undergraduate seminar discussion of key texts, to postgraduate students on the MA in Film and Television Studies (2014–15) who provided a sounding board when I was trying to restructure the whole project. Philip Payton has been endlessly supportive and encouraging of this project, which meant more than he could know, and Gemma Goodman has been my intellectual companion, and friend, throughout—thank you so much. Mom and Dad instilled a love of

Cornwall, and Dad identified 1960s cars for me. To Johnny and Ned, in particular: thank you for putting up with me in the last few weeks of writing. I know I was a grump.

Last, but absolutely not least: Kathryn, thank you for keeping me going with emergency childcare, email humour, sewing chat and cups of tea at moments of crisis. Heather: your humour, companionship and care packages sustained me through the year of research leave. I can't believe we've never met! We must put that right, now that I wrote that f****r!

And Helen—you suggested that I write a book about Cornwall many years ago. I did. Thank you, always.

R.M., 2018

Introduction:
A Journey into Cornwall

This is a book about the picturing of Cornwall in the moving image. At the same time, it is about much more than the representation of one particular place. In its concern to identify and draw attention to the audiovisual strategies—the 'grammar'—by which one region has been realized on screen, it is also a book about the wider significance of landscape on film and television, in both theoretical and political terms. The moving image has been central to Cornwall's ability to be imagined, or even seen at all, and how places are made and remade in visual culture impacts directly upon them, often in significant material and economic ways. In the case of places on the literal and metaphorical periphery, unpicking the process of that making allows the possibility of change to become visible. In *Picturing Cornwall*, I trace the history of one region's construction on screen, from the beginning of cinema to contemporary emplaced film practice, in order to argue for the importance of paying attention to the materialization of region in the moving image.

Cornwall

My earliest memories of Cornwall begin with a long, long car journey, usually through the night, from the landlocked English Midlands to the outermost, south-westerly coast. In particular, I remember being woken from my cosy bed, made up on the back seat (before the days of rear seat belts and child car seats), for the most exciting moment: I had to be awake for crossing the Tamar Bridge from Devon into Cornwall. It was dark, so there wasn't much to see except, of course, for the sign that said 'Welcome to Cornwall', signalling that we had arrived somewhere else. This was before the time of dual-language signs, so a key visual signifier of difference was absent. It was also before the improvement of the A30, the major trunk road down the Cornish peninsula. It was all about the bridge, about the crossing over and the passing of the sign, even though that was just a moment in an eight-hour drive. Simply in the journey, then, Cornwall was already figured for me, as for most other non-Cornish British people, as remote, different: somewhere else.

Cornwall is the most south-westerly county of England, a peninsula, almost entirely bounded by water: the English Channel lies to the east, the Atlantic Ocean to the west, and the River Tamar marks the boundary with Devon, and with England. Save for a short stretch of land, Cornwall is separated from England. It is also a region with its own language, flag, and cultural and ethnic identity. While Cornish is said to have been last spoken in the late eighteenth century by Dolly Pentreath, the Celtic revival of the late nineteenth and early twentieth centuries brought the language back, and it was officially recognized under the European Charter for Regional and Minority Languages in 2002. It is taught in schools across Cornwall, although government funding for the Cornish language was rescinded in 2016.[1] The Cornish were finally recognized as a national minority under the Council of Europe's Framework Convention for the Protection of National Minorities in 2014, and Cornwall has its own black and gold tartan, invented in 1960 (Kennedy and Kingcome 1998: 52). The ancient flag of St Piran, a white cross on a black background, thought to represent white tin/black ore or rock, was adopted as the national flag during the late nineteenth century (Payton [2004] (2017): 272). Tin, and to a lesser extent copper and silver-mining, along with china-clay excavation and export, have been Cornwall's key industries together with fishing and agriculture, and the development of mine engineering in the region put Cornwall at the centre of the international mining world until its decline from the mid-nineteenth century (Payton [2004] (2017): 217). There is a global Cornish diaspora based on emigration of Cornish miners and engineers, especially in Australia, South America, Ireland and the USA (see Payton [2004] 2017, 2007).

As mining died out Cornwall became Britain's first post-industrial landscape, the engine houses and stacks of the mining industry scattered across the region, crumbling and appropriated as romantic ruins for the tourist industry that developed in its wake. Work at the last mine, South Crofty, ended in 1998. The china-clay industry remains important in mid-Cornwall though, as we shall see, it has rarely figured in the picturing of Cornwall as place (see also Goodman 2016). Cornwall has fought for its right to independence from England on the basis of Athelstan's establishing, in 926, of Cornwall as a separate and distinctive Celtic territory (Payton 1992: 46), through groups such as Mebyon Kernow

('Sons of Cornwall') and the Cornish Nationalist Party. The boundary between Cornwall and Devon/England, and the Polson Bridge over the Tamar near Launceston in particular, is the site of frequent conflict—for example over recent discussions about the merging of the two counties to make a parliamentary constituency of 'Devonwall'.[2] While the other Celtic peripheries of Britain, with which Cornwall has both geographic and cultural connection, have 'nation' status and devolved parliaments, Cornwall, despite an ongoing campaign, remains tied to and dependent upon England in a complicated and contested relationship.[3]

The Cornish coast, with its mild microclimate, dramatic rocky coasts and picturesque villages, has been one of England's most desirable holiday destinations since the end of the nineteenth century when railway travel opened it up to travellers beyond the very rich. Nevertheless, it remains one of the poorest counties; as I write, for example, the food bank in Camborne, an inland post-industrial town, is on the verge of running out of food. Screen Cornwall has supported and encouraged the growth of tourism as Cornwall's major industry after mining (the '*Poldark* effect') and tourism has led to the cementing of short-term, minimum-wage service industry employment and few opportunities for young people, who have left the region in search of employment in increasing numbers.[4] Kennedy and Kingcome note the ways in which former miners are now employed as actors to play their previous roles in a pastiche of the lost industry:

> For the Cornish the combination of heritage and tourism has serious and demoralising implications. There is the uneasy sense of living in a theme park, where sites are misappropriated, preserved and commodified by others for others; whilst the economic base and familiar landscapes of the living community are under pressure (1998: 54).

What is more, the economic focus on Cornwall as a tourist theme park is understood to have stifled other economic development such as fish processing and quarrying (1998). Closely related to the rise of tourism has been the growth of second-home ownership, particularly on the coasts, gradually pricing the majority of Cornish people out of property purchase and creating a significant divide between the romantic coast and the post-industrial inland towns and villages (Kent 2003: 124).

It has been shown that Cornwall has a closer relationship to Brittany in France, for example, in terms of language, culture and geology, than it does to England. Cornwall's regional identity, then, has been the site of its contested relationship with England, the basis for its connection to Europe and its global connectedness via ancient international sea trading and the export of mining expertise.⁵ At the same time, Cornwall's relationship with Europe at a macro-regional level is complex: while Cornwall received some of the highest proportions of EU funding in recent decades, like other such regions, Cornwall voted 'leave' in the 2016 Referendum on the European Union, partly on the basis of disputes over fishing quotas and territories imposed by the EU.

It is in respect of this contested relation to the national that I draw on Michael Hechter's formulation of 'internal colony' in my understanding of Cornwall throughout this book (1999). Hechter proposes that 'the lack of sovereignty characteristic of internal colonies fostered a dependent kind of development which limited their economic welfare and threatened their cultural integrity' (xiii), noting that this term 'has been largely reserved for regions that are simultaneously economically disadvantaged and culturally distinctive from the core regions of the host state' (xiv). Hechter does not, however, include Cornwall alongside Scotland, Ireland and Wales in either the 1975 or 1999 editions of *Internal Colonialism*. In fact, he explicitly excludes it, on the grounds that:

> the Celtic region of Cornwall became largely assimilated to English culture by the mid-seventeenth century. It was not until the seventeenth century that the English state began to seriously implement policies of cultural intolerance in the peripheral regions. Thus, the relative weakness of Celtic ethnicity in nineteenth and twentieth-century Cornwall is due, in part, to the fact that the integration of this region into the English economy had occurred prior to 1600 (64).

Modern Cornish historians dispute this narrative (see, for example, Payton 1992: 30–32), seeing Cornwall as having been subject to precisely the cultural and economic domination and exploitation by the centre that Hechter sees as critical to an internal colony. He says:

> Peripheral industrialisation, if it occurs at all, is highly specialised and geared for export [c.f. mining and fishing in Cornwall]. The peripheral economy is, therefore, relatively sensitive to price fluctuations in the international market and lags behind the core in terms of wealth (1999: 9–10).

This precisely describes the decline of mining in Cornwall in the nineteenth century (Payton [2005] 2015, 2007), as well as its contemporary economic position; similarly, Cornwall today can certainly be understood to 'reactively assert its own culture as equal or superior to that of the relatively advantaged core. This may help it conceive of itself as a separate "nation" and seek independence' (Hechter 1999: 10) as a disadvantaged group in the internal colony/core hierarchy. It is my suggestion that events since 1999, and the increased historical and political awareness of Cornwall's identity and contested relation to the nation, make its inclusion as an 'internal colony' both appropriate and important as a rhetorical move.[6]

The View from the Bridge

The Marxist theorist Theodore Adorno argued of the culture industry that

> [i]n a supposedly chaotic world it provides human beings with something like standards for orientation, and that alone seems worthy of approval. However, what its defenders imagine is preserved by the culture industry is in fact all the more thoroughly destroyed by it. The colour film demolishes the genial old tavern to a greater extent than bombs ever could: the film exterminated its imago. No homeland can survive being processed by the films which celebrate it, and which thereby turn the unique character on which it thrives into indeterminable sameness (1991: 89).

One might understand this critique of the picturing of place in popular culture as staging a distinction between an experiential perspective (the 'homeland') from 'inside', and the symbolic violence performed by the outsider view, mediated by 'colour film' and condensed, simplified and distorted by the 'tourist gaze' (Urry 2002). Edward Relph's notion of insideness and outsideness to place is evidently useful here:

> From the outside you look upon a place as a traveller might look upon a town from a distance: from the inside you experience a place, are surrounded by it and part of it. The inside–outside division thus presents itself as a simple but basic dualism, one that is fundamental in our experiences of lived-space and one that provides the essence of place (1976: 49).

This idea has already been taken up in relation to Cornwall by Bernard Deacon, who mobilizes it in relation to early Cornish perceptions of place which contrast with the romanticized tourist image being built by artists, writers and other visitors in the late nineteenth century (1997).[7] I want to unpick Relph's inside–outside typology a little further, then, in relation to these ideas and its potential in relation to understanding the specificity of moving images of place. He suggests that, through 'novels and other media' (1976: 50) it is possible to 'experience places in a secondhand or vicarious way, that is, without actually visiting them, yet for this experience to be one of a deeply felt involvement' (52) and this, it seems to me, is a valuable frame through which we might understand the precise construction of moving images of place. How, for example, is an affective experience, one 'of a deeply felt involvement' with place, produced through sound and image? Relph goes on to break down the category of 'insideness' into a distinction between three categories of 'behavioural', 'empathetic' and 'existential', which offer a useful taxonomy through which we might distinguish between the different ways in which place is presented on screen. 'Behavioural insideness', for Relph, comes from 'being in a place and seeing it as set of objects, views and activities arranged in certain ways and having certain observable qualities' which are seen and experienced by the visitor (53). We could see this as corresponding to the documentary observation of a place through the moving image, and Relph suggests that continuous with this is 'empathetic' insideness, 'a fading from the concern with the qualities of appearance, to emotional and empathetic involvement in a place' which enables an individual to understand a place as rich in meaning and to identify with it (54).

This shift from outsideness, to behavioural and then to empathetic insideness with place, provides a sociological architecture onto which we might usefully map a moving image grammar of place, from the panning long shot of the travelogue to the close observation of custom, costume and character, to the production of moving images and sound which immerse us in place in powerfully affective ways. One might, then, think about how this framework could operate ideologically in relation, for example, to John Caughie's concept of the 'documentary gaze and dramatic look' in film and television (2000), or how Andrew Higson's idea of the view of 'our town from the hill' in British film dramas of the 1960s (1996) might be elaborated and further refined in relation to Relph. Throughout *Picturing Cornwall* I draw upon Relph's taxonomy of outsideness and insideness to think about how moving images of Cornwall drift between both perspectives, across genres, but also how the empathetic, vicarious insideness upon which they have, historically, insisted in the project to produce Cornwall as available to view and consume, contrasts with the 'existential' experience of place produced in amateur film and contemporary screen practice in Cornwall.

It is evident, then, that I wish to avoid any sense of an essentially different view or knowledge of place based on some idea of an ethnically authentic Cornishness; in using the term 'insider', I wish to indicate a connectedness to place which comes through significant and meaningful experience of it over both time and space. While not a native 'insider' myself, I am also not an 'outsider' to Cornwall. It has been the location of my family home for thirty years, and a family holiday destination for eighty or more. Through my parents, I have briefly occupied the troubling position of 'second-home owner'. While I have a long-standing experiential relationship to the region, then, I do not have an embedded native connection to it, and in terms of ethnographic method my writing position is probably best described as that of a 'participant observer' (Gray 2003: 83). This point matters, because *Picturing Cornwall* draws on Relph's formulation in structure (it begins with the outsider and the view, and ends on the view from within) but also in argument. *Outsider* views of place underpin the dominant aesthetic through which mainstream screen representations of Cornwall have proceeded and developed, but these picturings have also sought consistently to produce a vicarious sense of 'being there', of being located *inside* the region. The creative practice explored in the final chapter offers a quite different view from within, one based upon a long-standing, rather than temporary and short-term, relation to place. It is this distinction—between representations resulting from an experiential, existential (rather than essential) insideness, and the construction of a vicarious, empathetic sense of insideness for the purpose of emotional affect—which I wish to highlight in structuring the book in this way. I remain, I think, caught precisely between the two, looking both ways from the bridge: a critically useful positioning.

A Note on Method

In the broadest terms, this book approaches its objects of study—mainly films and television programmes—through the close analysis of the audiovisual text and through discursive and archival contextual analysis. I consider the ways in which sound and image make meaning in conversation with each other, and with the broader context in which they were made, as well as with a contemporary context in which place and landscape are perhaps more politicized than ever before. In this respect, the scholarship I consider above, from a wide range of fields, has provided a model for this interdisciplinary project, along with two other frames that have been of methodological significance. First are calls from within Film Studies, by Sue Harper (2010) and Stella Hockenhull (2005, 2008), for greater attention to be paid to the relationship between the moving image and the other visual arts.[8] Some of this work has demonstrated the generativity of considering film aesthetics in dialogue with other visual arts for moving beyond discussion of the literal incorporation or quotation of paintings in films. *Picturing Cornwall* develops work on art and film, considering the significance of painterly representations of Cornwall for its life in the moving image (see Moseley 2009, 2013a, 2013b). In this way, I complicate this field by thinking about a particular regional landscape and its use, in conversation with other visual arts, to produce particular forms of affect contributing to the perpetuation of its problematic place-image.

Second, and in relation to this, Shields's *Places on the Margin: Alternative Geographies of Modernity* (1991) has been formative for this book, both in its attention to the political significance of thinking about the construction of geographical and cultural peripherality, but also in its development of the concept of 'place-myth', 'the socially maintained reputation of a place or region' (14), a concept which has been enabling for this inherently intermedial project. Shields emphasizes 'spatialization', 'an intellectual shorthand whereby spatial metaphors and place-images can convey a complex set of associations without the speaker having to think deeply and to specify exactly which associations of images he or she intends' (46). These place-images

> come about through over-simplification (i.e. reduction to one trait), stereotyping (amplification of one or more traits), and labelling (where a place is deemed to be of a certain nature). Places and spaces are hypostasised from the world of real space relations to the symbolic realm of cultural significations. Traces of these cultural place-images are also left behind in the litter of historical popular cultures: postcards, advertising images, song lyrics and in the setting of novels (47).

'Collectively', continues Shields, 'a set of place-images forms a place-myth' (61). While not mentioned here, the moving image must, I suggest, be considered as a key instance of 'the litter of historical popular cultures' from which place-images are formed. The concepts of 'place-image' and 'place-myth' offer a wonderfully flexible and politically alive framework, because Shields understands them as discourses formed at the intersection of a myriad of visual, aural, oral and written forms. In this respect, I mobilize these terms throughout *Picturing Cornwall* in order to signal, for example, the interconnectedness between the moving image and painting, photography and advertising images, both those which are directly discussed and those which that discussion invokes for the reader, as they participate in both the mythologization of place and its deconstruction in engaging with this book. Within my adoption of Shields's formulation of place-myth as a way of understanding the screen construction of Cornwall across time, then,

I have understood the place-images which constitute it as always in dialogue with painting, photography and advertising, with other visual forms and with each other. This is the reason for the book's title: the word 'picturing' is intended to indicate the multiplicity of visual ways in which place-images are constructed, the connection between the still and the moving image, and the ways in which all of those pictures contribute to our own imaging, imagining and reproduction of place, to our fantasizing of region. Cornwall has featured in the moving image since the first days of cinema. Early industrial and promotional films, newsreels and cinemagazines, fiction films, amateur and home movies, television serials, documentaries and lifestyle programmes of every genre have drawn upon the dramatic landscape of the far south-west of Britain for both subject matter and picturesque setting. The consequence of such screen longevity and ubiquity, though, is the necessity for selection and omission. There is one key site of 'everyday' screen Cornwall to which I have not been able to attend: local news and current affairs programming. Programmes such as *Spotlight News* represent an important body of moving image picturing of region 'from the inside', though a picturing which is also in dialogue with the wider administrative 'region' of the South West and with the national, through the particular organization of broadcasting in the UK. As I could not devote adequate space to this enormous body of programming which includes but is not limited to Cornwall, and as there is research under way in this area, notably by Nick Hall, who has written about Westward Television's documentary unit (Hall forthcoming 2018) and who is also, among other projects, working on a history of regional television criticism in local press, I have chosen to exclude it here.

The Organization of the Book

The book is organized in relation both to forms of narrative, and to audiovisual motifs relating specifically to the regional landscape, its place-myth and its screen picturing. Across the book as a whole, I identify and trace a particular audiovisual rhetoric through which Cornwall has been visible on screen, and argue that the place-image which has been developed through that grammar, in dialogue with its construction in the visual arts and in literature, has predominantly worked to focus attention on the edge of Cornwall—on the periphery of the periphery. The consequence of this over-emphasis on the 'edge' is that the inland territory has been representationally 'emptied out'; the deep irony, on the other hand, is that the material result of the focus on the edge has been the exorbitant rise in price of coastal property and the movement, to the 'invisible' and largely impoverished inland territory, of the majority of native Cornish. So while inland Cornwall remains largely unseen, it is manifestly not empty, and in this respect the book aims to intervene in the picturing of region on screen, to demonstrate its political and economic significance, to make the centre visible.

Chapter 1 situates Cornwall in a scholarly frame, positioning *Picturing Cornwall* in relation to the key fields of study in which it intervenes: Cornish Studies, work on landscape in film and television and on place in the moving image. This chapter also explores the significance of the book's focus on 'region', and its critically regionalist approach, one which is intended to challenge the hegemony of the national as an analytical frame in studies of screen media. Chapter 2 considers the travelogue form, from the first Great Western Railway film of the region, *Scenes in the Cornish Riviera* (1904), to Andrew Kötting's *Gallivant* (1996), exploring the persistent construction of Cornwall as 'view' for the incomer. This sense of the Cornish landscape as a source of spectacular visual pleasure establishes the ground from which both the dramatic and documentary aesthetics examined in the chapters which follow have developed, as well as representing the key visual rhetoric to which some of the Cornish image-making discussed in the final chapter responds. Chapter 3 turns to romantic fictions of Cornwall, looking at the ways in which the region's place-image has been developed and exploited from romantic screen dramas of the silent era, through the wartime positioning of Cornwall as a site of difference within unity, to *Poldark* (BBC, 2015–). Across this chapter, an audiovisual rhetoric of immersion and affect emerges as the characteristic device through which the Romantic potential of the regional landscape on screen is harnessed in drama. Within this aesthetic, the intermedial figure of the woman at the edge of the cliff takes shape as a motif through which Cornwall as romantic periphery has functioned as a site of both anxiety and potential, particularly in relation to gender and modernity. Chapter 4, which explores the broad category of 'landscape documentary', shows the ways in which this figure persists across generic and narrative forms, even in the arts documentary. In the final chapter, I turn to examples of screen Cornwall by local practitioners, to think about the film language through which Cornwall has been pictured from 'inside'. Through an exploration and analysis of amateur Cornish film of the 1930s and contemporary Cornish film practice, the book ends in a consideration of the potential and difficulty of picturing Cornwall in more experientially based ways which might complicate, challenge or resist the mainstream insistence on a tourist view. To return to Adorno's provocation, then, my concern in *Picturing Cornwall* is to stage the moving image culture industry's concomitant preservation and demolition of place, asking how Cornwall might exist outside of its mainstream construction on screen.

I

Landscape, Region and the Moving Image

Cornwall is a peripheral region physically, culturally and economically, and in general terms has been constructed through an ongoing discourse of Romantic tourism as a 'pastoral' site, a discourse, as Gifford notes, which constructs a space of 'retreat' in juxtaposition to the supposed complexities of the city and the present (1999: 46). In the course of this construction, Cornwall's industrial history and post-industrial economic position are appropriated as 'traditional', 'Romantic' and 'tragic'. The significance of the past in the present is persistent in the Cornish landscape, in the form of granite tors, standing stones and the ruins of Cornwall's tin- and copper-mining industrial history visible on moor-top and cliff edge. As Ian Bell has noted in his work on travel narratives and national identity, this has been a particularly consistent production of rural Englishness:

> The comic postcard England of rural tranquility, village bobbies and red-faced councilors seems curiously intact to the urban traveller, and its persistence is an ironised reminder of an alternative ideological fantasy, a version of the pastoral still identifiable in the remote periphery, one of Virgil's Georgics still available in the remote southwest of England (1995: 21).

The ideological fantasy of pastness and simplicity at the periphery noted here has also been a profoundly white one, and Cornwall's construction on screen attests to and perpetuates this 'retreat' from contemporary urban diversity. Bell writes of Devon, here, as 'the remote southwest of England'—the 'southwest' a 'region' within which Cornwall is usually included—and within a national frame, in relation to constructions of 'Englishness'. How, though, has Cornwall been understood in its specificity, outside of its relation to England?

Cornish Studies

Most scholarship on Cornwall has either come out of the Institute of Cornish Studies (University of Exeter) at Penryn, or has been published in the Institute's series *Cornish Studies* (University of Exeter Press). Deacon and Payton (1993) offer an excellent analysis of the development of Cornish culture, beginning with the construction of Cornishness as 'mining and Methodism' following industrialization in the eighteenth century. At this moment, they argue, when Cornwall was acknowledged as the world leader in deep metal-mining (63–64), this new discourse overlaid 'an older, vernacular Cornish culture'. The Cornish Celtic revival of the late nineteenth century, which focused on Cornwall's Celticity, Catholicism and links to Brittany, looked back to a moment of heightened political power in the Middle Ages and would underpin the establishment of the pressure group and language society Tyrha Tavas in 1933 and Old Cornwall Societies across the region. For Deacon and Payton Cornwall has, above all, been produced for and by the south-east of England as:

> a place of retreat, simplicity and innocence, peopled by bucolic, smiling villagers. It is a place to be 'discovered', to 'fall in love with' and then to cherish—preferably in the state it was when first found. It is essentially a tamed countryside that is nevertheless 'deep rural England' (72).

This, they suggest, is linked to idealized ideas of the past as 'heritage', and thus as a museum of potentially saleable heritage artefacts. Similarly, Deacon has argued that 'Cornwall is a product of the gaze of artists and tourists, anthropologists and novelists ... the Cornish are constructed; they have little role in the construction' (1997: 7), linking this construction of region directly to the uneven relationship between Anglicized centre and Celtic periphery in which 'travel writers, visitors, painters, novelists and poets ... have "discovered" Cornwall' and then reproduced it through their own images (8). Deacon is concerned to challenge this by looking at insider voices, and I continue this project in the final chapter of the book, which attends to amateur film of the 1930s and contemporary film practice in Cornwall.

Deacon describes the evolution of Cornish Studies, in the context of a turn away from grand narratives, from a narrow but important focus on local history and culture, an interest in revivalist Celticity in the 1970s, and in nationalism in the 1990s, to a more cultural approach which looks to questions of representation, for example in literature and tourism discourses, and to post-colonial theory (2002). Noting the importance of Cornish Studies in the context of calls for a devolved Cornish assembly and European Objective One funding (31), the importance of looking outwards, Deacon argues that:

> the politics and economics of exclusion and division, the promotion of 'difference' in political, cultural and economic terms, and the search for identity in a consumerist society—are broad cultural issues and ones that are equally important in studies of contemporary Cornwall. For example, the commodification of Cornishness is an area that desperately requires more interdisciplinary attention (37).

Picturing Cornwall responds to that call, hopes to be 'alert to the multiple representations of Cornwall that exist both now and in the past' (38), and addresses the need for work in Cornish Studies to appear in wider arenas, reaching larger audiences.

James Vernon provided one of the earliest scholarly engagements with the cultural positioning of Cornwall in the national frame (1988), and explored the ambivalence of Cornwall's relationship with England, noting that it 'had always existed on the margins of Englishness, both a county of England and a foreign country' (153). Interestingly for my project here, Vernon notes the imperial dimension to England's positioning of Cornwall as a dark, foreign land, linking the work of the Newlyn painters, who came from outside Cornwall to establish an artist 'colony' in the fishing village, as echoing this discourse (159). Kennedy and Kingcome also note the focus of the Newlyn artists at the edge, while de-industrialization and china-clay mining increased in the interior: '[e]verything was cosy on the Riviera' (1998: 51–52).[1] In addition, a number of scholars have examined the growth of tourism in Cornwall following the decline of the mining industry, drawing out the repeated deployment of discourses of foreignness, romanticization and commodification which have disguised the region's poverty and erased its industrial heritage.[2] Vernon invokes Spivak's work on the post-colonial to discuss the internalization of the discourse of Cornwall as a land of myth and romance, arguing that 'the continual traffic in the tropes and narratives of the Cornish and English national imaginations perpetually undercut[s] the attempt to map Cornwall and England as discrete nations' (154).[3] Accordingly, this book could be considered as an exploration of the ways in which film, and more latterly television as a 'window on the world', can be understood as apparatus of colonization (see Wheatley 2013).

While Trezise's *The West Country as a Literary Invention* (2000) approached Cornwall from a wider regional perspective, which, as he acknowledged, is threatened by a more general notion of 'the West' of England (14), his discussion of the meanings of 'moving westwards' and the tradition of romanticizing it (15) remains important to understanding the picturing of Cornwall, even as a distinct region within it. Westland's *Cornwall: The Cultural Construction of Place* (1997) was an important development in the field, identifying the conventional terms in which the region has been imagined, reproduced and understood: 'inbred, savage Cornwall, the bumbling country Cornwall, the "foreign", exotic and potentially dangerous Cornwall' and remote, romantic Cornwall (1). Within this collection, Deacon's work on outsider and insider views of Cornwall and the centrality of mining and Methodism to the region's self-construction after industrialization and the divergence of representations between 'West Barbary' and 'Delectable Duchy' have been formative to my work (1997). Westland's own work on Cornwall as a 'passionate periphery' in romantic literature (1995) and Helen Hughes's work on Cornwall in du Maurier's *Jamaica Inn* consider the relationship between regional Romantic landscape and gender (1997).[4] Gemma Goodman and I have explored the ways in which recent television dramas located at the Celtic periphery have shifted focus from an alignment of landscape with the female body, to the body of the romantic male hero as a post-colonial site (forthcoming 2018). This multidisciplinary work has begun to build a picture of Cornwall's wider cultural construction, but at its centre remains a void: there has been little attention to moving images of Cornwall, despite the centrality of screens large and small to the envisioning of Cornwall.[5] *Picturing Cornwall* addresses this absence, and complicates work on landscape and place in the moving image in order to build a politically informed framework for the analysis of region in the moving image.

Theorizing Landscape in Film (and Television)

Lefebvre, drawing on P. Adams Sitney, offers the now canonical account of the use of landscape in film, drawing a distinction between narrative and spectacular modes of landscape in the cinema (2006a). Sitney had previously identified the elision of landscape from scholarly discussion, describing it as 'virtually an unconscious issue of film theory' (1993: 103). Sitney points out that 'the moving camera and the panoramic sweep' had since the 1890s 'reflected in a stylised manner the movement of human eyes over the field of vision' (107), and that the long shot (already present in painting and photography and, by 1908, including the aerial shot) would, with the development of editing, become an establishing shot (108). He also indicated the importance, since the 1950s, of the zoom lens for cinematic landscapes, making smooth transitions and trajectories from long to close shot in one camera setting, and across enormous distances (111). Sitney's identification of the Western as a genre 'predicated upon dramatizing the situation of individuals in a distinctive landscape' is crucial, and will emerge as significant for the analysis of landscape in moving images of Cornwall (109).

Lefebvre's theorization of the role of landscape in the cinema hinges upon its relationship with narrative. He draws on Eisenstein's notion that landscape is 'the most flexible in conveying moods, emotional states and spiritual experiences' (1987: 217, quoted in Lefebvre 2006b: xii) to argue that in order to function in this way, landscape 'must obviously distinguish itself from mere background space or subservient setting where action and events take place' (xii). Lefebvre argues that the spectator can operate either a narrative or spectacular mode of viewing, in which 'contemplation of the setting frees it briefly from its narrative function (but perhaps, in some cases, only for the length of a thought)' (2006a: 29). Landscape, then, can be made the focus of the image by the spectator, even where its primary function is narrative setting. This he describes as 'impure landscape'. In contrast, landscape can be 'intentional', deliberately drawn attention to, for example by the deliberate citations of paintings, or by the repeated use of long shots, or by montage (30–33). The visual indication of point of view, followed by a subjective/long shot also encourages attention to setting. He gives the example of transition shots:

> that indicate in the narrative a spatio-temporal change in the action; they are sometimes accompanied by an optical effect (fade in, lap dissolve, etc.) but can be made just as well with a straight cut. They can occur at various points in the film, including at the beginning and at the end where they serve to indicate the spatial boundaries of the diegesis (33–34).

This observation is—ironically, given his neglect of it—especially interesting in relation to television, with its characteristic series and serial forms, repeated opening sequences and segmentation. As I have previously argued of *Poldark* (BBC, 1975; 1977) it is in precisely these moments that the Cornish landscape is emphasized on television. In the short serials *Echo Beach* (Channel 4, 2008) and *Delicious* (Sky, 2016), Cornwall functions symbolically as pathetic fallacy, drawing on a place-myth which renders it a site appropriate to romantic melodrama, with landscape used as narrative setting and 'spectacular' scene transitions (though *Delicious*, which bears a significant narrative similarity to *Echo Beach*, was significant as the first television drama of Cornwall to be set exclusively inland, in which views of viaduct, river and field constituted a notable shift in the television representation of the region).

In contemporary comedy-drama films such as *Blue Juice* (Prechezer, 1995) and *Saving Grace* (Cole, 2000), Cornwall functions as a site of alternative lifestyles and mysticism, and the moments of personal epiphany in these films speak to the intensity of connection between selfhood and regional landscape. The long-running dramas *Wycliffe* (ITV, 1994–98) and *Doc Martin* (ITV, 2004–) also use the Cornish landscape as narrative setting, making significant use of it as spectacle in title sequences and scene transitions. While these moments offer spectacles of regional landscape, thinking about them as television is suggestive for exploring the application of Lefebvre's theory to this adjacent medium. In both programmes, the title sequence remains the same over several series and years; landscape here surely operates quite differently for the regular television viewer than it does for the viewer of a film. Each episode of detective drama *Wycliffe* opens and closes with the same sequence of iconic shots of the Cornish landscape, focused around mine, cliff and moor. Over a repetitive, dramatic string melody, the camera pulls back from a shot of a rock at sea to frame it through a cave opening, an image which dissolves to the eponymous detective in profile with the sea behind him as he turns towards the camera. A thumbprint becomes the contour lines on a map, an aerial shot swoops round a cliff, the detective drives across a lonely moor and the sequence ends on a shot of him on the phone in front of an engine house, towards which he walks. The final shot of each episode finds the hero in a classic 'prospect' pose on a clifftop promontory at sunset.

Similarly, the unchanging titles of *Doc Martin* are based upon a 360 degree time-lapse pan around the cove of Port Wenn and across standing stones, cows and a beach, as if all of Cornwall were visible and encapsulable from the camera's fixed point. The landscape is unchanging over time except in relation to daily and seasonal rhythms: day to night, high to low tide; the circular structure of the sequence is echoed in the repetitive, vaguely jazzy theme music. The pan comes to rest, finally, on a view of the cove from the sea, then pans around the cove to Martin's new practice, up on the cliffside. In place of this sequence, the beginning of the pilot episode dramatizes the centre–periphery relationship by beginning *in media res* with panoramic aerial shots of the coast as Martin flies from London to an interview in far-flung Cornwall. As *Picturing Cornwall* will demonstrate, these sequences are metonymic, in both form and content, of the audiovisual grammar of place that has developed across the long twentieth century. However, over the course of the characteristic weekly, seasonal and annual repetition of television, the initial spectacularity of these landscape sequences, which frame and divide episodes, drains away, fading into prosaic familiarity. In this way, the specificity of the broadcast television text reinforces the picturing of Cornwall not only as unchanging over time, but also as always, already constituted through a few, distilled and familiar place-images.

In my view, Lefebvre's primary contribution to the discussion of landscape and the moving image resides not simply in his distinction between landscape's possible modes as narrative setting or as spectacle, as the primary subject of the image (2006a: 23), but also in his emphasis on the potential ambiguity of landscape's function, its ability to hover between the two (27). His argument about the flexibility of landscape, which takes the example of dispute over the role of landscape in the paintings of Joachim Patinir (c.1480–1524) (24–25), depends largely on interpretation by the spectator (48) and it is here that the potential of landscape's ability to operate between setting and spectacle can be foregrounded. Lefebvre argues that this '"impure" landscape, whose existence we cannot clearly attribute to a director's intention', is its 'principal mode of existence in cinema and it plays an important role in our experience of films' (48). When viewed through the politicized, critically regionalist lens I suggest here, landscape refuses a role as mere narrative setting, and is persistently called forth as an ideological space, even as it remains specific as place. Higson has argued of British New Wave films that because they 'are promoted as realist, landscape and townscape shots must always be much more than neutral narrative spaces. Each of these location shots also demands to be read as a real historical *place* which can authenticate the fiction' (1996: 134). I want to suggest that such a reading is not dependent upon a moving image text's claim to realism, but rather that, from the perspective of 'impure landscape', the historical and political specificity of place in the moving image might always be in play. This approach has something in common with eco-critical approaches which seek more embodied perspectives in which the removed viewpoint is displaced (Kerridge 2013: 223), and with Ingold's suggestion that we consider using 'taskscape' as an alternative to landscape:

> a word to remind us, when our surroundings seem to be laid out for our gaze, that our perception of them is not comprehensive, but is a function of the activity we are engaged in, work, or leisure. Perception is conditioned by the specialization that a task involves (Ingold 2000: 195, quoted in Kerridge 2013: 225).

Harper and Rayner have edited two collections of essays on the subject of cinema and landscape, drawing attention to the significant work of national representation performed by landscapes on screen (2010: 24). In *Film Landscapes* (2013), they note the displacement of the term 'cinematic landscapes' by 'moving images of place' (1–2) as indicative of the development of the field of inquiry in a short period of time, and of the turn to forms beyond fiction film.[6] While these volumes remain crucial in establishing historically attuned attention to landscape on screen, one of the key aims of *Picturing Cornwall* is to challenge the overwhelming focus on the national that is characteristic of Film Studies' attention to landscape, by turning towards the regional as a lens to disrupt the discursive primacy of 'nation'. Further, the generalized opposition between city and country, one of the 'large metaphors' of cinematic landscapes (Lukinbeal 2005: 14), which draws upon Williams (1985), is sharpened in *Picturing Cornwall* to focus on the precise ways in which one place has been figured as 'lost to modernity', but also on the moments where this discourse has, if temporarily, been overturned. Thinking about the instances in which particular countrysides are figured as outside of the modern helps us to think about the material and economic effects of a place-myth that positions a region as beyond change and development.

Existing scholarship almost entirely ignores the fact that landscape has represented a significant part of the television image, too, and there has been little attempt to theorize the particularity of its use on the small(er) screen. While Higson's account of the functions of landscape on television is now out of date (1987), given the shifts to high-definition (HD) and widescreen formats noted by Wheatley (2011, 2016), it remains useful. Higson notes that landscape functions as space, place, spectacle and metaphor in cinema (1987: 8), while television's characteristic focus on 'chat' rather than extended narrative means (in 1987) that outside of the classic serial, where 'authenticity is displaced by spectacle', landscape operates differently on television (9). His suggestion that the aerial landscape shot on television also expresses an 'ideology of presence' (9), and that this is profoundly linked to tourism (10), remains relevant, but his discussion of the 'relatively avant-garde' film *So That You Can Live* (1982), shown in Channel 4's 'Eleventh Hour' slot, is especially helpful for *Picturing Cornwall*. He writes about:

> a film about the complex changes in the lifestyles of those living in the South Wales valleys, and affected by de-industrialization. While landscapes here can be read as spectacle, as discourse space, and as dramatic space, they are also separated from other materials and

explored both as landscapes and as texts to be read. Here, the camera *does* linger on the landscape ... and, although the high vantage point often threatens to contain and use the landscape only as spectacular object of the gaze, voices-over direct the attention of the viewer to an historical reading of the landscapes. It is possible then to read the ways in which the land has been shaped by relations between capital and labour, that is, shaped according to a particular class perspective, and an aesthetic code and economic logic (12).

Higson suggests a potential reading in which landscape as place on screen might come forward in politically inflected ways, despite colonizing spectacle, as a result of the operation of sound in relation to image. Is this, however, only possible in an avant-garde film text? *Picturing Cornwall* complicates this position by thinking about generic differentiation within television texts, asking, for example, how aerial shots of the Cornish landscape operate in *Poldark* (BBC, 2015–), compared to a documentary serial such as *The Fisherman's Apprentice* (BBC, 2012), in which there is a directly stated political and educational aim. Does the documentary impulse necessarily mean that spectacle surrenders to education?

Wheatley (2011, 2016) draws on Lefebvre (2006a) in her analysis of landscape programming on British television in the context of developing HD technology, pointing to the recent burgeoning of series which ramble through rural landscapes in search of, and dwelling on, the perfect view (2011: 234). The great leap made by this analysis is in its attention to the specificity of the television landscape image, its slow pace and contemplative attitude, the 'quiet wonder' encouraged by these programmes, which, she argues, 'is perhaps rather more suited to cosy, televisual images of landscape' (244). Wheatley's identification of the spectacular mode in which landscape is used in these television programmes does, though, also remain framed by the national and, in Chapter 4, I turn to landscape programming of Cornwall to think about how a grammar specific to region, rather to the nation, which has developed intermedially and over time, operates in recent landscape programming of Cornwall. What is its relationship, for example, to the affective, immersive rhetoric characterizing romantic dramas of place?

Place and the Moving Image

The work discussed above established the importance of paying attention to landscape in the moving image, and adjacent to and growing out of that new field has been the development of work on the representation of place in the moving image (predominantly, in cinema). Much of this work remains within the frames of the national, the urban and generalized notions of 'the rural' which, note Fowler and Helfield, are profoundly attached to ideas of 'the past', a formation critical to Cornwall's construction on screen (2006: 6, 12).[7] Work on the representation of Scotland, Ireland and Wales in film seems to offer a natural starting point for thinking about moving images of Cornwall, given their shared status as romanticized Celtic peripheries of Britain.[8] McArthur's call in *Scotch Reels* (1982) for attention to 'indigenous' as well as 'outside' representations of Scotland is an important one, and much of the work on Irish cinema places emphasis on representations of self in a post-colonial national context.[9] Petrie's claim in *Screening Scotland* that 'the construction of Scotland as a peripheral and remote place far from the heart of metropolitan British culture, an imaginary space in which a range of fantasies, desires, fears and anxieties have been projected' (2000: 8), is especially relevant to the Cornish case, as Petrie acknowledges (32).[10]

However, the fact that Cornwall occupies a contested position in relation both to 'the national', with its own ancient claim to independent nationhood and as yet unsuccessful lobby for a devolved parliament, as well as dispute over the importance of Celticity to its identity, means that there are important ways in which its (also fraught) status as region calls for a different approach. In this respect, Hill's work on *Cinema and Northern Ireland* (2006) is closest to my project here, given Northern Ireland's contested, colonial relation to England; as I do in *Picturing Cornwall*, Hill looks beyond the feature film to amateur, travelogue and newsreel films to think about the construction of region on screen from within as well as without. Noting the 'disproportionate skew towards the urban' in this field (2014: 1), Hallam and Roberts look to the spatial turn in Film Studies. They ask questions which *Picturing Cornwall* is also intended to address, such as 'What role do moving images play in the social and political production of space? To what extent can film function as spatial critique?' (8); this work, too, makes the leap beyond fiction film. Hallam's research shows the ways in which different film genres correspond to different practices of spatial mapping (176), and she argues that newsreel 'views' of place contrast significantly with amateur film recording of the same events. Her argument that 'the view aesthetic of the newsreel serves primarily national, rather than local, interests of identity and belonging' (180), and the analysis of amateur film presented in the final chapter of this book, confirm this.

At the boundaries of this field there have been suggestive acknowledgements of the importance of the particularities of place on screen, beyond the limits of the city and the nation. Dina Iordanova's work on Balkan cinema, for example, has raised the question of representation in relation to a peninsular place often seen as marginal to Western Europe, but also 'as a crossroads or a bridge across cultures' (2001: 6).[11] This description is resonant with Cornwall's positioning as a geographically and culturally peripheral peninsula that, nevertheless, remains profoundly connected through culture, language and the diaspora to other sites around the nation and the globe. Schoonover's work on Sardinia in cinema is particularly attuned to my project in *Picturing Cornwall*, in terms of both aesthetic and political perspective. Noting the use, in Italian cinema of the 1960s and 1970s, of Sardinia as a remote, mythical, natural space which sits in contrast to urban Italy, Schoonover points out that it simultaneously represents a lack of placeness, standing as elsewhere and nowhere, as a 'disarticulation of spatial particularity' (2016). He connects this trope of the region's representation to historical context, to a moment just before gentrification, and, drawing on Brunsdon's work on empty spaces in film (2007a), to the prospect and potential of capitalist real-estate speculation. 'Empty space' in moving images of Cornwall, too, sits ready for purchase and development as the object of the tourist gaze (Urry 2002). Similarly, Gopinath, in writing about the representation of the region of Kerala in India in relation to gender and sexuality, provides a useful model of understanding the potential of 'region' as an analytic category to 'bypass the national and to disturb ideas of national authenticity and purity' (2008: 341): region as a space of resistance.

Phillips has taken up Lefebvre's interest in the 'impure' landscape image in his work on Japanese genre film of the 1960s, suggesting that we need to think about the treatment of space and time in the moving image in a more historicized way (2011: 215). While Phillips frames his analysis in relation to a national cinema, his account of landscape in the moving image is extremely attentive to the historically and culturally specific meanings of the Shimokita peninsula of Honshu. James's work on the Scottish Highland landscape in cinema is an important development, proceeding from the recognition, in a context of globalization, of the importance of paying attention to the representation of 'subordinated minorities' in their relation to the nation state (2006: 186). Most significant, perhaps, is the collection *Regional Aesthetics: Mapping UK Media Cultures* (2015). In the introduction, Franklin suggests that 'region and place have come to be even more intrinsic to people's sense of self due to the disorienting and dislocating effects of this rapid cultural diffusion' (Franklin 2015: 2), and the collection demonstrates how 'media (particularly local, regional and grass-roots forms) can increase consciousness of place' (3). In particular here, Perrins's work on the production of different 'Wales' from within and without, in mainstream and amateur film, offers a wonderful model, if necessarily within a national rather than a regional frame, for work on place in the moving image. The final chapter of *Picturing Cornwall*, which looks at film practice 'from within', proceeds with this same approach to the possibility of a 'regional poetics' in mind. In more general terms, *Picturing Cornwall* is aligned with the approach taken by Rhodes and Garfinkel, and their concern to wrest 'place from its status as mere setting and narrative "support"' and to focus on 'the generative structures, aesthetic conditions, and political implications of the profilmic, drawing background to foreground, periphery to centre' (2011: x).

This field demonstrates that it is not just landscape in general but places in particular which matter on screen. Within it though, there has been a considerable emphasis on urban space, on film, on fiction and on mainstream production, with rural and peripheral places, television, non-fiction, amateur and independent work significantly under-attended. In this respect *Picturing Cornwall* makes an important contribution to the interdisciplinary conversation; this book considers television and film in tandem as adjacent in a wider field of visual arts, looking beyond fictional storytelling to think about promotional film, newsreels, cinemagazines and amateur film, as well as contemporary documentary. Work on the newsreel form, in particular, remains scarce and it is my intention that this book should be understood as making an argument for attending to it more carefully and more frequently in thinking about the history of the moving image, particularly in relation to place.[12] It is for this reason that I integrate discussion of newsreel and cinemagazine films throughout the chapters, juxtaposing them with fiction films, documentaries and other moving image works in order to stage productive, discursive relationships.

Key ideas in early and more contemporary research on landscape are helpful in complicating existing work on moving images of place. Schama (1995: 6) notes that landscape is more a product of imagination than of geography. Following Williams (1985), scholars have frequently noted the pastoral myth of the rural idyll or retreat, in juxtaposition with the city as a place of business and economy, while the countryside is seen as apolitical and classless.[13] In relation to this, Little argues that 'dominant representations of the rural can conceal problems and mask difference', and notes a need to recognize 'the power relations through which dominant representations are produced and consumed' (2002: 11).[14] Filming, and viewing, the landscape makes, remakes and reasserts these power relations. The act of perception is one of power and control, and contemporary theorists have developed this notion considerably. Hawkins, for instance, points to work in the history of art, including, of course John Berger's *Ways of Seeing* (1972), which has understood landscape painting of the eighteenth and nineteenth centuries as an expressive site in relation to 'power, social justice and conflict', whereby aestheticized landscapes are understood to hide the realities of life in the countryside (2013: 193).[15] *Picturing Cornwall* is interested throughout in the proprietorial and colonizing gaze at the regional landscape inscribed in its screen texts and paratexts, and in the construction of and relations between outsider and insider views of place. As Howard has noted, contemporary research shows that the perception of landscape is not only visual, but also occurs through sound, touch and smell (2013: 43). If, as Wattchow argues, landscape becomes place only through 'immersion by the insider' (2013: 88), can landscape ever be place on screen? How, specifically, might such a sense of particularity of place be produced through moving image and sound? How might tactility and even perhaps olfactory experience be conjured on screen? What is at stake, ideologically, in the attempt to reproduce insideness?

Cornwall: Place/Region/Territory?

Of course, Cornwall is both a place and a region, but there are political implications to both terms and some unpacking is required to frame the way in which I use them throughout the book. Commentators have often understood Cornwall as disadvantaged by its subsumption within the wider governmental administrative region of the 'South West', and in this respect the argument for understanding Cornwall as a 'region' in its own right is an important one. Thomas has explored the complexities of Cornwall's regional positioning and the threat to its territorial integrity, citing the loss of Cornwall County Council in local government reorganization, the 1993 proposal for a formal 'South West' region with Bristol as the capital, and the collaboration with Devon to attract European funding, 'Devonwall', as critical moments (1994: 140). She charts the designation of Devon and Cornwall as NUTS II and the subsequent failed application for Objective One funding in 1993 as a result of the linkage with Devon (which hid Cornwall's economic disadvantage).[16] The later designation as NUTS II UKK3 (Cornwall and Isles of Scilly) within UKK (NUTS I, South West), led to successful bids for EU funding in 2000–06 and 2008–13.[17]

While the now common understandings of place are that it 'is space to which meaning has been ascribed' (Carter, Donald and Squires 1993: xii) and that it is bound up in a sense of identity (Rose 1995: 88), perhaps in this case we need a term which is more politically charged? Doreen Massey's work, for example, has suggested that 'place' is often subject to exclusive claims which attempt to fix meanings, producing a place as bounded, authentic, singular, fixed and unproblematic—as static, unchanging and outside of development (1994: 5). This is a problematic position in relation to Cornwall, in its contested and, as we shall see, routinely archaicized relation to the nation, and this is why Massey urges us to understand 'place' as unfixed, contested and multiple, constructed in relation to connections with what lies beyond, as open and porous (think: Brittany, emigration and the Cornish mining diaspora) (5). While Massey's work has been taken up particularly in relation to gender and power, one might also consider it in relation to class and sociocultural location: who has the privileged and determinant perspective on place? As Massey has noted elsewhere:

> who is it who has these romantic views of place if not those who have the ability to leave? Consider the novels written of the northern home by those who have migrated south, songs sung by the migrant about the place they have left ... such views may not be held by those confined to the place, or by those who more actively participate in its affairs (1995: 65).

Below, I explore some of the intricacies of nomenclature in relation to the extreme south-west periphery of the UK.

Urry's work on place has been as important as his work on the gaze at it, and his research is inherently bound up with ideas around travel, tourism and questions of economic and cultural power, revealing the structural relations which underpin the positions of tourist/local (1995). In this respect, an understanding of Cornwall as a place of commodification through tourism and its construction as 'consumable' on screen underpins the book as a whole.[18] There is a fascinating if relatively limited body of work on the construction of region, for instance Brace's analysis of the ways in which regional identity has participated in the construction of British national identity (in which the south-west is almost entirely absent, as it is on national weather maps, raising the question of its relation to the national) (1999), and Russell's influential analysis of the construction of the North of England, *Looking North* (2004).[19] In the 'unequal relationships between the northern periphery and the metropolitan core' (1), Russell recognizes that other significant regions including '"the South-West", "East Anglia" and perhaps, above all, the ill-defined and oft-ignored "Midlands" have been marginalized within the regional hierarchy by the sheer power of the North's sense of place and by the dominant discourse of the "North–South divide"' (9). Russell also looks at self-image and self-expression alongside external views, as do I. Both Brace and Russell frame their discussion of region in relation to the nation and to Englishness, and inevitably, given the significance of centre–periphery relations in representation, *Picturing Cornwall* often produces the same framing. Maintaining a sense of the play between region as simultaneously contiguous with and disrupting of the national is critical here.

Urry (1995: 152) notes the critiques that globalization leads to cultural homogeneity, and that privileging the local is potentially isolating and one-sided, while noting that globalization can, in fact, increase local distinctiveness (154). Pointing to visual culture's role in aiding globalization in relation to place (2013: 264) and the significance of place to belonging and identity (265), Bowring offers 'region' as a useful 'point of negotiation' between the global and the local, in that it both transcends particularity but also privileges local distinctiveness over global idea flows (263).[20] Hettne and Söderbaum define a region as 'firmly rooted in territorial space: a group of people living in a geographically bounded community, controlling a set of natural resources, and united through a certain set of cultural values and common bonds of social order forged by history' (2002: 39), though in the internal colonial case of Cornwall we might want to question the issue of 'control' over its natural resources. Such ideas of region are also, of course, easily appropriable by capitalist consumer culture (think: Cornwall as the land of pasties, ice cream, smugglers, piskies and sandcastles). The work of Lefaivre and Tzonis on architecture (2003), upon which Bowring draws, has been central to the formulation of 'critical regionalism' as an approach which could challenge 'romantic regionalism' and mediate between the local and the global, questioning both, and Bowring also presents critical regionalism as an approach which assumes the difficult relation of centre–periphery and offers a way of defamiliarizing landscape and disrupting relations of sentimentality (2013: 268). As Tzonis argues, 'regional' is out there, waiting to be found, where 'regionalist' is made, with the aim of helping to construct group identity (2003: 13).[21]

Hettne and Söderbaum note that the 'new regionalism' can operate either to challenge or strengthen the notion of the nation state (2002: 33), commenting that 'regions are social constructions, and to observe and describe regionalization is also to participate in the construction of regions' (36). In this respect, I use the term 'region' in *Picturing Cornwall* in awareness that in the very act of writing about it, I contribute to its construction, but I do this deliberately in relation to Cornwall's ongoing demand for recognition of its distinctive identity and its call for political devolution in line with the other Celtic nations of the UK. I intend this book as an act of support in relation to a place which continues to suffer economically and culturally from its positioning in a centre–periphery hierarchy. This is a place that, through continued location shooting for film and television, the related growth of second-home ownership and the perpetuation of tourism as the primary development industry in the wake of the decline of the mining and fishing industries, remains one of the poorest places in the UK. At the same time, my use of 'place' and 'region' should be understood as 'critical' in Lefaivre and Tzonis's sense, resistant to stasis and open to elsewhere, development and change. I use the term 'territory' interchangeably with 'place' and 'region', and it is intended to carry both an emphasis on physical geography, but also to be suggestive in relation to questions of power and control.

The critically regionalist approach to place in this book offers a way of thinking about geographical relationships outside of national boundaries (acknowledging, for instance, the ancient and ongoing connection between Cornwall and Britain's other Celtic nations, and with Brittany, and the connection, through mining and emigration, with a Cornish diaspora in Ireland, Australia, South America and the USA [Payton [2004] (2017), 2007]). It seems more important than ever, in the contemporary geopolitical landscape, to find ways of understanding place outside of the boundaries of the nation state. A critically regionalist viewpoint can allow us to see, for example, Cornwall (from 'within') as a place of global connectedness, modernity and change (ancient and ongoing industry and ports) rather than (from the outside 'centre') as an archaic, remote place of tradition and stasis. Perhaps the most significant turn represented by *Picturing Cornwall* is its attention to a critically regionalist understanding of place on screen. This book was begun at a critical period of instability, at micro- and macroregional, national and global levels, taking in devolution (Scotland, Wales and Northern Ireland [1998]; Cornwall's ongoing call) continued across the recognition of minority status for the Cornish (2014), the 'Devonwall' debate (a live issue in the lead-up to the 2017 UK General Election), anxiety over increased immigration in the face of Russian military incursions in Ukraine from 2014, the war in Syria, the Referendum on Scottish Independence (2014), Brexit (2016), and President Donald Trump's threats to build a wall between Mexico and the USA (2017). The introduction of a politicized, critically regionalist sense of 'place', then, to the discussion of landscape on screen, seems particularly important now.

2

The Outsider and the View: Travel, Tourism and Film

The meaningful use of landscape has not been the preserve of the fiction feature film. Landscape has been significant, too, across the documentary forms of film as well as television, from newsreels and cinemagazines, promotional and industrial films, as well as documentary, lifestyle and reality forms of television, to amateur film. This chapter explores the audio-visual construction of Cornwall as regional place across actuality forms from the beginning of the moving image, in order to complicate Lefebvre's suggestion that landscape in cinema operates mainly as narrative setting, and occasionally as spectacle (2006a: 29). It does this by considering the idea that the regional landscape never 'vanishes' (29), is never 'freed from eventhood' in film and television (22), but is always political. I aim to make a contribution to work on early film, suggesting ways of approaching moving image forms that have rarely been the focus of scholarly attention, as Ruoff has noted (2006a: 14). There is a remarkable lack of scholarly work on both the newsreel and the cinemagazine, which were for decades a regular and significant part of the cinema bill. McKernan, whose own writing and gathering together of work on newsreels is a key exception (1992, 2002), comments in his introduction to Crosby and Kaye (still the only work to attend to the form), that the cinemagazine 'needs to be recognised collectively as a significant and influential part of moving image history' (2008: xii).[1] I hope to contribute to the project of bringing attention to the important role played by these under-attended forms, the impulse of which, like later television documentary forms, was both education and entertainment; indeed, Crosby's own essay on the cinemagazine describes it as 'the "colour supplement" of the cinema' (2008).[2] *Picturing Cornwall* approaches the newsreel as a form which has made a significant contribution to the construction of a specific regional place-myth and the tourist economy it has supported. Accordingly, I analyse it alongside and in relation to actualities, drama and amateur filmmaking. In attending to the newsreel and cinemagazine in this way, I hope to encourage further critical and theoretical scholarship on their relationship to other forms of both film and television.[3]

This chapter spans more than a century of moving image history and as such is necessarily selective; I have chosen indicative examples across a range of genres and moments, and accordingly there will be omissions (though not, I hope, consequential ones). The structure of the discussion across Chapters 2 and 4 (which considers television landscape documentary) certainly suggests teleology; it makes visible the establishment and development of actuality genres and their subforms across audiovisual media, through a focus on the representation of a specific region. This development is placed in socio-historical context through reflection, for example, on the growth of the travelogue in relation to the history of technological advance, the resurgence of this genre in the twenty-first century, and the emergence of avant-garde documentary forms such as *Figures in a Landscape* (Shaw Ashton, 1953) in the context of mid-twentieth-century modernism. At the same time, the chapters reveal a particular form of looking at and representing Cornwall which emerges and crystallizes across the development of these forms and which the rest of the book traces through other audiovisual constructions of Cornwall: the conjoined tropes of the outsider and the view, along with an audiovisual grammar of region which developed in tandem with the continuing evolution of public and private transport, tourism, and the moving image.

Mobility and the Moving Image

Scholarship on early cinema, on visual culture, on place and on tourism, has explored the significance of the conjunctural development of motorized forms of transportation—train, car, plane—alongside photography and moving image technologies, providing contextualization for the emergence and development of the travelogue genre explored here.[4] In *The Haunted Gallery: Painting, Photography, Film c.1900*, Nead includes a section, 'Cameras and Cars', in which she points to the 'long and tangled relationship between these two technologies of modern motion ... both were instrumental in bringing about a shift in what might be described as modern vision and in reconfiguring conceptions of subjectivity in relation to time and space' (2007: 133). 'While the flaneur is a central figure of modernity, so too are the train passenger, car driver and jet plane traveler. Their arrival changes the nature of vision', suggest Urry and Larsen (2011: 162), identifying this change with the emergence of that they call a 'tourist glance'. Nead's point, that the motor car 'relocates the history of twentieth-century visual media in the countryside' (134) and locates modernity there as well as in urban spaces (153–54), is critical for my project: to examine the audiovisual exploration of a peripheral rural space enabled and established at this moment of possibility in which modern forms of transportation and the moving image came together. The continuing relevance of the suggestion that 'a nostalgic and conservative image of the national past was effectively created out of types of movement made possible by the latest forms of modern technology' (134) is illustrated in this chapter's exploration of moving images of region. The audiovisual picturing of Cornwall always already stages the encounter between tradition and modernity, at the level of form as well as content.

Cornwall and the Tourist Gaze

The conjunction of new modes of travel and the moving image has a particular resonance and significance, however, in the case of moving image constructions of Cornwall, in that it coincides with Cornwall's de-industrialization. Deacon and Payton note that, in the late 1890s, sections of the Cornish intelligentsia 'broke ranks' to support the development of tourism in the hope of rebuilding the local economy via Great Western Railway's (GWR) investment in seaside hotels and advertising (1993: 70), revealing the reconstruction of Cornwall, predominantly from outside the region, as a romantic, picturesque and mystical place. This was an imagining supported by late nineteenth-century Celtic revivalism, enabling Cornwall's 'otherness' and 'difference' to be emphasized through, for example, the celebration of the by-then extinct Cornish language, ancient traditions and feast days, and the region's ancient and ongoing connections with Brittany (72–75). It was this Celticizing consolidation of Cornwall's construction as 'a romanticised periphery' (Deacon 1997: 7) that underpinned the promotion and development of the region's tourist economy (Lowerson 1994; Thornton 1993). As Perry (1999: 95) and Thomas (1997: 121) have both pointed out, this construction of Cornwall was a powerfully pre-industrial one, which elided its significant industrial heritage (Perry 1999: 95) as well as the region's considerable international reach through engineering and emigration (Payton 2007).

Thornton has charted the development of coastal tourism in Cornwall, both before and after the coming of the GWR in 1859 and the launch of the Cornish Riviera Express service in 1904 which, he comments, 'cut the journey from Paddington Station, London to Penzance to a remarkable seven hours. For the first time, Cornwall was remote to English middle-class demand, but "accessible in its remoteness"' (1997: 63). GWR, he notes, took a 'pro-active role in the development of Cornish tourism. Eventually it played a considerable part in shaping an image of Cornwall that survives to some extent even today' in constructing a 'Cornish Riviera' (63).[5] Lenman (2003) demonstrates that as post-industrial Cornwall became more accessible as a destination for artists and tourists, local photographic companies were recording Newlyn School paintings before they were transported back to the 'centre' of Birmingham or London, where the impact of their romanticized images of Cornwall was 'greatly increased by reproduction, not only in art journals but also in mass-circulation papers like *The Graphic* and *The Penny Magazine*' (102). While there was a long-standing history of literary representations of Cornwall which initially established this place-myth, the development of photography and then the moving image, alongside increased access via public and, eventually, private means of transport such as the car, not to mention the aerial views possible from aeroplanes (as well as, differently inflected in the case of the modernist painter Peter Lanyon, the hang glider [Causey 2006: 8]) and most recently, in *Poldark* [BBC, 2015–], the drone), have been instrumental in producing Cornwall as the object of a desiring look at place.

Urry (2002) establishes the role played by Romanticism in the development of the tourist gaze, noting that its effects 'were to suggest that one could feel emotional about the natural world and scenery', leading to the establishment of 'scenic tourism' and sea-bathing (20). Crucially, Urry distinguishes between what he calls the 'romantic' form of the tourist gaze, a search for authenticity 'in which the emphasis is upon solitude, privacy and a personal, sort of semi-spiritual relationship with the object of the gaze', for example, 'undisturbed natural beauty' (43), and the 'collective' gaze which 'necessitates the presence of large numbers of other people' (for example at National Trust properties or seaside resorts such as Blackpool) (1995: 138). Urry points out the importance of photographic representations, postcards, guidebooks, television and, later, the Internet in producing the internalized, romantic, ideal representations of the views upon which tourists gaze (2002: 78, 90). He reflects upon the idea that the development of moving images and motorized transport have produced a 'mobilised tourist gaze', one which is significantly different from the detailed, two-dimensional image produced by a stills camera, and more akin to 'the on-rushing images encountered on TV and film' (152). Urry goes on to suggest the notion of the 'tourist glance': 'the capturing of sights in passing from a railway carriage, through the car windscreen, the steamship porthole or the camcorder viewfinder' (153). *In The Tourist Gaze 3.0*, Urry and Larsen consider more fully the impact of the growth of audiovisual recording and representational technologies, rethinking the tourist gaze as a performative, embodied, framed and framing practice:

> What is sought for in a holiday is a set of photographic images, which have already been seen in brochures, TV programmes, blogs and social networking sites. Much tourist photography involves a ritual of 'quotation' (2011: 179).

Urry and Larsen's argument here speaks directly to a critical contradiction in the production of Cornwall's place-myth, one upon which the tourist economy of the region remains dependent and which hinges on precisely the conflict between the conditions of the preformed romantic and collective gazes. While Cornwall, as this chapter will show, has been constructed primarily as the object of a (privileged) romantic gaze, based upon the individual's commune with the sublime beauty of nature, this construction has circulated predominantly via film and television programmes, through which the virtual tourist gazes, collectively, at the romanticized regional object, its remoteness and accompanying promise of solitude (and thus exclusivity). Ironically, 'the more its adherents attempt to proselytise its virtues to others, the more the conditions of the romantic gaze are undermined' (Urry 1995: 139). In the case of Cornwall, the enormous popularity of programmes such as *Poldark* and *Doc Martin* (ITV, 2004–) has brought crowds of people to usually deserted filming locations such as former mining sites in the more remote parts of West Penwith, and has increased the buying up of property in coastal villages including Port Isaac.[6] While the tourist industry is bolstered by the promulgation of a romantic gaze at sublime, authentic Cornwall, at the same time its dependence on a collective look and consumption threatens the possibility of the visitor encountering it.

The Internal Colony and the View from Outside

Deacon has argued that Cornwall's construction as a romantic periphery has been 'a product of the gaze of artists and tourists, anthropologists and novelists ... The Cornish are constructed; they have little role in that construction', a construction which has come from the process of 'discovery by the centre' (1997: 7–8). Drawing on Relph (1976), he goes on to explore what he describes as 'insider' voices that contributed to the production of Cornwall and Cornishness from the 1770s to the 1840s. While I return to Relph's notion of the 'inside' experience and expression of region in the moving image in the final chapter of the book, here it is enough to suggest that the tourist gaze at Cornwall in dominant moving image constructions produced from the centre for the purposes of industrial promotion, tourism and education of various kinds, reproduces such 'outsideness'. It is the look of the outsider at a 'view' of place, even where the attempt is made to reproduce insideness vicariously (through, as we shall see, the use of immersive camera positioning, movement and image composition). It seems significant, then, that the tourist gaze at Cornwall was enabled and developed predominantly by the coming of the railway and moving images in tandem. As Lynne Kirby points out in *Parallel Tracks*, there have been significant connections between railways and imperialism:

> Insofar as the train has always been an extension of an imperialist vision, of the hegemonic expansion of an economic and cultural power, a principle of incorporation and arrangement and of the discipline of heterogeneous territories, its function has been that of coherence, order, and regularity. In general, the train is a vehicle that imposes sense on what modern Western culture sees as irrational: nature and tradition (1997: 27).

Extending this argument to the relationship between the railway and the moving image, it is possible to frame the exploration of travelogues of region in relation to the incorporating, organizing and delimiting role they play in relation to the production of place-images. As Kirby notes, the conjunction of railroad, cinema and tourism produces 'a subject conditioned to desire the token possession of an inaccessible place through vision' (41). While Ruoff points out that '[f]requently episodic, travelogue narration offers an alternative to hegemonic narrative forms in both the documentary and the feature fiction film' (2006a: 2), travelogue narration might also construct and reinforce hegemonic picturings, and experiences, of place. The coming of the railway—and the moving image—to the de-industrialized 'difference' of Cornwall with GWR's Cornish Riviera Express in 1904 organized the wild, remote territory of Cornwall into an accessible, procurable and potentially securable space for (the rest of) England.[7] As Hibbert noted of the Home Grand Tour via GWR's Holiday Line in the *Great Western Railway Magazine*, '"The Cornish Riviera" [was] the Empire's most famous holiday centre' (1914: 186). My contention is that the notion of the tourist gaze can be conceptualized most usefully for Cornwall in relation to the 'outsider' look at place theorized by Relph, specifically in relation to the region's status, especially after the crash of the mining industry, as an 'internal colony' (Hechter 1975). Conceptualizing Cornwall's peripheral relation to the centre in this way provides a frame through which it is possible to make a politically inflected reading of the history of its construction in moving images and their paratexts. In the conjunction of modern modes of travel and moving images of Cornwall, we can observe the development of a politically significant description of regional place-image that continues to inform its place-myth. The early coincidence of moving images, new modes of transport and the growth of tourism produced a focus on the coastal edge of the geographic terrain—the periphery of a periphery—which has continued to dominate the place-myth of Cornwall. The resultant 'emptying out' of the terrain, in which the centre falls away and out of representation, produces a set of exclusions around poverty and industry which have cemented a place-myth in which Cornwall remains rural, picturesque, archaic and unchanging. It is this place-myth that helps to maintain tourism as the primary (and troubled) regional economy. In the remainder of this chapter, I examine the construction of this place-myth in actualities of Cornwall since the beginning of the moving image.

The Travelogue: Visiting Cornwall

Cornwall has long been one of the classic British holiday destinations, but it is not fully synonymous with the notion of 'The British Seaside', a phrase conjuring up deckchairs and knotted hankies, sandcastles and ice creams, piers and promenades, amusements and saucy postcards. This is the 'liminal' seaside, which 'puts the "civilising process" temporarily into reverse ... and conjures up the spirit of carnival' (Walton 2000: 4; see also Allen 2008). In Williams's *The English Seaside* (2012) for instance, a book of photographic portraits of English seaside places published by English Heritage, it is enlightening to consider the sections in which Cornwall does and does not appear. In Williams's sketch, Cornwall is NOT: Punch and Judy, donkey rides, piers, beach huts, chalets and caravans, deckchairs, public conveniences, model villages, amusements, helter-skelters, carousels and crazy golf. As he points out of this popular imagery of the Victorian seaside, by the 1960s, the 'most prosperous visiting publics were already disappearing to Cornwall, France and increasingly Spain' (11), thus constructing Cornwall as somewhere 'foreign', even exotic. Williams's book does picture Cornwall, however, as: Atlantic breakers and pebbles (19), a huer's hut[8] (24), wrecked fishing boats at Newlyn (38), painted signs for pubs and the Witchcraft Museum at Boscastle (22, 61), the Camelot Castle hotel at Tintagel (102), the 'romantic House in the Sea' and miniature suspension bridge at Newquay (103) (a site/sight which, as we shall see, is a persistent image of remote, Romantic Cornwall), piracy, wrecking and smuggling

(189) and art galleries (197), images which speak clearly to Cornwall's dominant place-myth of raw, natural beauty, romance, Celticism and art. Cornwall, here and elsewhere, figures as far away, different and, perhaps, more middle-class than the 'ordinary' English holiday. Similarly, it is not part of the British modernist seaside, outside of the Tate gallery at St Ives, a site already associated with modernism in the arts as well as with the picturesquerie of other Cornish fishing towns.[9]

Cornwall's distance from London and other metropolitan centres made it timely and expensive to travel to, even after the advent of GWR's Cornish Riviera Express service in 1904, and much of its appeal, with the exception of the resorts of Newquay and perhaps St Ives, has been built on the circulation of place-images of tiny, isolated fishing villages (Polperro, Looe, Boscastle, Port Isaac, Cadgwith), remote and unspoiled coves (Bossiney, Kynance, Porthcurno) and spectacular, dramatic coastlines (Tintagel, the Lizard peninsula, West Penwith). Such images combine in a wider place-myth based upon romanticism, Celticity, mystery and, above all, difference, distance and the vague possibility of danger. The crossing of either Brunel's railway bridge or the 1962 road bridge from Plymouth in Devon to Saltash in Cornwall marks the breaching of a border between regional territories and the sense of crossing into another country, entering a different place. Walton notes of the holiday in general that 'the journey itself was an important part of the holiday experience, developing its own folklore in families and communities, born of shared anticipation and tribulations and punctuated by the observation and celebration of familiar landmarks' (2000: 73). My own (aspirational, working/lower-middle-class) family history is filled with the mythology of the oft-made journey to Cornwall, almost one hundred years of stories about travelling south-west on holiday from the English Midlands, handed down orally and in the form of photographs and postcards (Figure 1).

Most of these stories centre on the length and difficulty of this journey which takes the classic form of the monomyth, with its obstacles (breakdowns, traffic jams), magical helpers (kindly locals, other motorists and holidaymakers) and finally, the return home which would ultimately become genuinely circular when the family relocated to one of the most remote parts of Cornwall (Campbell [1949] 2008). The story has different generational versions and inflections: 'before we had a car' (my grandparents: the train, the motorbike and sidecar, fetching still-warm milk from the farmer whose field was being camped or caravaned in, before the 1950s); 'before the M5 motorway' (my parents: country lanes, the overnight break in the journey, sleeping in the car, before 1977); and finally, 'before the [improved] A30' (everyone, before the late 1980s). The long overnight

Figure 1 A century of family holidays in Cornwall

journey, remembered from childhood. As an adult, talking sweetly to my old Mini, begging it not to overheat going up the hills on the A39, as my boyfriend and I road-tripped to Cornwall, listening to music (Crosby, Stills, Nash and Young, acid jazz) played from a cassette recorder on the back seat; looking out for the hilltop copse of trees at Broadwoodwidger on the A30. Much later, then married, breaking down on Bodmin Moor in the dark with a large dog and a two-month-old baby, and being rescued. The persistent commonality in these stories lies in the distance and difficulty of the journey made to the longed-for, saved-for, dreamed-of prize: a stay in Cornwall, with its quietness, wildness, isolation, lack of pollution, sea swimming, the (dangerous) intensity of the sun 'because the air is so clean!' and wonderful, fresh food (including fish bought on the beach and the iconic cream tea, taken in an orchard or garden). The difficulty of the Cornish journey is even present, in microcosm, in tales of the struggle down the precipitous cliffs and the reward at the end (the sought-after beach 'only the locals know', or that 'you can only get to by boat, unless you're prepared to climb'). These family place-images are also clearly 'outsider' views, constructions of place that conjure it as a wild, difficult to access, magical land of plenty and escape.

In discussing the democratization of travel produced by the development of railways, Urry notes that:

> [s]tatus distinctions came to be drawn less between those who could and those who could not travel, but between different classes of traveller. In the twentieth century further distinctions became drawn between different modes of transport (air, sea, rail) and between different forms that this took (scheduled/package air flights). But also as geographical movement became democratised so extensive distinctions of taste were established between different places. Where one travelled to became of considerable significance (1995: 130).

Cornwall has been constructed, as my personal examples and analysis of travelogues of Cornwall will suggest, as precisely such a 'distinctive' British seaside destination in Bourdieu's sense, a place which might offer the tourist something different, an experience freed from the bustling crowds and deckchairs associated with resorts such as Blackpool, Scarborough and Great Yarmouth (1984).[10] While the British seaside resort exemplifies Urry's formulation of the 'collective' tourist gaze, remote, romantic Cornwall is constructed in my accounts, among others, as the object of the more individualized tourist gaze, and these positions, as John Walton suggests, may also align with a certain social class (2000: 20). While Urry's account of the distinctions of travel here does not include the car, access to which, in the early period of my study, was extremely privileged, as Walton notes of seaside holidays in the interwar period, increased car ownership and the motor touring holiday allowed a certain class even greater access to this 'remote' Cornwall via the motor touring holiday (78). He argues that:

> Up to the Second World War at least, the working class presence at the seaside was most marginal in the small, picturesque seaside resorts, remote from population centres, where artists might congregate and the families of professionals and unconventional industrialists spend long, relaxed summers in beach games and long walks ... These were, increasingly, the preferred retreats of the more aloof and better-connected middle-class families, helped by the flexibility of travel which the car increasingly provided (56).

Much of Cornwall, in its remoteness from main metropolitan centres, retains this feel of a certain kind of exclusivity, one related to ease of access by public transport. Outside of the main resorts served by rail, Cornwall is often still perceived as 'tricky' to explore without a car. The map given inside the cover of the 1928 edition of *The Cornish Riviera* (Mais 1928) shows the limits of the railway's coverage of the region at the moment of its publication, leaving much of Cornwall, beyond the resorts constructed as main tourist destinations, and served by GWR and local railway, far less accessible to the car-less visitor from afar. The overarching picture of Cornwall in literary travelogues of is one of Celticity and creativity, legend, magic and mystery, antiquity, separation and difference.[11] Cornwall's powerful place-myth, in which landscape and feeling are linked in persistent pathetic fallacy, has been supported and developed through photography and the circulation of postcards but, most widely and persuasively, in the moving image travelogue.

Newsreel and cinemagazine film of Cornwall was often slanted towards tourism; in the 1930s, young women feature heavily in tourism-oriented film of Cornwall, as in *Belles of Cornwall* (1936), a feature on young people holidaying at Carlyon Bay, in which girls clad in two-piece swimsuits signal liberated hedonism in the sunshine. *Going Places: Tintagel* (1937) offers a rather different portrait of the young, modern female tourist, showing a visit to the ruined castle associated, in myth, with King Arthur, focalized through two female hikers. While the ostensible focus is on the spectacular coastal landscape displayed in panning shots and picturesque views framed through the castle's stone doorways, and the suitability of Cornwall as a tourist destination for female friends, its inclusion of the young women as part of such views is part of a visual tradition of Cornwall which pictures the woman as both spectacular and precarious, at the very edge of the region.

Open Air Theatre (1955) presents the Minack Theatre at Porthcurno, presumably to the motoring or walking tourist, as just 'an 8 mile journey from Penzance ... rapidly becoming one of the highlights of a Cornish tour'. The amphitheatre, on the edge of the cliffs of the Penwith peninsula, also featured in *Love Story* (Arliss, 1944) and, accordingly, the film has a magical, romantic orchestral score of strings and woodwind, interrupted by gull cries. Here, the Cornish coast is associated with the romantic sublimity of nature, and with art. A high-angle panoramic shot of the coast moves in towards the cliffs 'scented with thyme, coloured with heather and bracken', down onto the rocks and back up to the clifftop in a gesture which was becoming archetypal in the representation of this region. 'Here it is that man can feel the immensity of nature, think his deepest thoughts and shout aloud his greatest words,' proclaims the narrator, whose mild American accent suggests an acknowledgement of Cornwall's international appeal.[12] Already, here, is the intimation of emotional and intellectual epiphany at the edge, which would become, as we shall see, a persistent trope of dramas and documentaries of Cornwall. Similarly, *Kynance Cove Cornwall* (1957) presents glorious colour aerial footage of one of Cornwall's most remote, spectacular and beautiful beaches, again to a sweeping, romantic string-led orchestral score. 'Along the distinctive Cornish coastline, unparalleled for sheer, savage splendour ... it presents a spectacle constantly breathtaking,' says the narrator, and the voice-over makes reference, too, to mysterious Cornwall in the legend of the haunted Kynance Gate, invented to ward off those who might discover smugglers. Beginning with a high-angle shot from the clifftop of the cove and cottages, Kynance is presented here predominantly through a moving camera which pans to frame and hold particular iconic 'views' of the cove, punctuated with held shots which look down onto the beach or at the clear turquoise water to articulate the view of the visitor.

This chapter takes a historical journey around Cornwall with the film travelogue. The trip is not presented as a chronology, but rather is organized around genre and place, as well as around the different modes of transport by which these moving image expeditions have taken place. I begin with those films marked most clearly as travelogues, including those sponsored by the railway industry and those made and shown as part of cinema newsreel and cinemagazine programmes, concluding with the personal, artistic journey of *Gallivant* (Kötting, 1996). There is frequently a lack of generic discreetness (industrial films often include elements of tourism and travelogue, for example), but such examples are illuminating when considered in relation to the historical development of this genre of region. A number of the films and programmes discussed here coincide with the earliest period of moving images, during which the travel film was an important and ubiquitous genre. I begin here, then, with an examination of key writing on the travelogue genre and its relationship to theories of the aesthetics of early film.

Travel Films, Spectacle and the 'View Aesthetic'

In his influential 1981 essay 'The Cinema of Attractions: Early Film, its Spectators and the Avant-Garde', Tom Gunning noted the importance of travel films and topicals in very early cinema's 'harnessing of visibility' ([1981] 1990: 56), and argued for cinema before 1906 to be understood as 'less a way of telling stories than as a way of presenting a series of views to an audience, fascinating because of their illusory power ... and exoticism' (57). In particular, Gunning noted the importance of both the close-up as an attraction in its own right, and early film attractions' direct address to the cinema audience, in which display and exhibition took precedence over narrative absorption (59). Some years later, in response to the neglect of non-fiction in the reconsideration of early film, he proposed an elaboration of the theory of early cinema attractions via the 'view' aesthetic, which he described as the 'Urform of early nonfiction film' that characterized actualities of natural and social history from around 1906 to World War I (1997: 14). Drawing on comments by Grierson about early forms of documentary, he argued for recognition of the distinction between the 'descriptive' mode of early actualities, in contrast to the 'interpretive' rhetorical and discursive mode of later documentary film (12, 22). For Gunning:

> the most characteristic quality of a 'view' lies in the way it mimes the act of looking and observing. In other words, we don't just experience the view film as a presentation of a place, an event or a process, but also as a mimesis of the act of observing. The camera literally acts as a tourist, spectator or investigator, and the pleasure in the film lies in this surrogate of looking. The primary indication of this mode of observation lies in the clear acknowledgement of the camera's presence (15).

Early view films, in Gunning's scheme, present views of both places and activities or processes, including the local custom or festival; in the latter, the temporal organization of the now multi-shot film becomes important, alongside spatial logic (16–17). Gunning notes in quite general terms that in the early view film we see an 'aesthetic that would remain remarkably consistent in travelogue films of future decades' (15). In *Picturing Cornwall* I argue, as Gunning does for the 'cinema of attraction' in the avant-garde and other genres ([1981] 1990), that the descriptive 'view' aesthetic of both place and process, in which 'the act of looking and observing' is mimed, can still be clearly identified in newsreel and cinemagazine forms into the 1960s. It is evident, too, in later television documentary forms in which, for example, the 'phantom ride' of the early view film has developed into the swooping helicopter or drone shot, or the nauseating Steadicam shot from within a boat. Later, Gunning would trace attempts 'to overcome the limits of the traditional picture and its frame' (2006: 34), and again it would be the movement of the moving image which would be important: from the panoramic views of early travel films (either a view taken from a panoramic viewpoint or via the panning movement of the camera itself, mounted on a tripod, or taken from a moving vehicle, as in the case of the 'phantom ride' produced by mounting the camera on moving vehicles, commonly trains [35]). For Gunning, such moving images allowed not just a broader view but also travel into the image—a literal travelling shot which surpasses borders and may produce a thrilling kinaesthetic effect of travel at speed (36).

Pantenburg describes the pan, the 'paradigmatic gesture of the "landscape film"', as 'the gesture of the landscape surveyor' (2012: 130), and similarly, Daniels sees the elevated viewpoint as 'encouraging the act of survey'

> in two senses: to view and to take stock ... the act of seeing is remarkably proprietary and reactionary. The elevated position allows the appropriation of the English rural landscape. ... The elevated position also allows the viewer to be distant from dissenting voices of contested interpretations of either rural landscapes or the nation. Further, the surveying gaze indicates objective detachment, reinforcing the authority of the claims to knowledge embedded in the images (1993: 130–31).

The pan, from a point of elevation or even from the air, is characteristic of moving images of Cornwall, and these theoretical positions identify the potentially controlling, delimiting and privileged function of this shot. I suggest that an examination of the specific organization and reproduction of such 'travelling' images of region might enable the identification of a moving image rhetoric of camera movement (and sound) which describes and maps place in ways which have become reified. In this way, the act of looking, aligned with the act of describing in the travelling moving image, has crystallized a mode of looking at regional place—a kind of 'audiovisual grammar of region'—which is politically and economically consequential, and which makes landscape meaningful beyond narrative setting or spectacle (Lefebvre 2006a); this trope is traced throughout the book.

Gunning explores the connection between the 'view' aesthetic of early film, the tourist viewpoint and the travel genre more fully, arguing that '"foreign views" portray not only a distant site but also a particular point of view, one from outside the land viewed' (2006: 25). He also makes the connection between moving image views and earlier forms such as lantern slides, photographs in stereoscopes, and postcards, as well as later amateur photography (27). Indeed, as Gaudreault has suggested, early moving image 'views' such as those produced by the Lumière brothers 'belong as much if not more to the history of photographic views than to the history of cinema' and emphasize the significant connection between photography (including, I suggest, postcards and a longer history of landscape painting) and the moving image 'view' (2006: 92). A key aspect of Gunning's argument is the production, by these means, of 'colonial' images that 'provide searing illustrations of spectacle as appropriation, as the traditions and inhabitants of the unindustrialized world were posed for the contemplation of citizens of the modern world' (2006: 29). He does, though, also note the potential for resistance contained in the return of this look by its object (1997: 23). Such spectacularizing images are evident, too, in travel films of the de-industrialized internal colony of Cornwall as, in the aftermath of the decline of mining, it was appropriated by naturalist, *en plein air* artists gathering at Newlyn, and later at St Ives, keen to capture Cornwall and its noble, fishing peasantry in paint. Indeed, vestiges of this colonial, appropriative tendency remain present in the most contemporary of programmes, as Chapter 4 shows.

The inscription of such a 'colonial' point of view is a common theme in writing on the early travel film, as noted by Musser (1990: 123), Ruoff (2006a: 2) and, in a more extended way, by Jennifer Lynn Peterson, who picks up on the possibility of resistance noted by Gunning. Peterson's analysis of filmed scenes of the American West sponsored by railroad and other transportation companies in the early years of the moving image (2006: 79) are especially resonant for an analysis of Cornwall, which, as I will argue, has functioned analogously as Britain's 'Wild West' as well as its 'Deep South'. In her analysis, Peterson asks us to consider which aspects of a landscape stand in for a 'vast region' such as the American West (80), a question picked up by *Picturing Cornwall*. Her *Education in the School of Dreams: Travelogues and Early Nonfiction Film* (2013) asks questions about genre, aesthetics and ideology that also inform this book, and this chapter in particular. 'As a form of landscape representation', she says, 'travelogues engage questions of territory, nationalism and political power', representing 'a new kind of visual imperialism, achieved through travel practices and the visualization of travel' (8). While Peterson reads against the grain to find evidence of resistance or subversion in, for example, the returned gaze of the surveyed to challenge the racist, colonizing images they contain, her analysis also offers a useful observation through which to understand the 'picturesque' framing of region in travelogue films presenting a series of 'views' of place. Comparing notions of the sublime and the picturesque, which she suggests might be understood as a 'commercialized form of the sublime' (179), Peterson notes that the picturesque is typically understood as a politically retrograde form, suggesting that it 'relentlessly aestheticizes the world, depoliticizing it and structuring it in terms of a set of reductive conventions that can be easily understood' (179). The picturesque, she argues, can operate to mask conflict, such as that which might emerge from the production of colonial or racist moving image representations (202); perhaps we might consider the romanticized picturing of the ruined Cornish mine stack and engine house, typical of moving images of Cornwall, through this lens.

Dubow's work on the complexities of colonial vision also reflects on the significance of the picturesque, but rather than seeing it as papering over conflict, or as reflective of colonial settlement, she makes the case that the picturesque is, rather, constitutive of it. Dubow argues that 'foreign' space cannot be fitted into the incomer's visual regime; the picturesque produces foreign space as manageable. This is 'the phenomenal force of the colonial picturesque: the desire to call perceptual meaning into existence; to bring the colony into view'. For Dubow, then, we need to understand the colonial picturesque 'not as something which, in the four sides of its pictorial frame, represents a real space, but as something practically productive of "place"' (2000: 98). Cornwall, too, as internal colony, is pictured repeatedly as a place of both sublime and picturesque views, of potential danger and horror, but also of romance and beauty. We might, then, for example, understand the panning shot of the Cornish coast—a key element of the audiovisual grammar of this particular place—along with the intertitle-card and the voice-over narration, as a speech act which attempts to bring the sublime limits of region into the bounds of a vision which it exceeds.

Seeing Cornwall by Train

As Musser has pointed out, the railway film was an important early subgenre of the travelogue, tying industry to the cinema, which functioned as 'a useful form of publicity' (1990: 127–28). GWR's very early collaboration in the 16 minute film *Scenes in the Cornish Riviera* (1904) seems to be the first extant actuality footage of Cornwall and begins, appropriately, with the arrival at Plymouth of the Cornish Riviera Express, the first non-stop train from London introduced in that year. The Cornwall Railway and Brunel's bridge over the Tamar had opened in 1859, with the line going from Plymouth to Falmouth; there had been a railway line between Truro and Penzance since 1852. While the Cornwall Railway was nominally independent until 1889, Roden argues that it was effectively a branch of GWR from the mid-1870s (2010: 80–81). GWR had been trying to attract tourists to the region since the 1890s (Burdett Wilson 1987: 24), but in 1904 the beginning of the daily express service connecting London with Plymouth, the publication of A. M. Broadley's GWR book *The Cornish Riviera* and the production of *Scenes in the Cornish Riviera*, along with the commencement in the previous year of a pioneering motor omnibus service linking Helston and Lizard, the most southerly point of Cornwall, to which GWR had decided not to extend the tracks (26), marked the beginning of a concerted and long-term effort by the railway company to publicize its new service which made the far south-west of the country accessible from London.

The film begins with an intertitle-card presenting the words 'First stop, Plymouth. The longest daily non-stop on the world.' The card is bordered top and bottom with 'GWR' and 'The Holiday Line' marking stops along a railway line, and identical frontal illustrations of a railway engine decorate each side of the frame, drawn so that the smoke from the trains' boilers resembles ice cream cones.[13] This opening image brings together an emphasis on technological marvel, travel innovation and the distance of the region—on a global scale—with the construction of Cornwall as a far-off destination for leisure, pleasure and tourism. Following static shots of the engine being changed over and leaving Plymouth that emphasize the height and length of the train in contrast to the people on the platform, the next intertitle-card is 'Entering Cornwall. Royal Albert Bridge, Saltash.' The film begins, then, with a deliberately extended and dramatized moment of transition between places; the journey to this point has been long and the engine must be changed ready for the next lengthy stretch, and now the spectator is taken across a physical border—Brunel's marvel of engineering bridging the River Tamar, by means of a phantom ride from the front of the engine. The crossing is presented in a series of travelling shots edited together as the train goes onto and across the bridge and into Saltash station, the first in Cornwall. There is some slight movement of the camera, probably from the motion of train, and the shots have been chosen to give the best possible view of the bridge, and of

Saltash beyond, but much of the crossing is from the dark interior of the bridge. The train's arrival in Saltash is followed immediately by a panning shot of the bridge over the river from the Saltash side, looking back at Devon, giving the impression that the journey across the Tamar on the phantom ride didn't give enough of a 'view', obstructed as it was by the supports of the bridge.

From Saltash, *Scenes in the Cornish Riviera* takes the cinematic tourist on a journey around the picturesque coastal destinations served by the GWR, from Looe to Polperro and across to Newquay, then back across to Falmouth via Truro and from there down to the remote outpost of the Lizard ('England's Most Southerly Point', though yet to be titled as such), newly accessible via motor omnibus. The scenes filmed in the fishing villages of Looe and Polperro are presented by means of long shots of the asymmetric jumble of cottages and warehouses which border the harbours, seaweed drying on the walls, craggy cliffs, crashing waves, seagulls and fishing boats, moored and leaving the harbour (in an edited sequence of shots which show process and narrative as well as place). These views are juxtaposed with 'local colour' shots of woven crab pots, and fishermen chatting and pointing both out to sea and at the camera, acknowledging the film's tourist gaze. At the same time, as also noted by Peterson of early film of the American West (2006: 80), tourists are already pictured here, engaged in the archetypal coastal holiday activity of skimming stones at the water's edge. Arriving at 'Newquay', the focus is predominantly on the tourist, holiday experience in what would become one of Cornwall's most popular and populous resorts: the bay is shown from behind the railings and benches of the promenade, and we see people playing with dogs and walking with prams, children playing at the water's edge, digging in the sand, playing leapfrog and playing up for the camera. The sublime, romantic and picturesque aspects of the Cornish coast are not forgotten here, though; we are reminded of them by a shot of the tiny 'House in the Sea', accessible via private suspension bridge, which still features in Williams's pictorial account of the English seaside (2012: 103). The visit to Falmouth shows river trips but also the business of a crowded port and harbour, including a marching infantry troop being filmed from the side of the road—Cornwall, while distant and a site of leisure, is also constructed as participant within the nation and its defence, as the repeated figuring of Cornwall in relation to World War II, discussed in Chapter 3, suggests.

It is en route from 'Falmouth to the Manacles' that we begin the exploration of remote Cornwall beyond the railway, via omnibus, filmed coming over a little bridge towards the camera, followed by a shot of people wandering towards the camera in a picturesque village lane lined with thatched cottages. These images seem to capture both tourists and local people, as children gather outside open doors to gaze at the camera and the bus remains just visible in the bottom-left corner of the frame, marking the presence of sight-seers in a leafy hamlet with a pond, as well as the subtropical vegetation of palms and gunnera which indicates the climatic difference of the region. At 'The Manacles', a panning shot right reproduces the sight-seer's gaze from cows on the hillside and out to the sea and some of Cornwall's deadliest rocks, site of many shipwrecks. The presence of such an outsider sight-seer, atop the headland and gazing out towards the Manacles in a classic 'prospect view' (see Moseley 2009), underscores Gunning's sense that the 'view' aesthetic of early actualities also mimics the act of looking (1997). GWR's new bus service to Lizard is clearly promoted in 'Scenes at the Lizard'; parked before a serpentine workshop where the local stone is worked into headstones, vases, bowls (and, more latterly, barometers, clocks and miniature lighthouses for tourist souvenirs), the driver is seen encouraging people to board. Pictured from the side, no doubt to best display the GWR lettering, some passengers wait already seated and others embark, while a liveried driver leans against the bonnet. As we see the bus depart, local children run after it and, alongside local men and a pony, two men on motorbikes race up the street and past the camera; the bus brings the tourists, real and cinematic, to Lizard Point, where a shot of crashing waves and the fishermen's shed in the cove is followed by a pan left and up to show the lighthouse up on the clifftop. While Cornwall is pictured here as remote, rural and potentially dangerous, with rough seas and treacherous rocks, the tourist is reassured that modern forms of transportation, not least the civilized service offered by GWR, have arrived, and that the wilder parts of the region can already be safely explored in 1904.

Following these scenes, in a cut from a panning shot right and out to sea (but just before we lose sight of land, preserving the continuity of the journey along the coastal edge), the travelogue takes the viewer through Penzance to Land's End, to finish at the seaside town and artist colony of St Ives. In Penzance, the film tourist explores through a slow phantom ride from the front of a moving vehicle, travelling along the wide road beside the promenade between Penzance and Newlyn, with its hotels and seafront weather shelters. A bicycle, people with dogs, horse-drawn vehicles and a road sweeper cross before the camera as it moves forward; a panning shot around the inner harbour shows that this is a busy seaside town. We are treated, too, to a long shot of the romantic castle on St Michael's Mount, which more than fills the frame, then to a more distant shot of the island from Marazion beach, where men sit and skim stones at the water's edge, and then further evidence of Cornwall's persistent ancient rurality, a 'Cornish Cottage—1000 years old'. 'Scenes at Land's End. The last and first of everything in England' is not the final stop in this GWR journey around Cornwall, perhaps because it does not offer the picturesque, beachy fun of the film's finale in St Ives. Instead, reassured by a shot of the GWR bus in front of 'Land's End Hotel' that the company can take you safely to and from this most distant of tourist destinations, we are shown that our postcards and letters, even from this distant outpost of the nation, will reach those we left at home, by a shot of a stone postbox on the cliff edge at Land's End, unlocked and emptied by a postwoman, pictured sitting with her dog on the clifftop in the next shot, directly returning the camera's, and our, gaze, while she encourages the dog to approach it, and us. While Peterson argues that moments such as this, where the tourist gaze is returned by its object, are potentially subversive (2013: 145), I suggest that in this instance of exploration of a region positioned as an internal colony, it acts rather, or perhaps also, as a reassurance of the friendliness and familiarity of the locals who might be encountered on such an expedition. Peterson also notes:

> [i]t was a common strategy to show women engaged in outdoor pursuits in order to demonstrate how easy and enjoyable it was for all sightseers—even ladies—to engage in wilderness tourism. Thus, women can be seen as modernizing figures ... in early travelogues of the West (243).

It is notable that women tourists are powerfully present in early actualities of Cornwall, as well as in paintings, such as those of Dame Laura Knight (see Moseley 2013b), as I explore in Chapter 3. These instances of feminine presence at the regional periphery—with women often pictured perched precariously at a cliff edge, and here, in a modern, working role—certainly read as complex ciphers of modernity, in juxtaposition with images of tradition, rurality and myth.

The final shots of the Land's End visit contrast the image of a man, guidebook in hand, walking around a tiny whitewashed clifftop cottage to examine a plaque on its gable end, with a series of precipitous shots down to Atlantic waves crashing over rocks, a promontory and a rocky archway at Land's End, a number of immersive views of the 'Wreck of the "City of Cardiff"' and, finally, a shot of waves crashing on the rocks at the foot of a cliff, a springy grassy headland covered in sea thrift in the foreground. Again, this is an immersed shot, situating the viewer within the landscape, the slight pan up cutting away to 'St Ives' before we reach the horizon. This sequence of images is synechdochic of the film as a whole, and of the moving image construction of Cornwall in general, and begins to establish the regional audiovisual grammar explored throughout the book. Images which highlight the sublime extremity of the coastal Cornish landscape, which produce it as remote wilderness, are set side by side with picturesque shots (the ancient cottage, the village green) but also the civilized modernity of a modern bus and postal service which link this isolated regional outpost with the rest of the nation and with (urban) modernity. At the same time, a repeated attempt is made to position the viewer 'within' or 'inside' the view (Relph 1976), here in direct relation to the film's purpose as a tourist film of place, as the edge of the territory, accessible by GWR, is traced.

The final stop of *Scenes in the Cornish Riviera* is 'St Ives', introduced with a shot which pans right across the harbour, taking in the mass of fishing and pleasure boats, hundreds of masts, with stone cottages in the background. St Ives is presented as a picturesque site of local colour, the object of a colonizing gaze; dozens of children sit on a massive piece of boat machinery on the beach and play on a wrecked boat at the water's edge, returning the camera's curious look. 'The St Ives House of Commons' and 'The Quarter Deck' offer a fascinating, and revealing, conjunction of place-image: a shot of cottages and a narrow alley between them is taken from the beach, behind a lady artist who sits sketching on the sand, indicating both St Ives's status as an artists' colony and the modernizing, active presence of women. A pan right reveals her subject—a group of local men sitting and standing outside a building. A closer shot, from a different angle, shows them—fishermen, perhaps—sitting and smoking on a bench as younger men walk up and down and small boys play; this exemplifies Gunning's notion of the 'view' film's colonizing look at the inhabitants of, here, the de-industrialized tourist destination (2006). The final sequence emphasizes the liberated, beachy delights of a holiday in Cornwall: a shot of gulls at the water's edge, held so that we can watch the waves repeatedly come in and break on the beach, is followed by a side shot of a bathing machine being wheeled back up the beach, past ladies in deckchairs, to a row of other machines at the back of the beach. An intertitle-card, 'Enjoying the surf on the sandy beach', is followed by a series of long and then closer shots of two young women in bathing costumes, frolicking in the breakers with a dog, smiling into the camera and gasping as waves break over them and smiling direct to camera, the sun visible on their faces, their nipples clearly visible through their wet swimsuits. The final card mirrors the opening plate in design, but reasserts the point of the travelogue, declaring 'Cornish holidays are happy holidays. Go to Cornwall this year by G.W.R.'

Ruoff has argued that:

> [g]enerally speaking, the travelogue is an open form; essayistic, it often brings together scenes without regard for plot or narrative progression. During the hegemonic period of the studio system, the travelogue kept alive the loose narrative aspects of the picaresque in movies. Episodic narration offers an alternative to both the linear cause-and-effect structure of classical Hollywood cinema and the problem–solution approach of Griersonian documentary. The episodic narrative ... does not subordinate time and place to the regime of plot or story nor are its elements typically yoked to an argument. Description thrives (2006a: 11).[14]

In the case of the industrial travelogue film, for example those like *Scenes in the Cornish Riviera*, sponsored by GWR, the descriptive, episodic presentation of time and place may just be subordinated according to a different logic—that of the railway's path through the region, a logic by which some sites are highlighted and others entirely bypassed. Plotting a line between the picturesque holiday destinations accessible by rail, *Scenes in the Cornish Riviera*, in the first moving images of Cornwall, circumnavigates the region's interior territory, the sites of tin- and china-clay mining and of agriculture, to construct the region almost entirely as a peripheral, coastal place. While the journey is not consistently a linear, chronological tracing of the coastal periphery, the insistence on the return to the edge of the territory, for instance after zigzagging to Newquay on the north coast and returning to Falmouth via the briefest sojourn in the 'new' cathedral city of Truro, is a plotting that would become definitive of Cornish regionality. Here, then, we can observe the very beginnings of the making of the audiovisual place-myth of Cornwall, one that remains remarkably consistent to the present. This is formed in the inscription of an 'outsider' tourist view of place and the initial development of an audiovisual grammar of region: the juxtaposition of panning long shots of the coast, close-ups of waves, rocks and local faces, women perched at the edge of towering cliffs and picturesque shots of huddled fishing villages, an 'immersive' aesthetic. This would be elaborated through the travelogue, tourism and newsreel films of the following decades—and by screen drama, too.

Later railway films of Cornwall would elaborate and crystallize the place-myth established in *Scenes in the Cornish Riviera*, now with synchronized musical score and voice-over narration to reinforce their construction of place. Both *Cornwall—The Western Land* (1938) and *West Country Journey* (Sharples, 1953) articulate Cornwall, unsurprisingly, in relation to the lengthy journey by train. In *Cornwall—The Western Land* a steam train enters the first frame from right to left and departs from left to right in the final frame, producing a directional narrative of journey and return to and from the region on the Cornish Riviera Express. The opening images also take the viewer on a phantom train ride as the narration begins:

> Westward. Past the red cliffs of Devon to seek out Cornwall, the land where spring comes early. Where the farmer leaves his cattle out over night all winter. Where the botanist can find two hundred varieties of wild flower. To the land of cream and splits and pasties and saffron buns.

A long shot pans left from the sea and inwards, to a small town nestled in the cliffs, showing the Cornish Riviera train arriving alongside the beach, and materializing the tourist presence as the leisured classes arrive with their luggage and golf clubs. Already, here, Cornwall is articulated as significantly 'different', in climate, natural history and gastronomy, and this is confirmed in the voice-over narration, which continues:

> This is the corner of England that is hardly English at all. Washed on both sides by the Atlantic rollers, almost cut off from the mainland to the east by the River Tamar. To visit Cornwall for the first time is to visit a foreign country, a country of strange legend and tradition. Only two hundred years ago, the Cornish spoke their own Celtic language—the language of the ancient Britons.

Angled shots of 'foreign-looking' signposts (including 'Landewednack' on the Lizard peninsula), 'reminders of their bygone culture', are accompanied by a mournful oboe melody which signals this loss, and the association of the region with pastness. The continued presence of Cornwall's ancient history in the present is shown in a sequence of shots of stone circles, quoits, tombs and Celtic crosses as the region's internationally inflected cultural and spiritual identity is narrated in a detailed, voice-over account (Figure 2). The score changes to a rising and dramatic minor brass crescendo, which plays over shots of waves crashing on rocks, tiny fishing villages, coastguards and lifeboats as the narrator tells of fishing, shipwrecks and the danger of the Cornish coast. The score returns to a wandering, rising and falling woodwind melody as we visit coves, villages nestled in the cliffs, and fishing boats, while the narration presents the fishing industry as a non-profit, community endeavour. Cornwall's 'otherness', in this sequence, centres on its geographic, cultural and linguistic foreignness, a difference

Figure 2 Ancient, foreign Cornwall in *Cornwall—The Western Land* (Strand Film Company for GWR, 1938)

which is juxtaposed, visually and sonically, with its tourist appeal as a remote, peaceful, traditional region: the ideal site of leisure.

West Country Journey also begins with an evocation of Cornwall's difference, but this time that difference is constructed explicitly in relation to London and to Devon, both contrapuntal geographical nodes which have become central in the moving image definition of Cornwall as regional landscape. The film opens with a map that visually differentiates Cornwall (coloured yellow) from Devon (orange). Hubert Clifford's powerful score, suggestive of his experience as a composer for adventure films, makes a significant contribution to the construction of place-imagery in this film: rhythmic, rapidly bowed violins begin to conjure the train journey over this introductory image, and a bouncy, bright, brass melody is introduced which suggests dynamic movement onwards, and adventure, too. This title piece ends on a 'magical' harp flourish, and the high-horizon image of a brown, grey, dirty London fades up, attended by the sounds of traffic: smoking chimneys, rows and rows of closely crowded, identical buildings, interrupted by the occasional church spire or patch of faded green leaves, stretches as far as the eye can see. A slow pan left over this urban landscape begins, accompanied by voice-over narration: 'Summer on the sweltering streets. Dry crusts of stone, parching in the sun. Parched throats and hot pavements; sultry atmospheres and blistering tempers.' As the pan settles on the broad railway lines cutting diagonally across the image from top right to bottom left, washing hanging alongside them behind identical buildings in an image of repetition, dirt, drear, and overcrowding, the narration continues. 'There's only one answer: leave it.'

The stark contrast with this image of London is made in a cut to behind a family boarding a bright red train; the guard shuts the door behind them, and the narration continues in mimicry of a family discussion: 'Take a holiday! Where? Ooh, as far as possible—somewhere near Land's End ....' The next shot of the train clearly shows the lettering 'Cornish Riviera Express' across the top of the carriage as it starts to depart right out of frame. The voice-over continues, producing a verbal contrast with the previous monotonous and airless image of the city: 'where we can enjoy the sun, where we can cool our souls in the sea, get sand in our shoes and fresh air in our lungs'. A cut to a longer shot as the train starts to speed through the frame, like film through a projector gate, and away, is accompanied by the distinctive sound of the steam engine puffing. 'Somewhere like Devon or Cornwall. Let's try Devon.' A cut to a long shot of waves rolling onto rocks and a wide, sandy bay is accompanied by a shivering, dramatic violin piece which signals the change of location and produces a frisson in the contrasting mood. Devon is jolly brass melodies, amusements, buckets and spades, and diversity:

gently rolling landscapes, thatched cottages, agricultural bounty and 'savage, wild and untamed' moors. We see the train head inland, 'never far from the sea, but closer to the soil'. While there is mention of solitude, superstition and crooked tales, and while some of the imagery—of moorland, rocky tors, bent-over trees and screeching violin 'wind', hints at foreignness—is shared across the construction of both Devon and Cornwall in the film, the emphasis, in Devon, is gentle leisure and pleasure: cruises up the Dart, walks along the prom, bowls and retirement, in contrast to the wild, mysterious, resolutely coastal Cornwall it goes on to compose.

West Country Journey also takes the film tourist into Cornwall via the Cornish Riviera Express crossing Brunel's bridge over the Tamar and, from there, around the coast to a closing sunset at Land's End. A series of long shots of people playing in the surf and ambient sounds—of waves, shouts and gulls calling—increase in volume until we have an immersive auditory close-up which encourages the viewer to feel themselves present in the region, to have an almost visceral experience of being 'inside' place. Over shots of people sitting, and playing cricket, on a quiet, massive beach, where dramatic rock formations stand stark against a gigantic clear sky, the narrator tells us: 'You will find exhilaration in the surf that breaks and drags on the Atlantic shores. You will find the sun's magic on the shores of the West. If this was the only magic, if these were the only mysteries, they would be enough. But this is only the edge of the land, and this is only the fringe of the mystery.' As the narrator comments on the peripheral nature of these images, the film cuts to a shot of a woman and child wandering the beach towards us, beneath and between these massive formations. She takes the child's hand and begins to run with her after the others, out of the shot, and the narrator appears to comment directly on the image: 'Take your imagination by the hand … over the rocks and into the caves cut by the sea's tooth. There are other mysteries waiting for you.' The camera, and thus we, watch as a boy climbs through a rocky arch filling the screen, then tracks down, as he climbs, to capture his friends waiting below on the sand, watching them climb into a crevice in the rock which now fills the screen. This is a movement, repeated across screen Cornwall, that insistently brings us down and into the image, into the landscape, even into the geology of Cornwall, as a place of potential adventurous exploration. Here, a meandering, rising woodwind melody begins and this introduction to the region produces it as a place of mystery, adventure and exploration for all ages, a place-image which is articulated at the levels of oral and musical narration, camera movement, image composition and editing.

Following the theme of mystery and adventure, the film cuts to a shot down into a clear, colourful rock pool filled with green and red seaweeds as a 'magical' harp, brass and woodwind score accompanies the reading of a poem about the myth of King Arthur, in a hammy 'West Country' accent. Here, the brass in the score signals mystery with an insistent, staccato 6/8 phrase which ascends and crescendos dramatically on the fourth, dotted quaver, beat, dropping back again on the final quaver. A sequence of shots of ancient stone monuments across the region, from Men-an-Tol (where rickets might be cured), to Lanyon Quoit and the Merry Maidens (girls petrified for dancing on a Sunday), is followed by a pan left across Bodmin Moor, 'bleak with age', site of ghosts and sudden mists. 'This,' announces the narrator, on a shivering violin crescendo, 'is CORNWALL', and the film cuts to a long shot of St Michael's Mount, the music now less mysterious, and a little more romantic. 'And yet this too is Cornwall,' he continues, over a low-angle shot up at the castle, framed with bright red-hot pokers, followed by close-ups of semi-tropical flowers, yuccas and palm trees. 'The people here might well think themselves to be in Elysium, where there was no snow, no frost, no storm, no rain, but the cool west wind breathes there for ever.' This is gentle, romantic Cornwall, a key place-image both coexisting and contrasting with the previous articulation of drama, mystery and intrigue.

In the images which follow, Cornwall is art (a close-up of paints being mixed on a palette, an artist painting a jumble of cottage roofs), religion (place names recalling saints), foreign and feminine: 'she wears her houses with a foreign air, as if she had borrowed them from Brittany or Spain … then she puts music into the names of her fishing villages' as the names are read in accent. The film immerses the virtual tourist not just in the regional image, but also in its sounds, melodies, poetry and literature, textures, language and landscape. Fishing villages, boats and customs are shown in panning long shots and close-ups displaying the process of net-mending, and tanned, lined faces and hands. A woman paints the scene from the beach. Fishing is presented as a calling, a tradition, rather than an industry; over shots of boats on the beach of the tiny, picturesque village of Cadgwith, the narrator claims that 'the men of Cornwall find it hard to resist that call', a call to a skill 'handed down from father to son'. Fishing here is a tradition which is used not only to produce Cornwall as timeless and unchanging, but one which is linked to the mysterious and criminal activities of smuggling and wrecking: 'these men can tell of the days before their time, when the moonless nights were welcome too' says the narrator, and shots of painted pub signs, old men in front of stone cottages and the famous line from Kipling's 'A Smuggler's Song'—'brandy for the parson and baccy for the clerk'—link this place-image to its earlier construction in literature.

Cornwall in this film is both internationally connected, but also inward-looking:

> The men of Cornwall love their land, and are forever leaving it. In port, they scarcely stir as far as the next village, but they have sailed to the other side of the world and you will find corners in every Cornish harbour that are filled with figureheads, helms and pinnacles, the bones of old ships, the remnants of long voyages, adventure and memories.

The final narration presents such contradictory place-images in terms of the 'diversity' of the 'counties of the West', but it is precisely such contradictory imagery which produces an effect of stasis: outward-looking connectivity is counterbalanced by 'backward' rurality.[15] The film's final images are of waves crashing violently on rocks, accompanied by both ambient sound and an imitative brass sforzando. A solitary gull glides around the coast, attended by soaring brass and strings that build to a crescendo, and the film ends on a sunset image of the most peripheral rocks at Land's End, before returning to the opening map.

The earlier railway travelogue, *Cornwall—The Western Land*, is especially interesting for its brief but significant foray into Cornwall's inland territories, though even these moments are framed in relation to the region's coastal limen, which remains the focus of the film. The initial presentation of Cornwall as both foreign and reassuringly cosy is followed by two sequences which explore the region's mining heritage and here, on the verge of World War II, Cornwall's international industrial role is included in moving images focused on promoting the region as a tourist destination.[16] 'Most ancient of Cornwall's industries is tin,' announces the narrator, over shots of waves breaking onto rocks, accompanied by symbol crashes and the industrial sounds of mining. A rapid pan right from the sea to a ruined engine house on a remote, dramatic Penwith cliff continues up, up, up past more and more ruined mine buildings and along the clifftop skyline. In these images, we see the beginning of the romanticization of Cornwall's de-industrialized landscape which would reach its apotheosis in the phenomenal success of two different BBC adaptations of Winston Graham's *Poldark* novels, the first of which would be published eight years later at the end of the war. As the narration tells us that '[t]wo thousand years ago, Cornish men were trading in tin, and through the centuries they have handed down their tradition of mining skills', we see shots of the modern head-frame and miners emerging, as well as underground images, followed by further shots of waves crashing on the rocks: 'sometimes only a few feet of rock separates the miner from the sea above, and in heavy weather he can hear the thunder of the waves above his head'. While there is a nod to the (rapidly declining) contemporary mining industry of the region, the emphasis is on the dangerous proximity of the sea and the drama and romance of the ruined industrial remnants of mining at the clifftop periphery.

Given its later centrality in the place-image of Cornwall, the limited presence of mining in actualities of the region in the earlier period is worth consideration. Tin-mining, the region's key industry for thousands of years, was in significant decline in the twentieth century, but was the subject of a few educational, newsreel and cinemagazine films such as *Tinstone—How it is Obtained in a Cornish Mine* (1933). This film contains no shots of the mine buildings or the landscape and its imagery is darkly industrial, the frame crammed with metal, equipment and chains. Given the feminine address of *Eve's Film Review*, the film's comparison of the stamping machine to a domestic pestle and mortar is perhaps unsurprising. Similarly, in the later *Tin Mining* (1940–49), Cornwall is identified on a graphic map of world mining sites and the first shot is the industrial image of the pithead scaffolding. A pan down leads into an animated sequence in which the descent below ground is shown through superimposition and models, and the main part of the film details the mining process. *RSPCA Rescue* (1952) focuses on the danger of the post-industrial landscape through the rescue of a dog from one of Cornwall's two thousand abandoned mineshafts. *Cornish Tin Mining—Camborne* (1966) features no establishing landscape shots either, and focuses solely on the process and the local people who work the mine in mid- and close-up shots. The only exterior image is an extreme low-angle shot of the industrial metal pithead as the ore is hauled to the surface. These films do not even hint at the now-familiar romantic imagery of the ruined engine house and stack on the moorland clifftop. While the earliest extant newsreel on this subject, *Cornish Tin Mine Disaster* (1919), a 38 second, three-shot film taken after the Levant Mine collapse at St Just which killed many miners, does not initially appear to relate to the later ubiquitous *Poldark*-ization of Cornwall either, across its three shots—of the mining structure in the landscape (the head-frame rather than the engine house or stack which are yet to become iconic), the collapsed mineshaft and the final shot of miners looking on in distress—the construction of tin-mining as a potential source of tragedy and romanticization is evident.

Cornwall's other mining industry has been almost entirely absent from the region's place-myth. The 'Cornish Alps', as the distinctive conical white peaks, the by-product of mid-Cornwall's globally significant china-clay industry are known, and brilliant turquoise pools of the clay country would not represent a place-image of Cornwall save to the 'insider', although its otherness has made it a useful stand-in location for lunar or other 'space' landscapes in 1970s science-fiction films and television episodes (see Kent 2003: 116), as well as television car advertisements. *Pyramids of Cornwall—A West Carnclaze Study* (1929) demonstrates the process of extraction in great detail both visually and through intertitle-cards but, after an opening establishing shot, pays no attention to the clay landscape as 'view'. In contrast, *China Clay* (1964) opens with two sustained long shots of the 'Cornish Alps' against an intensely blue sky, followed by a slow pan across the landscape. The rest of the film is a classic process 'view', captured in mid- and close-up shots, including the export of the clay by ship from St Austell, in a return to the coast. The atypical opening of this film, in which the starkly spectacular landscape of the clay country is offered in a classic landscape 'view', stands out in this respect (Figure 3); it is only in very recent times that the clay country has been offered up as a spectacular landscape, in attempts to include the industry in the region's tourist landscape and economy through imagery highlighting its 'white beaches and turquoise sea', thus relating it back, once more, to the coast.[17] Where this essential part of Cornwall's historical, industrial interior landscape does appear, however, is in amateur film of the same period, as the final chapter of the book, 'A Different View', explores.

Unusually, then, in the history of moving images of the region, *Cornwall—The Western Land* moves next to a shot of the 'Cornish Alps'. The woodwind score here offers a slightly sinister, mysterious perspective on the images, and demonstrates the ways in which sonic cues can speak place-image just as strongly as visual ones, anticipating the later use of this landscape as 'alien' territory. While the narrator explains the use of china-clay in a surprising range of manufacturing processes, we see shots of slurry trucks being moved by miners in the quarry, with ambient, industrial sound. In Gunning's terms, this is a doubly powerful instance of the view aesthetic, where observation and display of both process and landscape are combined. The shift back to the coast is rapid though, as the narrator explains that 'china-clay is an industry unique to Cornwall, and so to the little ports of Fowey and Charlestown it has brought a new export trade'.

The rest of the film moves from regional custom in the toughness of Cornish wrestling, in which the male body is fragmented, spectacularized and regionalized in close-ups of face, half-naked torso and legs observed by the filmic tourist (stitched into the image through shots of local and tourist observers of this traditional sport) and back to the coast. *Cornwall—The Western Land* explicitly inscribes an outsider, tourist gaze throughout: we return to the region's edge with shots of a speedboat

Figure 3   The Cornish 'clay' landscape as view in *China Clay* (British Pathé, 1964)

bounding over the water, of tourist couples walking along a clifftop, and of the haymaking that goes on behind. The tourist's look is clearly inscribed within the shot and is made explicit to the viewer who shares it: we see the hikers look out at the landscape, then away from the camera before a cut to the haymaking which follows a shot–reverse shot logic. The score here is Celtic in feel, with Cornish bagpipes underpinning a woodwind melody which recalls the traditional Cornish folk tune 'The Furry Dance', a melody which subtly creeps into the score throughout the film. In these sequences, regional industry (mining, agriculture) has become the explicit object of the tourist's look, with the reassurance that these mundane, if picturesque, activities will not be the focus of a holiday here: 'Such is the Cornwall of the everyday. But come the summer, Cornwall and her people throw aside their daily routine to welcome a host of visitors.'

The film returns to the region's edge with pans from the sea and into villages and towns served by the railway, golf on coastal courses, yachting, and the allure of the beach. A group of girls walk down onto the beach at Newquay accompanied by gramophone jazz music, a shot of the beach and the sea ahead from their optical point of view is cut into the shot. This

Cornwall is the destination of the leisured classes of the 1930s, physical activity in the landscape tied clearly to health and pleasure, rather than industry (which remains the fleeting object of tourist curiosity). The film pursues this theme in a sequence of shots of family beach fun, swimming and body-boarding at the popular resort. A brass band 'seaside' tune becomes a more leisurely melody to accompany images of a couple sunbathing and cuddling, a close-up of women's backs, snoozing in deckchairs, seagulls taking off at the water edge and a pan right across a deserted sandy beach, up a cliff, and across the moor 'for those who like silence'. The film produces different Cornwalls for different kinds of visitor, but the film ends with an emphasis on the archaic, on a sense of loss, on the persistence of the ancient in the present, with an almost silhouette of a granite quoit and a mournful brass refrain which seems to anticipate the end of holiday, the fade to black and whistle of the retreating train.

While the question of how the visitor might access the more remote landmarks and moors which feature in *Cornwall—The Western Land* and *West Country Journey* remains unanswered, travelogues which appear around the growth of motor touring, and then in relation to the service from London to Cornwall by air, offer a less predetermined route around the region's edge, insisting just as firmly, however, upon its significance. Commenting on the different relationship to landscape afforded by travel by rail or car, Nead suggests that 'where the railway track presented the most direct route and was uninterested in the surrounding landscape, the road drew the motorist into a intimate and sensual relationship with the most ancient and picturesque parts of the country' (2007: 152). Ruoff formulates this in relation to film form, arguing that '[w]hile the train resembles classical Hollywood narration moving forward towards its fixed destination, the automobile stands for the episodic travelogue, where detour beckons just around the bend' (2006a: 7; 2006b: 229). While Ruoff is in danger of closing down the possibilities of the train travelogue as I have explored it, his argument does point to the looser (and significantly classed) access to place afforded by the motoring tour. Through travel by car, film of region is opened further to fantasy picturings of place that speak clearly of the more 'intimate and sensual' relationship to landscape noted by Nead.

Touring Cornwall by Car

The earliest moving image construction of Cornwall, a film sponsored by the developing railway industry, offered views of region in which local custom and tradition were pictured in their encounter with modernity in the form of train, motor omnibus, motorbike and tourist at a critical moment of conjunction between motorized travel and the moving image. The encounter of archaic Cornwall with modernity would resurface around the growth of travel by car and plane; Claude Friese-Greene's travelogues *Coves and Caves* (1920) and *The Open Road* (1925) have received virtually no critical attention outside of discussion of the latter's restoration by the BFI (Genaitay and Dixon 2010). Friese-Greene was the son of the early film pioneer William Friese-Greene and the inventor of the experimental and ultimately unsuccessful 'Natural Colour' film process.[18] The black-and-white *Coves and Caves* is presented as a motoring holiday home movie and was the fourth and final part of a film series, 'Beauty of Britain'. It could also be considered to be a precursor for the first part of *The Open Road*, an episodic journey in colour around Britain, designed to be shown weekly in theatres (Genaitay and Dixon 2010: 139). The episodic, serial construction of these travelogues is a clear antecedent of much later television landscape documentaries such as *Coast* (BBC, 2005–), *A Picture of Britain* (BBC, 2005) and others that use an episodic (and sometimes serial) format to divide the nation into (sometimes geographically contiguous and directional) regional sections for consumption by the armchair tourist for whom television still functions as 'window on the world' (Spigel 1988).

Coves and Caves is a short film constructed of brief portraits of selected tourist sites and activities around Cornwall, narrated by intertitle-cards. The places visited by the filmmaker and his female companion do not indicate the orderly progression of the journey by rail presented in the films previously discussed, but are suggestive, instead, of the more leisurely meander of the motor tour, stopping, between spectacular coastal views, at picturesque inland beauty spots less accessible without a car, such as the 'English' stately home Prideaux Place and a variety of village locations, including scenes of the fifteenth-century bridge over the Camel at Wadebridge and ancient Celtic crosses, presented in vignettes. A vignette is also used in a pan around the cottages and boats of Padstow harbour. The scenes in North Cornwall's Allan Valley are especially notable for their focus on movement in the image for the sake of movement: the movement of a water wheel attracts the gaze of, and mesmerizes, a baby. A woman with long loose hair walks along a woodland riverbank towards the camera, her hat in hand, while the shot displays the movement of dappling sunlight, leaves and water (Willemen 1994). These rather outmoded cinematic concerns have the effect of archaicizing the region, fixing it in the past as view (as does the use of iris in and out in *The Open Road*; see Peterson 2013: 143), and are a notable feature, too, of newsreels of Cornwall in this period.

The film's first shots, at Porth beach on the North Cornwall coast, present a familiar place-image of dramatic coastline rock formations, combined with holiday fun; 'Shrimping in the Cathedral cavern' presents a view of the beach through a cave to a silhouetted figure with fishing net, his trousers rolled up. An intertitle-card tells us that 'The limpid waters of the pool show anemones and weed at the bottom of the pool' and is followed by a shot into and across a rock pool, with something being thrown to splash into it and show movement in the image as a focus (Peterson 2013: 7) as concentric circles spread across the surface. The images in *Coves and Caves* are profoundly immersive, mimicking the tourist's gaze into pools, through caves and between rocks, and positioning the skyline high in the frame, if it is present at all, to position the viewer firmly with the landscape. In the scene titled '"The Banqueting Hall" One of Porth's many fine caves. It is 200 feet high and 60 feet wide', we watch a modern woman gingerly enter the cave, disappearing and then, by the clever use of a cross-fade, emerging ghostlike, only to disappear into another, apparently in the same shot. 'There is a second entrance from the sea. The dark space between the two is where you hold hands' explains the following intertitle-card, and such cinematic trickery functions, again, to align the modern female tourist with Cornwall's place-image of mystery and romance. In many ways, the most interesting and significant shot of the film is preceded by an intertitle-card inviting us to enjoy a visual prank created by the camera's potential for movement: 'There are many legends about mermaids in Cornwall. At first, we thought this was the reflection of one. Sold Again.' The accompanying shot shows a mermaid's reflection in a perfectly still rock pool—we can see its sandy bottom and seaweed clearly. The camera pans very, very slowly upwards to show a young woman with long hair and loose, flowing clothing, her hat abandoned beside her, sitting on the rock. Peterson (2006: 80) notes the way that while early travelogues of the American West 'do indeed represent the West as an Edenic garden ... they also upset the myth of the West as an uncivilized wilderness by depicting a region traversed by trains and peopled by tourists', a depiction through which 'the region was made to support contradictory myths in which the frontier co-existed with modernity' (81).

Not only does this moment in *Coves and Caves* explicitly inscribe the modern female tourist of Cornwall into the view, then, it also collapses her with the ultimate mythical and ethereal Cornish femininity, the mermaid. Peterson goes on to point out that while travelogues 'enunciate in the present tense ... [t]hey are also very much about the past, about a nostalgia for a mythologised past' (84) and this moment, along with the use of vignettes, makes the same point with lyrical efficiency. While, as we shall see, there are a number of points of connection to be drawn between constructions of Cornwall and the American West (and indeed, this is a link which was made explicitly in a cinemagazine item for *Eve's Film*

Review 652 in 1933, with *Britain's Wild West*), the conjunction of mythical and modern femininity in Friese-Greene's mermaid-tourist is combined with an 'in camera' visual gag in a way which clearly articulates the encounter between ideas of region as archaic with the modernity of motor travel and the moving image, coming down quite securely, in the fixing of the female tourist as picturesque mythical mermaid, in the past.

Away to the West! (1926) is illustrative of the early travelogue's tendency to produce Cornwall as an antiquated land of tradition, myth and mystery, and, further, clearly displays the emerging elements of a film grammar of region which would become definitive as they developed through the newsreel and into later films and television programmes. Part of another travelogue film series, Harry B. Parkinson's 'Wonderful Britain', it takes the film tourist through Devon and into Cornwall. The opening titles present an expressionist-styled painting of a dramatic rocky coastline, with gulls, which leads into a series of vignetted dissolving views of the picturesque Devonshire village of Clovelly. In a just a few shots a clear place-myth of the British 'South West' is communicated: this is a landscape of romance and emotion, one inspiring art and self-expression. The vignetted images are significant in constructing 'the West', from the opening, as a region of tradition and stasis, captured and preserved in an outmoded style of composition and framing which clearly marks the image as 'past', despite its clear signalling as a travelogue in the present (by, for example, the clothing of the people pictured within it). Irises (as in *Britain's Wild West*) and vignettes continue to appear in newsreels and cinemagazines, as well as in travelogues of Cornwall, quite late on and into the sound period, contributing to the production of the region as caught in the past. These devices, in conjunction with the archetypal, rapid, punning, received pronunciation narration of the newsreel and cinemagazine also underscored the region's conceptualization as an internal colony.

Away to the West! juxtaposes the silhouetted image of a glamorously attired woman looking out to the sunset on a clifftop, two men seated at her feet, with precipitous views from clifftops down to harbours and waves crashing on rocks (again, mimicking the tourist's peering look over the edge). Shots of Newquay's much-photographed and precariously located 'House in the Sea' follow scenes of a fancy dress parade, which include close-ups of locals dressed up as the Elephant Man, and as grass-skirted natives. A pan across a gull-filled Cornish harbour, and the intertitle 'For men must work ...', alludes to the link between Cornwall and artistic production, referencing both Kingsley's poem and Walter Langley's painting named after it to associate Cornwall with shipwrecks and tragedy. Scenes of fishermen working on their boats, mending nets and sorting the catch are intercut twice with dizzying shots down a cliff to waves crashing on rocks, shots which are repeated, in alternation with an image of a silhouetted figure on a cliff edge, before the final frame. A hand-written scroll with drawings of goblins and other magical creatures proclaiming the famous Cornish Litany, 'From ghoulies and ghosties and long-leggety beasties, and other things that go bump in the night, good Lord deliver us', ends the film, its final frame written 'Finis'. *Away to the West!* suggests Cornwall as a culturally distinctive, romantic tourist destination of traditional industries, quaint villages and customs, and dramatic landscapes, a place both mysterious and distant.

The later *By Cornish Coasts* (1934), narrated in the authoritarian but reassuring tones of C. E. Hodges ("Uncle Peter" of the BBC and London Evening News') has a direct tourist address and constructs Cornwall similarly as a picturesque, coastal, if foreign, place of mysticism and antiquity. Cornwall here is 'almost a land apart from the rest of Britain. It's a strange, lovely and mysterious land' peopled by 'a sturdy race of fisherfolk: simple, hard-working and lovable'. The construction of the Cornish as colonized, indigenous people here, is accompanied by a piano and violin score with a romantic, gypsy timbre and rhythm. Despite the inclusion of images of Cornwall's interior, viaducts, villages, clay mining, magic wells and prehistoric monuments, 'You never really get far from the coast in Cornwall,' reflects Uncle Peter, 'and you never want to', once again effectively reducing the region to the coastal periphery upon which its place-myth is predicated.

Friese-Greene's travelogue *The Open Road* is, as the title suggests, much more directly about travel by car than *Coves and Caves* and is perhaps most useful for the way in which it makes visible the explicit moving image construction of Cornwall as coastal and peripheral, in contrast to the other regions journeyed through. The film begins at the tourist spot designated as the last point of England, Land's End, journeying around Britain and ending, significantly, in 'a final setting [that] breathes the romance of London into every corner of the Empire' and spends by far the longest stay of the film here, constructing a resolutely 'tourist' London (Brunsdon 2007b). In this way, it situates the country's most far-flung region quite clearly as internal colony. The opening of the film pictures the car driving towards the camera and away from the sunset at Land's End and from there takes the audience to Lamorna, St Michael's Mount and St Ives before journeying to Devon, which appears here, as in *West Country Journey*, as more rural than coastal.

The scene at Lamorna is particularly fascinating for its presentation in relation to its identity as an artists' colony and thus as a key site through which Cornwall had already, by 1925, been represented in visual culture by painters such as Laura Knight and Lamorna Birch. Our 'view' of it is framed by a shot of the latter, pictured painting the scene in oils *en plein air*. The 'view' he paints, however, is quite evidently not the one before him, that we are shown in a repeated camera pan from the canvas to the right and out towards the sea, in a happy accident of set-up which functions on a meta level to draw attention to the lack of continuity between representation and the real. This is reinforced when viewed alongside *The Lost World of Friese-Greene* (BBC, 2006), a television documentary about *The Open Road* that retraced the original journey, juxtaposing clips from the film with contemporary travelogue footage. The first episode, 'Land's End to Weston-Super-Mare', presents opening shots from *The Open Road*, ending with the shot of Birch and the pan right, but dissolving to a present-day coastal shot of Land's End. The dissolve appears to complete the 1925 pan and thus neatly aligns the two time frames of 1925 and 2006; this is consolidated as presenter Dan Cruickshank gets into a vintage car and sets off, as does *The Open Road*, from Land's End, with the intention of tracing the people filmed or their descendants and to show 'how it hasn't changed'. Cruickshank follows the film's route and begins at Lamorna, where he drives the period car along the harbour and past the camera; a shot of the cove with a red boat in the foreground and tourists on the beach, accompanied by romantic violin music, is then followed with cut-in footage from the 1925 film: an iconic image of a woman with a *japonais* parasol on the rocks above turquoise water, a child sailing a toy boat, and red-headed children. These images, while they feature the reds and greens that dominate *The Open Road* (which Cruickshank tells us were deliberately sought out to show off Friese-Greene's Nature Colour process), are in fact taken from *The Open Road*'s trip through Devon. These nostalgic images of idyllic coastal Cornish holidays past are not even of Cornwall, but they are an aesthetic and atmospheric match for the Cornwall past and present which the documentary constructs. This innocent error is revealing of the chaotic, composite, 'outsider' moving construction of place, typical, as we shall see in the next chapter, of moving image romantic fictions of Cornwall, potentially troubling to insider experiences of place.

Cornwall by Air

Friese-Greene filmed from the air as well as while touring by car, and the shot of 'Trevose Head from an aeroplane' in *Coves and Caves*, taken from a plane flying low and northward along the coast, elaborates the still or panning shot from land but also anticipates the swooping aerial shots characteristic of the television dramas and landscape documentaries examined in Chapters 3 and 4. His *Across England in an Aeroplane* (1919–20) offered a view of the South West from 'Far above the world, in a region where there are no landlords, no profiteers and no politicians', and presented it as a place both innocent and lawless as it raced the Cornish Riviera Express ('doing her best') from the air. Plane travel could supersede both rail and road, this short film suggested, and the trope of 'Cornwall by air' would become, and remain, a significant one in the region's audio-visual grammar, marking, for example, the region's distance from the metropolitan centre of the nation in the opening of the fictional series *Doc Martin* and operating quite differently in documentary television. Newsreel films of the early 1960s publicized new services to and from the airports at Newquay and Land's End,[19] and Pathé's *Land's End Airport* (1962) (catalogued by Pathé, significantly, as both 'travel and exploration' and 'science and technology'), explicitly positions the most south-westerly airport in relation to its distance from London, beginning with footage of one of the capital's busy airports and the latest aircraft before offering the contrast of Land's End: 'Far from the crowded air above London, busy with air traffic, is a tiny airport called St Just at Land's End', a terminal where the place name is painted on the roof. The announcer acknowledges the need for the latest technology, but adds that 'here they have simpler methods to tell the pilots where to land' and that:

> all the tedious formalities of air travel seem to disappear here … no half-heard loudspeaker announcements worry the passengers that they might be left behind. St Just enjoys the personal touch: an airport employee beckons the passengers and they walk the few yards to the aircraft.

While the film is ostensibly about the modern facilities of St Just at Land's End, which boasts three planes and six thousand flights per year to the Isles of Scilly, the emphasis is on the old-fashioned planes which date from the 1930s, which offer 'some real flying' en route to the even further-flung islands, as we enjoy 'fly by the seat of your pants' aerial shots of the turquoise sea from the window.

Scilly Isles (1963) is a travelogue newsreel film, also catalogued as 'science and technology' (alongside 'sport and leisure' and 'travel and exploration'). Framed by the journey to a 'palm-decked archipelago that has kidded itself it's in a tropic clime', the film displays the turquoise waters surrounding the islands and makes much of the bright, saturated hues of the sky and flora throughout. While the islands are 'kidding' themselves about their

Figure 4   'Foreign' Cornwall in *Scilly Isles* (British Pathé, 1963)

foreignness, at the same time the film makes much of their distance and difference from the mainland, by contrast to which 'it's always pulsating Spring'. 'England is twenty miles and almost twenty centuries away ... unless you happen to see some ocean liner on the horizon, you can forget that this Old World coast faces the main shipping lines to America and the New World'; here, as in *Land's End Airport*, the association of Cornwall with outward-facing modernity is quickly recuperated in relation to its static antiquity. While Peterson observed, of early actualities of the American West, that 'this dialectic, in which a mythical wilderness meets dynamic modernity, worked to promote the West as a region that simultaneously signified the past and the present, a destination for both tourism and settlement' (2013: 237–38), the containment of Cornwall's role in relation to modernity can be understood in relation to its position as de- rather than unindustrialized and the impetus to shift into and maintain a tourist economy. On Tresco, where there are no cars allowed, the narrator comments that 'You'd expect a notice like this', over a shot of a sign in a window, framed by native daffodils, which reads 'English spoken here' (Figure 4).

A pan from beach to beach across the isthmus of Hugh Town on St Mary's settles on a tourist gazing, like us, at the view. This pattern, which inscribes the viewer as virtual tourist, is repeated throughout the film as it visits the different islands. The Isles are painted as a site of leisure, even for those who live and work there; over shots of bearded fishermen working on boats and builders repairing the outside of houses we are told that there is '[n]othing to do but paint the holiday boats and get ready for those visitors, who know what an "away from it" holiday can mean'. The single industry consistently associated with Cornwall, and with the Isles of Scilly in particular, is horticulture and, in particular, the early production of daffodils and narcissi, linked to the region's 'foreign' climate. The picturing of this process is such a consistent feature of early 'view' films of Cornwall, that it could be described as a genre of region: the flower film.

The 'flower' film emerges as a narrative of Cornwall, popping up in cinemagazine travelogues such as *Scilly Isles* as well as in amateur film. In *Flower Harvest—in Cornwall* (*Eve's Film Review* 308, 1927) and *Daffodils* (*Eve's Film Review* 355, 1928) we see the establishment of the paradigmatic narrative and images evident in greater elaboration in later examples, such as *Eve Helps the Flower Harvest* (*Eve's Film Review* 568, 1932) and *Flowers* (1937). The visual rhetoric is set in these early films: the viewer is taken to the Isles to follow the journey of daffodils and narcissi to the mainland as women young and old (but typically young and pretty) are pictured gathering the flowers in windy fields, trimming, bunching and packing them in sheds and greenhouses, ready to send them via boat to Penzance and GWR to Covent Garden's flower market. Despite the undeniably spectacular location, there is an absence of spectacular views of place in the earliest of these films, which are not tourist-focused, the 'view' instead focused exclusively on the harvest process and the role of women as workers for the audience of *Eve's Film Review*. *Eve Helps the Flower Harvest*, for instance, begins with a vignetted image of a daffodil field, and continues to use this device to frame picturesque images of women picking and carrying baskets of flowers across the rural island landscape (see Figure 5). The landscape 'view' is evidently linked to a specific tourist address.

Gunning notes of the 'process' version of the early 'view' film (clearly continued in the later newsreels and cinemagazines), that it is here that the view film moves most clearly towards narrative form:

> While rooted still in a descriptive approach, recurring narrative patterns are evident in many of these films. The most fully developed narrative pattern is the transformation of raw material into consumable goods.

Figure 5   Ancient Cornwall: the vignetted view in
Eve Helps the Flower Harvest (British Pathé, 1932)

In many of these films the narrative process moves from opening scenes of raw material through the various stages of production to culminate in a scene of delighted consumption ... within a comfortable or even glamorous bourgeois interior (1997: 17).

As an intertitle-card in the 1927 film tells us at just such a moment, 'flowers light up Eve's eyes'. The flower film, as a genre of Cornwall, articulates a political moving image grammar of internal colonization, in which the labour of the peripheral colony is presented as picturesque 'view' and its products are brought to the centre for its pleasure and profit.[20]

The flower genre is included in miniature in *Scilly Isles*, bringing a significant and spectacular splash of saturated yellow to the image. The mini flower film in this later travelogue follows the narrative and aesthetic of its newsreel and cinemagazine antecedents, following the flowers from their harvest by 'placid islanders', through packing and back to the mainland—here by plane, ending the film as it began, with a biplane 'from the springtime of aviation ... this is the only route in the whole of our modern world that still uses it, with an obstinate joy', once more producing Cornwall as ancient, stuck in the past and out of time. The viewer leaves the Isles, a 'paradise, where life has a different perspective and speed', to return to the 'modernity of the mainland', past a lighthouse perched on a remote rock (which the narration mistakenly identifies as the Lizard).

The late 1950s and early 1960s, through the (admittedly partial) lens of Pathé newsreels, was a period when Cornwall was pictured more generally in relation to modernity and technological advance, as well as in relation to ancient tradition and mysticism.[21] *Air Mail New Style* (1959) showed mail being delivered by planes from St Mawgan to HMS *Bermuda* in the Atlantic. *Tamar Bridge* (1962) showed the construction and use, for tourism and trade, of the new road bridge into Cornwall, described (in a typical confusion over Cornish geography produced by the desire to emphasize extreme peripherality) as 'not far from Land's End'. The bridge, the narrator tells us (with unintended irony), has 'put Cornwall well and truly back on the map for the family man who might have had second thoughts' about queuing for the ferry which the bridge has replaced.[22] In the same year, *TV from Space* documented the first transatlantic television signal, received via satellite at Goonhilly Down on the Lizard peninsula and broadcast via landline from Cornwall to London for broadcast on BBC and ITV: 'A few more Telstars in orbit,' the narrator suggests, 'and we could have all-round-the-clock world TV!' Cornwall's remoteness and peninsularity is, in this account, as well as in later documentary accounts of Marconi's contributions to global communication technologies, related to its role in modernity.

Westward Ho! (Rolfe, 1961), a colour travelogue 'spoken by Paul Rogers of the Old Vic Trust', offers a useful comparison between regional constructions of Devon and Cornwall, and in this film, sponsored by the British Travel Association, commercial travel by plane comes to Cornwall. The film is aimed squarely at the motoring tourist, and focuses on two couples as they explore these regions. The opening orchestral score hints at the Furry or 'Flora' Dance with the inclusion of a brief brass rendition of the melody, over shots of towering cliffs and crashing waves: this, clearly, is Cornwall, its dramatic place-image providing an irresistible opening for a film which deals with the wider 'west' of Britain. The journey begins with gentler music and gull cries as a middle-aged couple alight from a yacht in a peaceful, picturesque Devonshire harbour and climb into their Wolseley 6/110—a new, luxury, high-speed car—and the narration begins:

> Carefree days ... and that might so easily be you, landing in this sunny little harbour. If you like easy-going peace, where unchanging villages

provide a bewitching meeting place for unchanging countryside and an adventurous sea; but where in the world can this be?

Intercut with their journey, a young couple tour Cornwall. A glamorous young woman dressed in red descends from a small plane with the help of a smartly uniformed pilot, followed by a young man with weekend bags: 'And this could be you,' continues the narrator, 'if you like to be up and doing, filling every moment of an exciting holiday with sun-drenched memories. But where are we?' A new red Mini, a key symbol of early 1960s youth, urban modernity and technological innovation, waits for them outside the white airport building; they jump in and roar away, as violins in the score play 'The Furry Dance' to signal Cornwall, off across a wind-whipped, heather-covered moorland clifftop and away down a lane to explore the remote West Penwith coast. Presumably, this chic modern couple have arrived from one of the cities newly served by the service to Land's End Airport: 'It could only be one, unforgettable part of the world,' says the narrator. 'Follow that car, and find out. Follow it westward ... westward ... westward. Westward, until you come to—' Here there is a dissolve to a shot of the clifftop edge and a signpost which says 'Land's End': 'Land's End ... where that wilful sea rules the rocks.' Cornwall is resolutely and dramatically peripheral in this film, which focuses on the very edge of the region. The couple comes into shot, walking towards the cliff edge. 'Here, land and sea meet in true splendour.' A cut to the couple in medium shot, their backs to the sea, and the craggy rocks at Land's End visible behind them, shows them look up and to the side as the film cuts to a close-up of the iconic signpost. As gulls cry, the narrator continues, 'This is the westernmost tip of England, a thousand miles away from the north wind. Here King Arthur and his knights ruled their magic kingdom, now submerged, they say, among these crags.'

Cornwall, a destination for the adventurous, modern young tourist, is also a distant, archaic and mystical colonial land, one that 'belongs to you, this fabulous kingdom of ships and seagulls and quaint villages'. In the fishing village of Mousehole, shown first in a high-angle shot emphasizing its location nestled in a cove, the Mini drives around the curve of the harbour towards the camera, which pans to follow it in what will become a defining descriptive gesture within the regional grammar, emphasizing it as an edge. Mousehole is explored to the accompaniment of an accordion sea shanty and the narrator's incantation of the names of 'picture-book places ... names that read like fairy whistle-stops: Tintagel, Marazion, Polperro, Nampara, Lamorna, Lostwithiel'. Mousehole is fishing and art, but the focus is explicitly on the tourist's opportunities for consumption and pleasure, not the labour that provides them. Close-up shots of a fisherman working with his lobster pots for the camera, of the harbour sea gate mechanism, of boats and gear, are shown as the narrator continues, 'Time has stood still through sunny centuries here, where the sea yields such fresh succulence', as the fisherman takes a lobster from the pot and places it on the sand before the camera, which then frames the beast in close-up. The next sequence demonstrates the domestication and erasure of hard labour in travelogues of Cornwall. 'Watch out for those claws and you won't have a worry in the world!' proclaims the narrator, and a cut to a close-up of two lobsters is followed by a cut to one pink, cooked one on a bed of lettuce, perched on the harbour wall and pictured against the beach and fishing boats behind, dissolving to a close-up of meat being picked from the claw, then to a wider inside shot of a harbour restaurant where the couple eat and enjoy a glass of wine. 'Why is it that seafood tastes so delightfully different at the place where it was caught and brought ashore?' There is a pause in the narration as the man pours wine, as a romantic string waltz with hint of sea shanty plays, and we are encouraged to admire the views within and beyond. They clink glasses in cheers: 'Here's to the perfect holiday!' Cornwall's 'string of harbours pretty as a picture' are listed, as the film cuts to a shot of the harbour, then to an oil of a scene in the process of being painted, capturing Cornwall, literally, as a picture. The narration emphasizes the easy motoring access between picturesque coastal sites, 'all joined by 20 minute lengths of motor road. No wonder artists flock to Cornwall,' as a finger traces over a map and taps the next spot to be visited.

In contrast to Devon, predominantly winding country lanes and horse-drawn carts, thatched roofs, glamorous hotels and a leisurely, relaxed pace, Cornwall is for the young, active and adventurous who sail, walk and waterski at the coast. Over a wide shot of the coast, the turquoise sea and rocky islands, the couple walk towards the edge and we look out at the view with them: 'It won't be long, though, before you're back on the cliffs, watching the sea.' As they walk along the cliff at Boscastle, romantic string music plays and the narrator tells us that '[a]ll round the coast, you see this land–sea love affair at different stages', tying the dramatic coastal landscape to romance, as well as to dramatic narrative and adventure. The latter aspect of Cornwall's place-myth is crystallized in the narrator's reading of Kipling's poem 'A Smuggler's Song', over mysterious music and an echoy whistle and shots of a rowing boat coming ashore in the mist and pub signs including 'Jamaica Inn', a direct reference to the literary construction of Cornwall. The young couple walks into a panoramic clifftop shot and stops to enjoy the view; here, the potential tourist is invited to imagine themselves into a view in which youthful modernity is pictured in its encounter with ancient, timeless, mythical Cornwall:

Now you read adventurous history into each little craft and harbour, behind each cluster of loveliness you see cutlass drama. And you smuggle a new feeling of excitement, a thrill of what once was, into your memories of these valleys of rocks that reach, jump, wind or drop, sheer, over the granite clifftop, down to that unpredictable, ever-changing sea.

The couples encounter each other on their journey home, the Mini pulling ahead of the Wolseley on a coastal road; the film ends as romantic music is replaced, in an echo of the opening, by an orchestral version of 'The Furry Dance' over a wide shot of the craggy Cornish coast, its granite tors and deep blue sea.

This film presents a classic construction of Cornwall's complex and contradictory place-myth, but is also a clear articulation of its regional screen grammar. In particular, the use of the panning sweep around the coastal edge is a descriptive movement reinforcing peripherality as a key aspect of place-myth. While this gesture is an affective and affectionate caress of place, in its reiteration across moving image forms it also becomes a restricting and eternalizing trope which places emphasis on the region's timelessness, stasis and lack of change. Similarly, the repetition of the proprietorial 'prospect' view performed and observed by the tourist (and their viewer avatar) links the moving image construction of place to traditions in landscape painting, literature and travel writing, and contributes to the production of Cornwall as internal colony (Hechter 1975). *Westward Ho!* pictures Cornwall, as Peterson observed of actualities of the American West, as wilderness in encounter with modernity: the liberated young couple, she bikini-clad and he bare-chested, in their new Mini—the model of contemporary design innovation. The Mini was an affordable new vehicle for the masses, small on the outside but spacious inside, its revolutionary 'wheel at each corner' design saving space and producing a vehicle which was as at home in the city as it was on a touring holiday. The costume changes modelled by the couple in *Westwood Ho!*, and the display of what could be accommodated within it, are a clear demonstration of this, and the image of the modern young couple on a motor touring holiday in Cornwall would have been read as both glamorous and achievable. The film promotes tourism in the region, but also modern British design and engineering in the form of the Wolseley (which was used as a high-speed police traffic car in this period as well as an executive saloon) and the Mini, both built in the English Midlands.

Travelogue Redux

Gallivant is an independent film which revives and interrogates the travelogue form, combining contemporary footage of a journey, often accelerated or otherwise manipulated, with interviews, archive footage and soundtrack from dissociated sources. The film is an affective personal account of the artist/filmmaker's journey around Britain's seaside with his elderly mother Gladys and young daughter, Eden (who has Joubert syndrome, making her less likely to survive into adulthood), by motor home. While the journey by camper van is culturally associated with the liberated wandering of the 1960s hippy (and has a particular connection with the journey to Cornwall in the form of the annual 'Run to the Sun' in which classic Volkswagens head to the popular surfing resort of Newquay), the use of the motor home in *Gallivant* recalls its connection with the leisurely and yet also urgent end-of-days journeys of the retiree. The film often disrupts coastal mythologies; Eden's perspective on and interpretation of place, at the centre of the narrative, encourages the viewer to denaturalize myths of place as, for instance, when she complains to the camera in sign language about being tired and hungry on a 'romantic' windswept clifftop. The film's collage style and acceleration suggests that time is travelling too fast, while insisting on the ongoing significance of the past in the present through the use of archive sound and image.

The juxtaposition of untethered sources with the present journey can sometimes make meanings in conflict with established place-image, as in the film's presentation of Cornwall. The journey through the region begins in the centre of the most southerly village—Lizard. Accelerated, desaturated film shows people spinning around the signpost on the village green; the wind howls and gulls cry in auditory close-up, as if heard down a phone line, while someone from another time and place sings 'A sailor went to sea, sea, sea'. Aesthetically, this sequence is reminiscent of a 1970s holiday home movie, but the disjunctive sound makes it an unsettling 'memory'. At the precarious and windswept Most Southerly Point, someone looks out through the pay telescope. As tourists discuss the detail they can see of a ship at sea, footage of a silent peepshow and vaguely pornographic postcards is intercut with accelerated contemporary film of waves crashing onto the rocks at the point. The inserted clips are disruptive here, highlighting the very different meanings, dependent on place-image, of the pay-to-look device at the British seaside: the saucy postcard tradition of the south-coast seaside resort, for example, is out of place within the maritime tradition of the Cornish coast. This film is part of a different audiovisual tradition from the films discussed in this chapter, a reflection on generation, memory, travel, Britishness and regionality that uses disjunction to comment productively on the construction of place-myth. Some time later, on Mumbles Pier in Wales, Gladys and Eden think they're still in Cornwall, and we are encouraged, through their confusion over their location, to think about the meaning of regional boundaries.

Cornwall's role in modern communications is included in a visit to Goonhilly Down; a science-fiction hum drones under archive footage and sound from the first transatlantic broadcast and we see the microphone boom and the sound man in shot, as sound and vision accelerate to a dizzying pace, but the film moves rapidly into a discourse on Cornwall's place-myth of mysticism and folklore which is both critical and personal. Time-lapse clouds roll in from the sea, seen from a high point at sunset; the word 'truth' stands out at the end of the stream of voices and sounds. Film of a wet cobweb on moorland heather is accompanied by narration from an old scientific film: 'Here, with the film speeded up, we see the leaves unfolding from the plants. They look especially beautiful with the sunlight shining through them like this.' The film moves from the scientific and botanical to the reflective here; the film cuts to a shot of a quoit with sun flares coming through its gaps, sea and coast visible behind. The film accelerates, as the sound man approaches and holds the boom over it, as if to capture the sounds of the ancients: someone says, 'There's a cave somewhere, where Arthur and his knights are supposed to be sleeping and waiting to return in a time of need'; a violin hums quietly and continuously.

While this sequence critiques the association of Cornwall with mysticism and folklore, this aspect of its place-image is also used affectively to underpin the filmmaker's personal reflection on the journey at this moment, as he comments, 'The travelling was working well as a mental distraction and a means of understanding. By the time we passed Land's End, I was struck by an incredible sense of loss and yearning. Then, in St Agnes, I was told of giants, and years gone by.' Land's End is not shown, in a move which comments, through omission, on its overuse in film, but we hear of it in the context of his feelings of loss, over the image of the quoit after the sun has gone behind a cloud and the sound man has gone. On the clifftop at Chapel Porth, local people perform the myth of Bolster the giant and St Agnes, with enormous puppets worked by rods. The performance is accompanied by pipes, but a sinister, low-pitched electronic hum is constantly audible too. As the sun sets over the sea, the giant bleeds out into the sea. While *Gallivant*'s sojourn in Cornwall operates critically in relation to regional place-myth, it also depends upon it in the production of a deeply affective personal account, an audiovisual memorial to the present but fragile connection of humans with each other, and also with place.

Films picturing Cornwall by train, car and air set the timbre, content and vocabulary for the moving image representations of the region to follow, gradually developing into a generically specific shorthand set of audio-visual cues signalling place. Early travelogues established a place-myth of Cornwall in which timeless archaicism, romance, drama, mystery and danger coalesced in the production of a regional landscape peripheral to the 'centre' of London. A syntax of panning and static long shots of the coast, picturesque medium shots of both landscape and architecture, and close-ups of local faces and processes, traced and reiterated the safety and reassurance of the railway route around the edge of the region. In this way, the potential chaos of the unmappable, incoherent interior is bypassed, in a jaunt from cosy coastal village to lively seaside resort. In the next chapter, we will see how this emergent grammar of place has been harnessed to create a picture of Cornwall as an affective location for dramatic narrative, where an aesthetic of immersion, emergent early in Cornwall's screen picturing, delivers a sense of 'empathetic insideness' for the film and television viewer.

3

Screen Fictions

While some very early fiction films were set in Cornwall, only one of which is extant, it is in the predominantly British films made during and immediately after World War II, and in television literary adaptations, that Cornwall has been most visible in popular culture.[1] From the Gainsborough melodrama *Love Story* (Arliss, 1944), through *Straw Dogs* (Peckinpah, 1971) to the recent BBC serializations of *Jamaica Inn* (2014) and *Poldark* (2015–), Cornwall has been pictured almost exclusively in terms of Romantic regionality, as the setting for emotionally affective stories of love, mystery or horror; often, the romantic and the mysterious, or even frightening, are combined. As Orange notes, 'ruins elucidate the close relationship between romance and horror' (2008: 89), and in the case of Cornwall the ruined mine building at the very edge of the cliff encapsulates this dual potentiality, along with the unknown and unknowable moorland interior. This chapter explores the romantic Cornwall of screen fictions, a picturing dependent for its affective, dramatic effect upon the sites of cliff, mine and moor, and upon strategies of distillation and immersion.

Dramatic screen fictions of Cornwall have always articulated a distilled and condensed version of the regional place-myth, one obstinately focused upon the coastal edge. *A Tragedy of the Cornish Coast* (Northcote, 1912), the earliest fiction film of Cornwall available to view, is emblematic in this respect and demonstrates that the region's place-myth was already secure at this early moment, filtered through the contemporary popularity of the chase film and the Western. An artist, Tom, arrives in a Cornish fishing village to paint and falls for a local girl, Lucy, with whose family he has secured lodging. This does not sit well with a local fisherman, Henry, whose eye she has also caught and he kidnaps the girl, helped by two friends. Lucy's father enlists the help of Tom, the coastguard and other sailors, and the film, which becomes a chase narrative from the village across the sea to a rocky beach, ends with her captive there while Henry shoots at the rescue party.[2] The film pits the outsider artist against dastardly, gun-wielding locals (visually suggestive of smugglers or pirates), and the young woman is aligned with the regional landscape as the object of his admiring and acquisitive gaze. The Cornish are othered and romanticized in exotic, gypsy-esque costumes, with knotted headscarves and bold prints, and the frame, when not displaying the rocky beach and the sea, is crammed with the iconography of 'fishing village Cornwall' which would have been familiar from Newlyn School works of art in this period: wooden boats, hand-crafted crab pots, and stone cottages. The film is shot on location from an angle that positions the horizon extremely high, or in off-screen space, producing a deeply immersed and involving viewing position within the landscape. By the end of the film, the visual and thematic parallels between Cornwall and the American West are evident as the shoot-out continues in a rocky landscape. This comparison, continuing across the history of the region's picturing in the moving image, loosely aligns the Cornish with Native Americans and the incomer/outsider with the pioneer/cowboy, and a post-colonial perspective puts a rather different slant on the rendering of the dangerous and dastardly fishermen of *A Tragedy of the Cornish Coast*. In one of the earliest screen fictions of Cornwall, then, the region is irrevocably associated with romance, danger, art and the colonial frontier, and already begins to emerge as a place inviting the gaze inward, as a potentially immersive, affective landscape.

A dramatically concentrated picturing of region is often achieved through composite construction: the editing together of iconic sites and sights of Cornwall to construct a condensed screen place, regardless of actual geographical relation. This is the syntactic strategy most completely expressive of an 'outsider' view of region; to the empathetic or existential insider viewer (Relph 1976), a fiction such as *Love Story*, in which Porthcurno, Botallack and St Ives are constructed, through editing, as within walking distance of each other (and the Scillies are visible!), the melding of Cadgwith and Prussia Coves in *Ladies in Lavender* (Dance, 2004), or of Prussia Cove, Holywell Bay and Gunwalloe in *Summer in February* (Menaul, 2013), produces an incoherent and impossible picture of region; as Kent argued of *Wycliffe* (ITV, 1994–98), for Cornish audiences 'the inherent geography of many of the episodes seemed illogical' (Kent 2003: 117).[3] In her work on the cinematic city, Brunsdon has remarked upon both the composite nature of screen places, and the radical disjunction which can occur between insider experiences of place on screen, and those of a more general audience, noting that:

> [t]o reduce cinema to mapping the real is to deny the imaginative potential of the medium—but sometimes, to ignore the place of the

real can seem perverse. Place in cinema is made through the editing together of different spaces which may or may not have any pro-filmic proximity, and which may or may not involve a coincidence between location and nominated setting. Just as it can be made in different ways, place in cinema can also be read in different ways (2007a: 222).

Nevertheless, producing an *impression* of immersion in place, of a view 'from the inside', has been a key strategy across the history of moving image dramas of Cornwall. Across this long history, there is a tendency towards a high or off-screen horizon produced by camera position and angle, which makes for a strong sense of positioning within the landscape, in juxtaposition with the distant observation of it which has been suggested by Laviolette (1999, 2003) as typical of painterly picturings of Cornwall, and typical of paintings of sublime landscapes in which the (usually male) explorer gazes on the landscape from an elevated pinnacle.[4] This is the classic prospect view or positioning in front of a landscape (see Labbe 1998, Moseley 2009) which, as Berger noted in relation to Gainsborough's 'Mr and Mrs Andrews' (1750) (1972: 106–08), speaks possession and colonizing power. Such immersive aesthetics, which are often sonic as well as visual, with the sounds of regional landscape such as wind, waves and gull cries audible in close-up, produce a quite differently affective, intimate relation to place from the sublime prospect view or the picturesque frame, one which operates as an ostensible approximation of the 'inside' view discussed in the final chapter of the book. The analysis here tries to remain attentive to these questions of immersion, connection and affect as they are articulated in relation to the historical specificity of Cornwall as a dramatic location.

Cornwall's Romantic Landscape: Identity and Desire

In exploring the history of travelogues of Cornwall, some key aspects of an audiovisual grammar of region emerged. The insistence on the edge, and the concomitant emptying out of the interior territory, have organized the potentially chaotic otherness of Cornwall into a safe and easily navigable periphery, accessible by train, car and foot, with the strange, industrial interior marked as unknown and unknowable. The journey around Cornwall indicated here is preceded by the insistence on the journey into Cornwall as a place both familiar and strange, a journey that almost hysterically reiterates Cornwall as periphery to the centre of London (and, more broadly, England) in a dynamic of power that repeatedly figures it as internal colony. Attached to, and constitutive of, this relation is 'tourist' gaze at the landscape and its people (Urry 2002), and an associated vocabulary (the panning long shot, the picturesque mid shot and the affective close-up [Kavka 2008]), grammar and genre (the move from panorama to close-up, from raw material to finished 'picture' or product in the view film) which articulate the relation of nation to internal colony. If these are the characteristic strategies articulating Cornwall in actualities of region, how might they be mobilized and developed in romantic dramas of place? I want to begin with a consideration of the relationship between the Cornish landscape on screen, and war.

Nation, Region and War

Cornwall has had a recurring affinity for wartime fictions both contemporary and retrospective: a majority of films and programmes set in the region have played out against the backdrop of, in particular, World War II. What might be at stake in the repeated return to Cornwall in times of national conflict? I have written previously about the coast as a liminal space, and about the particular ways in which the Cornish coast has functioned as an unstable and leaky periphery, a site open to invasion, connection and change (Moseley 2013b). As I, among others, have commented, Cornwall has long been experienced, constructed and represented as somewhere 'other'.[5] Cornwall is a peninsular coastal county, with a number of major estuaries and historically important trading towns and harbours such as Hayle, Falmouth and St Austell.[6] While its borders are almost entirely watery, permeable, the route into it by land is narrow and limited in terms of both road and rail. The county's peninsularity then, makes it almost, but also importantly not, an island, nearly separated from mainland England by the River Tamar, a physical boundary repeatedly invoked to suggest the importance of territory in arguments for Cornish separateness. Petrie has noted, of representations of Scotland, the significance of the literal and figurative idea of the island, remote, isolated and cut off from the mainland, for texts which offer both utopian and dystopian fantasies of place (2000: 35), and these ideas are certainly present in moving image imaginings of Cornwall, while its physical connection to England maintains the centre–periphery dynamic as a central trope. The Cornish coast operates as a site of conflict over identity precisely because it is uncomfortably connected to England physically, and yet imaginatively divorced from it and therefore inherently unstable. In contrast, the other Celtic peripheries are wholly separated from England by their nation status, even where they share a land border.

Cornwall operates repeatedly as a potential site of meeting and connection, as a place where one might be drawn in, developed or drowned;

the peninsular periphery is a place of both possibility and risk. The coastline is a place of potential confrontation with self, with others, with greater forces. Despite the conceptual transformation of the sea and its shores that Corbin (1995) traces, as understandings of the seaside as a space of health and recreation have developed, the instability, uncertainty and anxiety associated with it since antiquity have remained residually powerful, erupting in comedy, horror and dramas of identity. Thus Cornwall's edges perpetually hold the potential for travel and exchange to, from and with literally other, as yet unseen and unknown, places, just as its own identity, as a place in relation to mainland Britain, remains uncertain, even to this day. Its peculiar positioning has made it a particularly meaningful space for the audiovisual articulation of narratives of identity, both national and personal. Regional identity, in screen Cornwall, is articulated less directly, through landscape and an immersive, romantic aesthetic.

The perceived foreignness of Cornwall is used repeatedly in British film and television to signal, intensify and connect representations of personal and national crisis, often questioning the categories of identity (national, personal, sexual, social) which they bring to the fore. The nature of its coasts, suffused with indeterminacy and potential otherness, along with the suggestion of mystery and danger that almost always attend Cornish-set texts, has made them a peculiarly resonant audiovisual space for representations of this kind, and this is perhaps why wartime and post-war narratives have featured so heavily in its audiovisual history, from films I have discussed before, such as *Love Story* and *While I Live* (Harlow, 1948) (Moseley 2009, 2013b), to the retrospective and precariously nostalgic television adaptations of Cornish-set novels such as *The Camomile Lawn* (Channel 4, 1992) and *Coming Home* (ITV, 1998). At the same time, as a number of scholars of British cinema have noted, wider 'rural Britain' played an important propagandist role in wartime cinema and Cornwall often functions metonymically in this respect;[7] as Bhabha has commented, 'the Difference of space returns as the Sameness of time, turning Territory into tradition, turning the People into One. The liminal point of this ideological displacement is the turning of the differentiated spatial boundary, the "outside", into the unified temporal territory of Tradition' (1990: 300). Cornwall becomes one with the nation at this moment. At others, its place-myth enables it to function as an anxious space of resistance (see Gopinath 2008).

I have previously discussed the connection between Cornwall and Brittany (Moseley 2013b), a connection which becomes revelatory in consideration of the French film *Cornouaille* (Le Ny, 2012), set, shot in and named after a peninsular region of south-west Brittany, an ancient site of settlement and exchange with Cornwall. The film is about memory and selfhood, love, haunting and horror, and, in its thematic concerns and aesthetics of place (crashing waves, immersion, precarious cliff-edge compositions) closely echoes the grammar of region suggested in *Picturing Cornwall*. *Cornouaille* points to the significance of the conjunction of physical geography and place-myth in determining a consistent moving image grammar of place, one which can cut across the typically attended question of national identity. The same questions were at stake in the lightly propagandist British wartime film *Johnny Frenchman* (Frend, 1945), a film about the *entente cordiale* in which Mevagissey 'played' both Trevannick, Cornwall and Lanec, France. This slippage demonstrates the ways in which regionality and regional identities might unsettle national ones, as well as the affinity of Cornwall for dramas of identity in crisis. Any south-coast British setting might have functioned as the location for a tale of the kind told in *Johnny Frenchman*, but the particular choice of a Cornish fishing village and its Breton counterpart, despite the evident drive to emphasize commonality over difference between ancient rivals at a time of international and domestic crisis, works to bring the underlying instability of national identity to the fore. The audiovisual and narrative construction of clear affinities between Brittany and Cornwall highlights regional and cultural formations and identities as potentially disruptive of national borders, rivalries and allegiances (see Moseley 2013b).

Cornwall, Nation and Gender

While Cornwall's liminal position at the edge of the national has typically operated as a resonant setting for wartime dramas of identity, in the immediate wake of World War II Cornwall was folded securely within the national by Pathé. Its newsreel films of Cornwall in and after 1945 worked towards national unity at this critical juncture (or at least towards a sense of difference within unity, as in the Gainsborough feature *Millions Like Us* [Launder and Gilliat, 1943]), rather than highlighting the region's potential foreignness.[8] It is only at this moment in the history of Cornwall's representation that it has been figured securely as 'home' in the mainstream moving image.[9] In these films, Cornwall is mobilized to represent the rural England that was fought for and which, in victory, has been preserved for the future, while echoes of the region's role in national security cling to the vulnerable coastal edge into the post-war period. The dramatic potentialities of the Cornish coast are harnessed in these films, which retain the key aspects of place-myth: romance and danger. At the same time, the uncertainty that so often hovers at the Cornish periphery crystallizes in particular around anxieties over the role of women in the post-war world, a concern also echoed in romantic wartime dramas of Cornwall.

Pathé's *Coast Guards* (1945) highlighted Cornwall's vulnerable position during the war. Over a dramatic orchestral score, the narration moves from the lonely coast in wartime to the idea that 'nature herself is the enemy'. The focus is resolutely on the edge of the nation, with images of the cottage at the very edge of the cliff and the coastguard's patrol of the coastal path. The film is dramatically immersive, with high horizons, extreme low-angle shots of coastguards against the sky, and shots that mimic the peer over the precipitous cliff and down to the sea; this is a visual grammar in evidence around screen dramas of Cornwall such as *Summer in February*. In the final year of the war, *Coast Guards* connected up the role played by servicemen (*sic*) in protecting the nation at this vulnerable coastal location, with the dangerous, mysterious place-image of Cornwall in suggesting that the smuggling of olden days is still an issue today on 'this lonely stretch of the Cornish coast'. Immediately after the end of the conflict, *Fishing Village* (1946) reflected on the propagandist role that newsreels could play in bolstering the nation's awareness of what it was fighting for. The opening shot, of a comb-bound book cover with the title of the film inscribed upon it over an illustration of a fishing boat at sea (echoing the style of an educational pamphlet), is accompanied by a dramatic (but wistful) brass and woodwind score which immediately fixes and romanticizes the eponymous 'Fishing Village'. A rapid, male, received pronunciation voice-over draws attention to the potential myth-making role of the newsreel, alongside its educational impulse, by asking the viewer, 'How would you like the story told, in poetry or in facts? If you like poetry, then this is lovely Newlyn, nestling beneath the cliffs that dip their feet in rough Atlantic waters.' These words accompany a panning shot of Newlyn from the hill above it, out towards the sea, and then shots of fishermen walking along the harbour wall to show the 'safest harbour in the West Country'. Two key and inextricably linked place-images of Cornwall, industry and tourism, are conveyed here in a striking instance of a newsreel film signalling an awareness of its role in producing place through romantic rhetoric by asking the viewer, 'And these men's hands ... do you want to watch the poetry of their gnarled and nimble fingers, or do you want to know the name of the thread they use?'

The book or pamphlet cover was a stylistic device used in a number of newsreel and cinemagazine films of Cornwall in this post-war moment, for instance in *Mullion Cove* (1946), which pictured the romance of a soldier and a Waaf preparing to settle back into civilian life after the war. The film opens with a book cover featuring a map of Cornwall, the film's title and director's credit, with a compass and old-fashioned galleon included in the design. The film focuses on the heterosexual romance between those who served (and the family they will go on to form), entangling this with a regional landscape discourse about what they (and the audience) have fought for, what might have been lost and what is now, newly owned by the National Trust, 'yours'. In this military romance, Cornwall is both romantic landscape and national territory; the music is strongly reminiscent of Hubert Bath's 'Cornish Rhapsody' score for Gainsborough's earlier hit, *Love Story*, with woodwind, rather than the high-pitched piano trill used in the original 'Rhapsody', mimicking the sound of gull calls. The film operates simultaneously as romance, travelogue and post-war propaganda, as the couple explore the harbour and beach, and he helps her over the rough ground in a gesture suggestive of a return to more traditional, pre-war gender roles. They sit to watch the sea on the cliff above, encouraging us to do the same after they leave, in an explicit articulation of the tourist's look at the view. In travelogue mode, the narrator refers to the smuggling of olden days, as the film moves from a shot of the romantic, rocky coast and pans, cutting to a closer shot and then to swirling waves on rocks.

Sailor's Return (1946) also pictures Mullion and follows a Wren returning home to help her father with his lobster fishing business. The opening shots show her walking the cliffs at Mullion in uniform as the narrator recounts her four years of navy service before returning to 'that little corner of the West she knows and loves so well: lovely Mullion, in Cornwall'. She sits and reclines in the sun on the cliff, and looks down; we are given her point of view, in a shot of the sea swirling over the rocks. As the camera pans across the view, and over shots of the cliffs, the narrator proclaims, 'This is the spot Pat's been dreaming of for the last four years. Because down there in the cove, lies enchantment.' Typically, the labour of fishing is presented here as leisure, and pleasure: its representation is hobbyist. The string-led orchestral score recalls a sea shanty and an extreme low-angle shot dramatically pictures her against the sky as she walks along the edge of the thrift-covered cliffs, a gendered shot which, in the screen history of Cornwall, signals anxiety. A close-up of her, in uniform, cuts to a close-up of her in a headscarf as she works the small boat with her father at sea. They pull up lobster pots, the music gentler now, more pastoral and romantic in character but still in the style of a sea shanty, and the narrator comments that now she has 'a real job to do'. Through a series of extreme low-angle shots, Pat is pictured as powerful at the edge, as a brave, modern woman who has defended the nation, in a similar fashion to the male heroes of *Coast Guards* (Figure 6). As she descends into the cove, though,

Figure 6 Wartime woman at the edge of Cornwall in *Sailor's Return* (British Pathé, 1946)

she exchanges one uniform for another, the dutiful, rural daughter safely returned to her family and her 'proper' role.

The changing position of women after the war was also noted in a fascinating newsreel item *Goat Farm* (1949), which while catalogued as 'trade and industry' seems to have had more to say about gender and, potentially, sexuality in the post-war period. The film pictures 'a couple of enterprising ex-service gels', who have started a goat farm in Duloe. The film explains that their impetus was the lack of milk delivery in a such a remote location, but the film seems more interested, visually, in picturing the Baroness von Kuffer and 'ex-Wren Morgan', her companion at their lonely caravan, commenting that the move 'from driving an army truck in the war to managing a lonely 26 acre farm in peace isn't everyone's idea of a change for the better'. In this instance, the unknowable interior of the region is a site of equally unknowable female identities. Cornwall is a romantic periphery which offers liberating possibilities in relation to gender, sexuality and selfhood, possibilities which feed into wider anxieties about the post-war roles of women who had worked hard outside as well as within the home as part of the national war effort. The existence of some of these films probably owes something to the proximity of Mullion to RNAS Culdrose, which played a central role in Cornwall's contribution to national defence during World War II, but they also resonate powerfully with wartime films of Cornwall such as *Love Story* and other romantic fictions of region. In all of these newsreel and cinemagazine films, Cornwall is pictured as a part of, rather than separate and other from, the nation, in a project of national unity in the wartime and immediate post-war period, and yet within them the unsettling potential of the Cornish coast still lingers. In these moving images of Cornwall, in both senses of the word, the figure of the woman at the edge, and the edge of the edge, functions in complex and contradictory ways in relation to women's changing role in the post-war period, and the wider project of resettling the nation through discourses of heterosexual romance and family. Newsreels such as *Sailor's Return* seem to function as a kind of answer to the difficult questions raised in British film drama of the same period.

Women's Cinema of Cornwall

In two cycles of romantic dramas, wartime Cornwall has been the setting for fictions in which anxieties around gender, nation and sexuality float at the surface. In a group of women's films of the 1940s and early 1950s and period films and television dramas of the 1990s and 2000s, British female identities around both world wars are explicitly addressed through their location on the distant Cornish periphery. Harnessing (and reinforcing) key elements of an established regional place-myth, this setting facilitates a kind of risky escape from or dalliance with the social mores associated with the English centre, understood metaphorically as a set of mainstream values, but also more literally, in that these dramas always construct Cornwall in relation to a rather differently liberated London.[10] These fictions of troubling gendered national identity have received little critical attention, mentioned in passing, if at all, in both accounts of British wartime cinema (Durgnat 1970; Armes 1978; Barr 1986; Murphy 2009) and works which deal directly with Gainsborough Studios' extremely popular and successful romantic and fantasy films addressed to a female audience (Cook 1997; Harper 2000).[11] The discussion here develops existing writing on British wartime and heritage cinema, as well as work on landscape and the moving image, arguing that an attention to the specificity of place, as well as to newsreel film allows for a more nuanced historical and aesthetic understanding of the audio-visual construction of region in relation to the national. These women's films of Cornwall directly address female desire and the liberation from social expectation afforded by war work and delayed marriage; the later costume films and serials look back, anxiously, to the same moment.

Mermaids

The mermaid is perhaps the ultimate figure of unstable femininity at the Cornish edge, central to the ancient regional folk mythology in tales such as 'The Mermaid of Zennor'. As we saw in the previous chapter, she appears in screen Cornwall, blended with the modern woman, as early as 1920 in the travelogue *Coves and Caves*. Neither fully human nor fully fish, crossing both literal and metaphorical boundaries, she is a strange, hybrid figure who has embodied the anxiety attached to desiring/desirable women in different historical moments and her comic screen incarnation in the post-war period condenses the concerns which are visible in the other women's films of Cornwall discussed here.[12] In two Gainsborough films, *Miranda* (Annakin, 1948) and its sequel *Mad About Men* (Thomas, 1954), the mermaid operates as a fantastical device through which anxious relations of national centre and regional periphery were articulated through post-war discourses around gender and resettlement. Through the comedy of *Miranda*, the Cornish mermaid come ashore, the nation was gently reminded of the potential threat to the centre embodied by the distant regional space of the internal colony, in the process of being released from the wartime discourse of 'difference in unity'. The London doctor Paul Martin (Griffith Jones) takes a fishing holiday to Cornwall without his wife Clare (Googie Withers). In a delightful reversal, it is he who is discovered and fished for by mermaid Miranda Trewella (Glynis Johns), who uses her siren wiles to talk Paul into taking her back to London with him as his patient.

From the outset, Miranda's outlandish and openly desirous (heterosexual) femininity is made evident. Miranda adores men, especially tall men with long legs, and she makes her admiration loudly apparent. 'Look at that beautiful man!' she declares of a guard outside Buckingham Palace, and when the Martins' butler Charles (David Tomlinson) carries her, she drapes her arms around his neck, comments on his muscles and whispers, 'Doesn't that give you a funny feeling? Are we going to your bedroom now, Charles?' Miranda infuriates wives and fiancées and temporarily messes up relationships. She even enraptures elderly spinster Nurse Carey (Margaret Rutherford). Miranda the mermaid is the emblem of the wild Cornish periphery and its potential to unsettle the centre, a disruptiveness which carries a particular resonance in the immediate and later post-war period in relation to the disruption of social roles and mores brought about by war, especially those related to gender. Miranda is foreign and animalistic (she speaks sea lion!), single, sexual, duplicitous and blunt about her desires. She is mythical and magical, but also a force dangerous to restrained English manners, and the perceived sanctity of marriage, and Johns's performance of Miranda, with her unusually husky, breathy voice and innocent directness, is in this respect perfectly contrasted with the restrained chic urban femininity of Googie Withers's Clare. Miranda resists attempts to paint her as Venus (after Botticelli), refusing to be contained within a conventional picturing of desirable (and modest) femininity from the sea. Ultimately Miranda does not represent a lasting threat to nation and family; like Cornwall itself she is merely a temporary foreign fantasy, as signalled by the comedic tone of the film, and, when her holiday in London comes to an end, couples are reunited. In an interesting twist, though, and one which reverses the conventional colonial sexual narrative, the epilogue shows that Miranda has travelled to Majorca, where a baby conceived during her London holiday has been born. The real mystery of the film, as ever, that of female sexuality, the mermaid's tail/le, remains unanswered: which of the men is the father, and how, exactly, was the baby conceived? The Technicolor sequel *Mad About Men* took advantage of the spectacularly colourful possibilities of the Cornish coast, but its main concern was to replay the comedy of liberated female sexuality established by the earlier film by having Miranda (Glynis Johns) help her distant cousin, non-mermaid Caroline Trewella (also Johns), to replace her unsatisfactory fiancé (who is mean with money, unimaginative and unromantic) with a more suitable (rich, attractive) match.

Women Artists at the Edge

The figure of the Cornish mermaid is a mythical articulation of wider anxieties attached to women at its periphery. I have already explored the way in which screen Cornwall has focused insistently on the coastal edge, and have begun to suggest the affinity, both geographical and emotional, of the liminal periphery for dramas of identity (see Moseley 2009, 2013a, 2013b). In romantic dramas of Cornwall, the precipitous edge is repeatedly attached to women characters, and particularly to creative, artistic women whose identities are both troubled and troubling. In contrast, location at the edge of Cornwall typically pictures male characters in classically powerful, controlled and controlling 'prospect' positions in relation to the land and seascapes before them (as in publicity images for *Poldark* [2015–]).

An abiding sadness attends the unstable figure of the woman artist at the edge, a character who often struggles with her disconcerting status as both wielder and object of the gaze, a creative figure who, like Miranda, encounters repeated attempts by other characters to fix her as 'art'. These women's dramas of Cornwall articulate the uncomfortable position of the 'new' woman, one repeatedly figured as ill or dying at the edge. The woman at the Cornish clifftop is a profoundly intermedial figure that demonstrates the importance of recognizing the meaningful relationships between the visual arts and the moving image, as noted and called for in recent years (Hockenhull 2005; Harper 2010; Moseley 2013b). Indeed, this figure and her story emerge as a trope of the wider Cornish place-myth and as a key element of vocabulary in its audiovisual grammar, and might even be proposed as a genre of Cornwall, in the same way as the flower film discussed in Chapter 2. Looking back over generations of family snaps, the impulse to photograph the woman at the very edge or top of the Cornish cliff is remarkable, the challenge to capture her as close to the very edge as possible without disaster. This is true, no doubt, of holiday photography at all dramatic coastal sites, in relation to adventure and spectacular daring, but Cornwall has a particular relationship to a gendered iteration of this cultural formation in its visual cultural history, one which brings together the woman as artist, as art and as a figure through whom historically specific anxieties around gender and society have been articulated, picturing her in ways which are filled with both possibility and precariousness.

Laura Knight's Clifftop Girls

Perhaps the most significant point of intertextual reference for this figure is in the work of the painter Dame Laura Knight. The 2012 retrospective of her work at the Penlee House Gallery and Museum in Penzance was the first time that Knight's Cornish works (and others) had been brought together and shown in the same space.[13] The insistence of her imagery, in the latter years of World War I when she was working between London and her studio in Lamorna, is striking. In a series of works made between 1916 and 1919, Knight painted young women, practically clothed and in a modern, almost bohemian style of dress (Knowles 2012: 61–63). Knight's women are sometimes figured alone, sometimes in pairs, and are posed sitting or standing at the very edge of the Cornish cliffs, looking out or down, in profile or facing away from the observer.[14] This was a significant shift from her earlier post-Impressionist works in Cornwall, which had featured families and children captured in movement as in 'The Beach' (1908) or 'Flying a Kite' (1910), painted in the Cornish countryside above Newlyn. In her later 'clifftop' paintings, the horizon is either extremely high in the frame, or non-existent. In either case, the sense of the enormity and presence of the sea is extreme, with little sense of 'freedom' in the frame despite the outdoor, cliff-edge setting, looseness of brush-work and vibrant use of colour. The latter was another departure in these works, both from her earlier works in Cornwall and from works of Newlyn School painters such as Walter Langley and Stanhope Forbes, who captured the fishing community of that village in muted tones of, primarily, grey and brown.[15] Women at the edge of Cornwall also featured repeatedly in the works of the Newlyn painters but, unlike Knight's clifftop girls, they are firmly located in a traditionally feminized space and attitude: they wait, inside dimly lit cottages or at the harbour-side, for news of their men at the mercy of the sea.[16] Lamorna and its colony of painters (which, along with Laura and Harold Knight included Dod and Ernest Procter, Lamorna Birch and A. J. Munnings) is around the coast from, literally and metaphorically peripheral to and slightly distanced physically and temporally, from Newlyn. Knight's choice not to make use of the horizontality of a landscape frame for these paintings means that the sense of space the former may afford cannot be exploited here, lending an almost claustrophobic feel to the images, despite their subject matter. The starkness and simplicity of the positioning of the figures in the landscape contributes to the immobility of the compositions—these are figures in contemplation of the coastal view that stretches before them, or of a more interior landscape, filling the frame.

These are modern young women, and the subject matter makes one think, instantly, of the 'new woman' of this period of immense national anxiety in relation to the Great War but also in relation to wider social change, as Ysanne Holt has discussed, particularly in relation to Knight's earlier, *plein air* nudes and the perceived isolation and 'spiritual purity' of pre-war Cornwall (2003: 99), noting that the:

> widespread preoccupation with bodily health and wholeness that is so insistent a feature of this period resonates through the 'figure in the landscape', one of the key visual themes here. ... Similarly, anxieties about urban degeneracy and declining standards of health, both physical and moral, helped shape coastal pictures of women gazing wistfully out to sea—whether the figure be a Newlyn fishwife or one of Laura Knight's young models reclining on the cliff-tops (5).

Knight's later clifftop women, though, are more anxious, uncertain figures; the framing, staging and composition places them precariously close to the edge of the precipitous Cornish cliffs, positioned, like Lissa in *Love Story*, Olwen and Sally in *While I Live* and Florence in *Summer in February*, on the verge of something significant, contemplative and yet uneasy. As a result of the framing and composition of the paintings, these are figures fully immersed in the Cornish landscape, engulfed and enraptured by its affect. Hockenhull has commented that 'the figure looking out to sea is a recurring image in painting, which created an emotional symbolism which was not lost on a war-time audience familiar with the dangers [that] faced the men leaving the shores of the British Isles' (2005: 59). This is certainly the case, and of course the wartime setting of the texts I am concerned with also makes this reading available, but in Knight's work, and in the moving images which are in dialogue with it, I suggest that the dominant aesthetic affect is the sense of precariousness and uncertainty which awaits the modern young women who watch from within them. In the moving image, this sense of deep immersion in place is repeatedly produced by a particular mobilization of the audiovisual grammar of Cornwall that positions characters, and the viewer, securely in place. Our lack of access to the full facial expressions of Knight's women contributes to the pervasive feeling of anxiety; the images bespeak a culture troubled by changing ideas around young womanhood, freedom, sexual morality and tourism. Cornwall, as a site of difference, possibility, danger and freedom, and the cliff edge as a liminal space, is the perfect setting for them. Knight wrote eloquently about Cornwall in the second volume of her autobiography, demonstrating her sense of its geographical and cultural difference, its perceived strangeness and liminality and, indeed, its resonance in relation to the fragility of identity, to identity as somehow in transition:

> Cornwall is not like any other sort of country—it's no use trying to compare it with any other place. There are times when you think everything is quite ordinary; and there are times when you feel you are not properly you, but someone else whom you don't in the least know; and an atmosphere prevails which takes away any sense or belief you have ever had, and you don't know why, but you aren't in England any more (1965: 138–39).

Knight's thoughts on the place where she worked and painted her clifftop women are revealing. They are women on the verge, contemplative of the past, the future, of their very selves. They are, perhaps, modern sirens, Mirandas, perfectly liminal, poised at the boundary between land and sea, emblematic of the uncertainty associated with the coast and with identity, but rather more prosaic than overtly seductive in their loose, modern outdoor dress. These are twentieth-century female versions of the Rückenfigur associated with the nineteenth-century Romantic paintings of, for example, Caspar David Friedrich (1774–1840), perhaps most famously in his 'Wanderer above the Sea of Fog' (c.1818). As Melbye notes in his *Landscape Allegory in Cinema*:

the observing wanderer has his back to us, and so emphasis is diverted to the grand spectacle in front of him—a significant departure from anthropocentric landscapes of the past. This inclusion of a subject seen from behind ... was Friedrich's way of overtly establishing a human psychological association with the natural landscape. Again and again, he and other Romantic painters presented this form of contemplation as a spiritual alternative to churchgoing traditions (2010: 10).

Thinking about Knight's women as reworkings of this tradition, as modern female Rückenfiguren, opens up a productive interpretation of both these images and the later screen figures which echo their settings and composition as part of the wider Cornish place-myth. Knight's paintings of clifftop women certainly suggest the 'romantic' nature of the rugged and dramatic Cornish landscape. As a result of the specificity of their composition, staging and use of colour, however, they precisely do not divert attention to the 'grand spectacle' being observed, but rather focus attention on the women who look, and on the nature of their precarious relationship to the landscape. The women, as reiterations of the earlier Romantic Rückenfigur tradition, then, become allegorical figures, alluding to questions around modernity, liberation, travel and sexuality. Massey's work on the relations of space, place and gender are helpful here, particularly her sense that we must think in terms of 'space–time', of space as constructed out of social and historical relations (1994: 2). To understand the images of women at the edge in painting, film and television, then, we need to think about the particular conditions of production, temporality and historicity from which they speak. These images pose a threat to traditions of representation and relations to social space, and speak powerfully of a moment of transition in ways that carry across different socio-historical moments.

Knight's almost-narrative paintings of modern young women at the edge of the Cornish clifftop are, then, complex in the meanings they generate. As Holt notes, at the time of their production:

> [t]hese paintings were only really meaningful in terms of the receptions of a modern urban middle-class womanhood—a potential market for Knight's pictures in London galleries. Female spectators could imagine themselves inside the spaces of her paintings. They themselves might be the sturdy heroines posing heroically on the rocks, perilously perched at the point where culture meets nature, literally at the edges of the island. They might take up similar positions themselves on holiday visits to Cornwall and perhaps even find themselves decorating a postcard for sale to other tourists (2003: 19).

Here, she suggestively gestures to the afterlife of Knight's images in culture, their uptake in personal journeys of discovery, in souvenir production and, as I suggested earlier, in holiday photography. I propose that these images also have a resonant afterlife in British audiovisual culture, in screen fictions of Cornwall around the two world wars. Previously, I have discussed the use of this figure in television adaptations of *Coming Home* (where the original novel makes specific reference to Knight's work) and *The Camomile Lawn*, serial dramas set around World War II which focus on the sexual awakening of young women at a moment of profound change (Moseley 2013b) and which use the figure of the young woman at the Cornish clifftop as a cipher through which anxieties around gender and social change might be articulated. Writing on *Ladies in Lavender*, a British film set in Cornwall between the two wars, I explored the way in which the Cornish coastal landscape was used as a setting for the socially unacceptable passionate, romantic feelings of an older woman for a talented young Polish violinist, Andrea (Daniel Brühl), washed ashore on the beach below the house she shares with her sister (Moseley 2009). *Ladies in Lavender* is a film about unacceptable female desire and, in the classic operation of the melodramatic text, much of the unspeakable feeling of the drama is siphoned off into the *mise en scène* and, in the case of the Cornish-set romantic drama, into the affective, immersive regional landscape in particular, where it operates as pathetic fallacy. This is a film of high or absent horizons, of cameras positioned in dark caves and peering out from behind dark rocks, of sequences of slow motion and freeze-frame. These devices draw attention to the significance of a movement or gesture to capture them as almost-painterly screen memories: Ursula (Judi Dench) playing girlishly with seaweed on the beach, the sisters paddling at the water's edge, for example. The soundscape is equally immersive, with the crackle and hiss of waves retreating over pebbles and the crunch of footsteps on shingle high in the mix, quite apart from the wistful violin score by Nigel Hess which comes to signal both Andrea's passionate virtuosity and Ursula's quiet yearning for him.

The Cornish coast in screen fiction has been a site of potentially disruptive encounters with the foreign, the other, with desire and with the self. Here I explore a number of films that attend explicitly to the creative British woman at the edge, a figure, in contrast, persistently attended by instability, illness and death. I have written before of the immersive, affective use of the Cornish landscape in *Love Story*, a film set close to the start of the war and following classical composer and concert pianist Lissa Campbell (Margaret Lockwood) who, on discovering not only that she is unfit for war work but also has a life-limiting heart complaint, decides to escape the pressure of London for a remote corner of Cornwall. There, she says, she wants finally to be 'in life': 'I'm going out into the sunshine, I want to walk in the wind and watch the waves break over the Cornish rocks.' She meets Kit (Stewart Granger), a mine engineer who appears to be holidaying in Cornwall rather than contributing to the war effort in the services. Neither tells the other their tragic secret (Kit is going blind as the result of a blast during active service in the RAF), but they agree to a short romantic interlude without attachment or guilt. *Love Story* is the first screen site, beyond the early newsreel item discussed in the previous chapter, of the Cornish mine as a dramatic, romantic trope within the place-myth, and its presence results from the film's wartime project of incorporating regional identities within the national: 'some of the finest scenery in England', says Tom Tanner (Tom Walls), the elderly mine engineer from Yorkshire who has been drafted to 'pep up' mining for the war effort, of the Cornish landscape. When a blast underground goes wrong, extreme low-angle shots of the mine buildings, dark against the sky as the wind whistles and people wait anxiously for news, signal both tragedy and romance at the cliff edge in a way which anticipates the much later screen adaptions of Winston Graham's series of novels of Cornwall, the first of which, *Ross Poldark*, was published two years after this film's release. The incorporation of an industrial rather than a purely romantic place-image within the regional place-myth is further suggested when Tom brings flowers 'fresh from t'Scillies'. 'I thought they only grew cabbages there now,' Lissa murmurs regretfully, gesturing to the changes which have been brought by war and the need to 'Dig for Victory', with prosaic vegetables replacing romantic flowers in gardens across the nation, and evidently also bringing a concomitant change in a key genre of Cornwall established in the previous chapter.

From its first moments, *Love Story* suggests itself as a tragic story of loss. The opening notes of Hubert Bath's score, 'Cornish Rhapsody', a descending four-note arpeggio which then rises but falls again with determination into a minor melody, accompany credits rolling slowly over the image. A mobile view of the Cornish moorland, a massive sky and ancient stone hedges and buildings moves along a narrow lane away from the sea rather than towards it as one might expect. The film will make it apparent that this apparently 'final journey' has been filmed from the back of a donkey cart such as that which the main characters use to travel around the remote Penwith peninsula, and this explains the extremely slow pace of the receding travelling shot, which is hardly the thrilling phantom ride of those encountered in early view films. This opening feels distinctly like the end of a tragic film, and is filled with loss and regret at the retreat from the coast into the interior, rather than with the anticipatory joy which typically accompanies the journey into Cornwall or towards the coast (much as one feels at departing for home at the end of a holiday). The conjunction of music, credits, pace, direction and the ancient landscape travelled produces the film's opening as a last, lingering look at a much-loved place filled with memories, and in this respect casts a rather different light on the more upbeat ending of the film, reinforcing the temporary and fantastical nature of the romantic sojourn at the edge.

Lissa and Kit meet at the very edge of Cornwall, high on a cliff. The specificity of the film's landscape is initially signalled at the cut from London to the view of the coast from Lissa's hotel in Cornwall, which we enjoy with her. As the wind blows the curtains, signalling the fulfilment of her earlier wish, the final phrase of the chorus of 'The Furry Dance' is briefly audible in brass on the soundtrack.[17] The familiar folk tune immediately locates us in Cornwall, and is repeated in a high-angle shot of Lissa driving a donkey cart along a lane; we share her optical point of view out towards the clifftop as she drives along, singing 'The Floral Dance'. At the cliff edge, the camera pans across the coastal edge to follow her run across the clifftop and her pause there is a particularly powerful moment. Occupying a classic, powerful prospect position with the sea and the coast spread out before her, this is also a deeply immersive landscape image: the crash of the waves and cries of gulls are audible and the wind blows her hair as it does the grass at her feet. Unbeknown to her, Kit is climbing up the cliff below, and pretends to be clinging to the edge in desperation. After his joke is revealed, Lissa evades his advances, declaring 'I feel safer away from the edge.' With him, we watch her at the cliff edge as she listens to the landscape around her, turning it into music. We share his point of view as he tries to fix this view of Lissa in his mind in preparation for the loss of his vision, but we also share her experience of the landscape through the direct articulation of both her points of view and audition. This is completed later as she sits at the piano in the hotel's garden room, rehearsing the sounds of the clifftop, and Kit's words, turning them into Bath's 'Cornish Rhapsody', the film's theme. This meeting at the edge is fraught with contradiction and complexity: Lissa's apparently powerful, creative and controlling position as she composes at the clifftop, transforming the landscape into art, is simultaneously attenuated by Kit's attempts to 'fix' her as a view in his mind. Here, woman and landscape are fused as object of a romantic, tourist gaze, the connection reinforced in Kit's description of his activities in Cornwall. He is looking for 'Molly'—molybdenum—describing it as 'an attractive little piece I picked up yesterday'.

If the clifftop is a site of struggle for control for Lissa, in *Love Story* it also signals wartime 'gender trouble' (Butler 2011) around the figure of Judy (Patricia Roc), Kit's friend and Lissa's rival for his affections, an actress and director who is working at an outdoor theatre spectacularly located at the cliff edge.[18] Even before we meet Judy, she has been described by an elderly female resident of Lissa's hotel in terms which suggest that she is positioned outside traditionally acceptable bounds of femininity: 'She had a cigarette stuck in her mouth and trousers on.' Judy's is a risky, quite literally 'edgy', wartime femininity: she's in theatre and she is undomesticated (while frying mackerel, she carelessly drops ash from her cigarette into the pan); she also emerges as manipulative and deceitful in her play for Kit, thus ensuring that we understand Lissa as his rightful partner. *Love Story* is a drama of wartime gender anxiety: Kit's masculinity is in question—he appears to be failing in his duty to serve—and the thrust of the film is to restore his ability to fight for Britain. This plot operates in tandem with securing the romance which will maintain the values of monogamous heterosexual romance and family through this period of conflict and upheaval (as in *Mullion Cove*), and yet their reconciliation is unsettling.

The end of the film pictures Lissa in what we can see by now as a classic dramatic low-angle shot at the clifftop, watching a squadron fly out overhead on a mission as she fingers her wedding ring, and this should be an uplifting image, filled with hope for the future. Kit, following successful surgery, has returned to active duty and thus a less anxious gender equilibrium seems to have been restored. This final image, though, is significantly moderated by both the angle's emphasis on her literally and metaphorically precarious position at the very edge, and by the bittersweet memory of the finale-type opening of the film. The sense of anxiety and loss that suffuses these moments recalls the sense of fragility that surely accompanied wartime romance and, further, *Love Story* does not offer a hopeful outcome for Lisa's heart problem. 'I'm going to die,' she states simply, at the start of the film. Lissa's desire for creative and personal freedom is attended throughout by a sense of impossibility. Her moment at the clifftop as she looks, listens and experiences the landscape to turn it into music, into art, is tempered by the understanding that it is temporary, attended constantly by the anticipation of her death. Near the end of the film, it is her immersed and immersive performance of the 'Cornish Rhapsody' at the Royal Albert Hall—complete with an upward gaze as she plays the trills which signal gull cries, her apparent reimmersion in the experience of the Cornish landscape—which prompts her collapse, just as it did when she played the piece at the Minnack during Kit's surgery in London, at the edge of the landscape which inspired it. Through her composition, we re-experience the emotional affectiveness of Cornwall and of lost romance with her—and it is literally heart-breaking.[19]

The landscape aesthetics of *Love Story* insist upon the significance of such an immersive and emotional connection with the Cornish landscape.

Lissa's composition is the result of her sensory engagement with place, and the film emphasizes this by making us share her points of view and audition. Action, framing and camera position work constantly to locate the characters, and us, deeply within the landscape. We watch from the clifftop with Judy and Tom as Lissa and Kit dive off the rocks far below, the extreme high angle of the shot eliminating the horizon and filling the frame with the sea. The horizon is extremely high or absent both around them and in their optical point of view from the donkey cart, situating them securely within the landscape as they visit local sites of superstition, including a wishing well, the Merry Maidens stone circle and the Bargaining Stone—an ancient granite rock through which they shake hands to seal their affair. Kit explores the mine deep underground, and during a boat trip the horizon rises and dips behind them, producing a powerful sense of being 'in' the landscape, one which is reinforced as they row into a cave deep inside the cliff. This gesture of moving into the landscape is a long-standing part of the audiovisual grammar of Cornwall as a region, as we saw from the earliest moving images examined in Chapter 2, and in film and television drama of region it is harnessed to produce the landscape as deeply immersive and affective, here as an expression of depth of feeling in relation to desire and romance but elsewhere, as we shall see, the consuming and affective landscape can also signal threat.

While I Live, released four years later, clearly drew on *Love Story* in its story of a talented young woman composer Olwen (Audrey Fildes) who lives with her overbearing older sister Julia (Sonia Dresdel) in a grand house on the north Cornish cliffs. Haunted by her inability to finish her greatest composition, which Julia later titles 'The Dream of Olwen', she sleepwalks to the edge of the cliff and, startled by her sister's call, falls to her death. On the twenty-fifth anniversary of the tragedy in 1947, during a radio broadcast of the piece which has been finished by another composer, a young woman walks out of the coastal mist in the garden and into the drawing room, playing along perfectly with the broadcast up until the point at which Olwen had stalled, whereupon she faints. The woman is an amnesiac, but Julia and the butler/groundsman Nehemiah (Tom Walls) believe her to be the reincarnation of Olwen. She is, in fact, Sally Grant (Carol Raye), a married journalist from London who has suffered some kind of nervous breakdown while researching a piece on Olwen which, like the musical composition, 'just won't come right'. Olwen's composition, like Lissa's in *Love Story*, forms the score of the film and is introduced as the opening credits roll over a shot of waves rolling onto a wide, rocky beach. As the credits conclude, the camera pans left across the bay to find Olwen sitting atop a rocky promontory, presumably using the Cornish coast as the inspiration for her composition, a 'tone poem' with unsettling chromatic elements which is suggestive of the combination of romance and threat which underpin its place-myth. The perpetual motion of landscape and music in this title sequence, and the constantly wandering, anticipatory woodwind of the underscore, perfectly expresses the disquiet attached to the regional landscape, a dis-ease signalled too in the mist which creeps into the house from the sea, and the 'Cornish dust' which has dirtied Sally's shoes. The text returns almost hysterically to the tone poem, which is stuck in Sally's head. As she sits at the clifftop from where Olwen fell and listens to the sounds of place which inspired it, she tells Peter 'that melody brought me here'. Later we discover that, overwrought and struggling with her writing, her husband away from home, the music played on the radio and, in a daydream, she travelled to Cornwall. It was non-domestic, creative labour that prompted her strange episode: 'not being able to think, brought me here'. Nehemiah is the repository of screen Cornishness in the film, the only accented main character, a 'layer-on of hands' and a figure described by modern Land Girl Christine (Patricia Burke) as 'soaked in superstition'. Nehemiah reminds us that the Cornish 'have queer ideas and strange notions' and, for much of the film, is the figure through which Cornwall operates as a site of superstition, supernatural mystery and potential horror.

The main part of the film takes place in 1947, during the immediate post-war period of struggle and resettling as men and women returned from service and society began to adjust, as newsreel and cinemagazine films of this moment indicate. The film explicitly connects Sally's episode with the potential anxiety suffered by the professional working woman and, in the alternative explanation of reincarnation or haunting (Sally was born on the day of Olwen's death and has dreamed of the house since childhood), connects the hysterical post-war woman with the figure of the tortured female artist at the cliff edge. Madness and/or illness, it seems, attend the non-domestic, creative post-war woman, with the remote Cornish periphery a resonant site of possibility and threat perfect for its dramatization. Both women are pictured there, Olwen at the moment before her death and Sally as she hypnotically retraces Olwen's steps, and the same precipitous extreme high-angle shots to the rocks below reproduce both women's optical point of view and offer the viewer a deeply affective and unsettling kinaesthetic experience of regional place. As in *Love Story*, part of the struggle experienced by the woman at the edge is ownership of the creative gaze: Olwen is a talented composer, yet she struggles to maintain control over her work—she can't finish it and her sister dominates and names her work which, ultimately, is completed by another composer after her death. She is finally fixed as a painted image over the fireplace in the room where she worked, female artist become art. Sally, similarly, is a writer, but unable to cope with the modern demands of labour both inside and outside the home, loses her grasp on reality and escapes into a resonant, parallel identity, one which is fully creative but also unhappily located in domestic space.

Summer In February, a dramatization of a romantic relationship among the Lamorna artists around the outbreak of World War I, is a self-consciously intermedial text drawing on the work of Laura Knight (Hattie Morahan) as well as upon the equine and traveller paintings of A. J. Munnings (Dominic Cooper). 'A True Story' of the romantic relationship between Munnings, Florence Carter Wood (Emily Browning)—the sister of Joey Carter Wood (Max Deacon)—and Captain Gilbert Evans (Dan Stevens), the agent of Colonel Paynter (Michael Mahoney) who rented his land and property to the artists, the film's primary interest is in the psychic and creative struggle of Florence, who has run away to Cornwall to study in the colony at Lamorna alongside her brother. From its initial romantic premise, the film descends gradually into horror and death at the cliff edge and, in its aesthetic, demonstrates the ongoing relationship between visual cultures of Cornwall in relation to this earlier moment of conflict in relation to gendered and national identity. This film returns repeatedly to the figure of the woman at the edge, both in direct quotation of Knight's clifftop girls but also in a literalization of the film's dramatization of the physical and psychological possibility and precariousness experienced there by its central female protagonist. *Summer in February*, a title which refers to the GWR publicity which indicated the delightfully unseasonable Cornish weather but which also encapsulates the sense of disequilibrium which suffuses the film, emphasizes Florence's state of arrest between her desire to be an artist and her frequent positioning as part of a paintable 'view'. In this respect, the film shows the continued parallel between the landscape and the female body as subjects for the male artist, contrasting this with Laura Knight's painting of, and egalitarian relationship with, her model Dolly (Mia Austen).

The film's opening sounds and images inextricably connect the anxious subjectivity of the Edwardian woman poised on the precipice of modernity with the powerful affect of the immersive Cornish landscape. At the same time, they speak to the longer history of the regional place-myth-making in visual culture through a densely signifying opening sequence. The opening credits appear over a black screen, accompanied by the repetitive sound of waves and then a sudden intake of breath, as a woman's face, appearing to wake suddenly from a dream, fades up to fill the screen in extreme close-up. A cross-fade to a slow pan directly merges woman and landscape as it follows the waves and their spray crashing onto a beach,

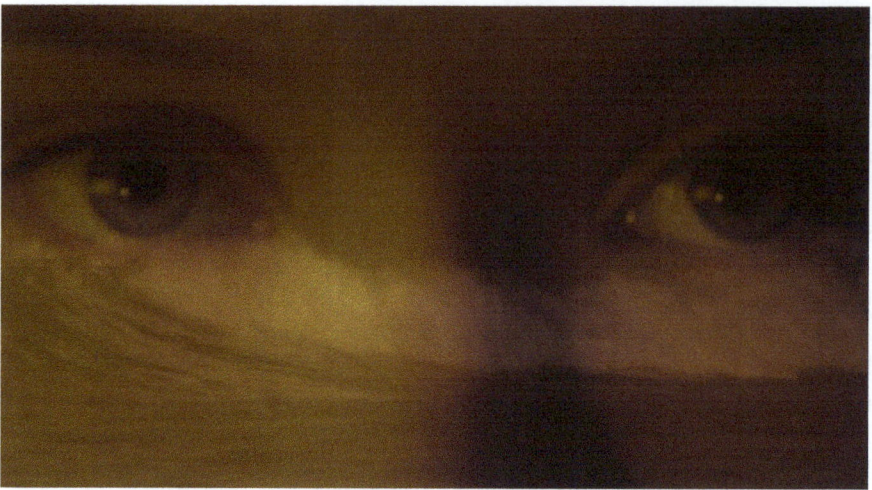

Figure 7   Woman as landscape: *Summer in February* (Menaul, 2013)

their sound dominant over a quiet, legato piano melody which fades into the sound mix (Figure 7).

The following dissolve is to a slow pan left, slightly ahead of two horses galloping across a wide beach. The effect of this is to show the expansiveness of the landscape, which becomes a series of horizontals of massive sky, and a strip of sea and sand with reflective water rivulets and dark jagged rocks at the left of the mobile panorama. The score is gradually filled out with woodwind as we begin to hear the shouts of the riders, and a cut to a closer shot of gulls at the water's edge is followed by an optical point-of-view shot through binoculars, effectively producing a vignetted image. Two elderly women are birdwatching from the cliff, and their mobile gaze through the viewing device lands on a woman artist who is painting a reclining female nude model on the beach below (Figure 8).

This shot encapsulates the long history of picturing Cornwall across the visual arts, in its merging of the history of artistic production in Cornwall, the use of an outmoded framing device in early moving images of place which produced the region as perpetually 'past' (here in relation to a strikingly 'modern' view of Cornwall), and the deliberately intertextual juxtaposition of these points of reference in a period film which tells the story of the figure which has haunted that history, and recurs into the present through the film itself. In a further elaboration of a shared narration of region, the opening shot of *Summer in February* will later demand a rereading, just as the mournful opening of *Love Story* is contextualized by the narrative which follows. This shot, of Florence gasping for breath and

Figure 8   Intermedial Cornwall: *Summer in February* (Menaul, 2013)

opening her eyes, will in the course of the narrative be shockingly recontextualized as the precise moment of her death by suicide after drinking cyanide in her cliff-edge studio.

The film makes direct reference to Laura Knight's clifftop women through the use of compositions and colour identifying her paintings as key intertexts. On a grey and misty beach, Laura works on a painting protected beneath a bright red umbrella; other splashes of red also break the muted palette of the beach, on the model reclining on the rocks, and in the painting. As in this scene, ambient sound is always mixed high in the soundscape of the film, making the crash and rush of waves, the howling wind, rain, thunder and gull cries or even the hiss of lemon hitting hot coals inescapable, and productive of an affective, auditory sense of emplacement. The women talk about Laura's early romance with her husband, the painter Harold Knight, when they were fourteen and seventeen respectively: 'he taught me everything I know ... about painting' she tells Dolly, in a hint at the liberated sexual attitude which the film suggests is characteristic of the Lamorna group. Dolly offers a passing young man a finger wave, and he smirks. Modern female artist and model are pictured at the coastal edge in an intertextual moment which connects the female body with the landscape, and produces the kinaesthetic experience of landscape as both somatic and erotic. While the film presents one young woman's struggle with modernity, the film's intermedial strategy connects her to a wider moment of anxious change, initially signalled by an unabashed depiction of (female) nudity. Florence looks wistfully at, and then quickly away from,

Figure 9   Woman artist as art in *Summer in February* (Menaul, 2013)

Dolly's jiggling breasts as she runs up the beach with Joey.[20] While the film presents Florence's psychic struggle as directly related to the body and to sexuality, her first suicide attempt taking place at her wedding reception and her marriage to A. J. remaining unconsummated, this relationship is also clearly shown to be a struggle for control. While it is Dolly's role to be the object of the artists' gaze, and Laura's to wield it, Florence struggles constantly to reconcile the attempts of others to picture her with her own desire to do the picturing. A. J. persistently tries to frame her as the object of his painter's gaze, static astride a horse in the woods or immobile in his studio (and the film uses framing and composition elsewhere to emphasize this, see Figure 9), while sneering at her own ambition as an artist.

It is Florence's desire for 'a room of one's own', as Virginia Woolf would describe it in 1929, in conjunction with her affair with Gilbert, consummated in the ramshackle studio he finds for her next to the cliff path, which reveals struggle for independence and self-definition, rather than sexual psychosis, as the root of Florence's dis-ease. As he presents his painting of her on horseback, 'Morning Ride', in London, she looks between it and his other portraits, of an exotic gypsy woman and of Dolly, half-naked on the beach, and the camera simultaneously zooms in to and dollies out from her face in close-up in what is now a classic device, post-Hitchcock, to signal disorientation and distress. She is just another one of A. J.'s women. 'Do you know who you are, deep down?' she asks of Gilbert. The desirable, eroticized body, whether male or female, is frequently aligned with the landscape view in *Summer in February*. 'She's very paintable,' says A. J. of

Figure 10   Florence at the edge in *Summer in February* (Menaul, 2013)

Florence, as he looks out at the seascape before him. Similarly, when Joey takes Florence outside on her arrival in Lamorna, she looks out into the darkness and declares, 'Oh Joey it's perfect. I can't wait to see the view. And you know A. J. Munnings!' And later she will seek out Gilbert and sit to watch him fish, man and landscape combined as view. As Gemma Goodman and I have argued of the recent television adaptations of both *Poldark* and *Outlander* (Starz, 2014–), a drama set in the Scottish highlands (Goodman and Moseley 2015, forthcoming 2018), and as I explore further below, the conjunction of the eroticized male body with the spectacular landscape has been a significant trope in recent film and television dramas of region in ways which draw attention to continued conflicts around identity. *Summer in February*, by contrast, despite a nod to the desiring female gaze, remains on much more conventional territory in its alignment of the female body with both landscape and view.

Florence, then, is figured as one of Knight's clifftop women: she is the embodiment of the historically specific anxieties discussed above, and the trope of the woman precariously 'on the edge' is used in the film at times when she is at the height of personal crisis. When she considers suicide, she is shown teetering at the very cliff edge in a series of high or horizonless, extreme low-angle shots which frame her as a stark image of terror against the brilliant blue sky. This is the very articulation of the disquiet at the heart of the film, an animation of one of Knight's unsettling, almost-narrative, immersive paintings of young women in this period which also speak to the post-war newsreel images of women on the Cornish coast (Figure 10).

The cliff edge, whether summer house, studio or the open air, has been the repeated site of sexual liberation and anxiety, as I have previously explored in relation to television adaptations of popular romantic fiction in *Coming Home* and *The Camomile Lawn* (Moseley 2013b). In *Summer in February*, too, the studio where Florence tries to work, makes adulterous love with Gilbert, conceives, and finally commits suicide, is located precariously close to the cliff edge.[21] This vulnerable and exposed position is highlighted in shots emphasizing the battle to make progress along the edge against the elements, as the hut's broken shutter bangs in the wind and rain. In *Summer in February*, Cornwall may be a site of possibility and experimentation for the incomer, out of time and out of season with the rest of England, but it is also a site of potential disequilibrium, horror, despair and death (hinted at in the ghost poem which A. J. performs to a spellbound gathering, interrupted at the perfect dramatic moment by Florence's knock at the door on her arrival in Lamorna). Its landscape grammar is subtly expressive in this respect, from its palette to the unexpected diversion from its familiar use of landscape as either spectacular setting or peaceful transition between scenes. The film often makes use of the saturated blues, golds and greens of a recognizable 'tourist' Cornwall, for example in the title shot of Prussia Cove, and later, as the camera pans to follow characters as they walk around a promontory, emphasizing both the expansiveness of the landscape and drawing attention to the coastal edge in a movement familiar from the earliest moving 'views' of the region. At the same time, however, *Summer in February* also presents a Cornwall equally recognizable to the insider, a landscape of desaturated greys and greens, and of pale Naples Yellow. This is an expressive and communicative, as well as a naturalistic picturing of place, one which shows the region not just as a place of extreme contrasts, but also as a more prosaic site of damp misery, solitude and hopelessness. This is the Cornwall of the knacker man's journey, of the single, bleak glimpse of the sea in Molly Dineen's *The Lie of the Land* (2007), discussed in Chapter 4, as well as of the imagining of du Maurier's mysterious Cornwall on screen in, for instance, *A Picture of Britain* (BBC, 2005) as well as in the television adaptations of her *Jamaica Inn* (HTV 1983; BBC 2014).

The film makes sustained symbolic use of the Cornish landscape through decisions about colour, location and editing. When Gilbert visits Florence's grave near the end of the film, for example, the scene takes place at Church Cove, Gunwalloe. Geographically distant from the film's setting in Lamorna, this choice of location provides an appropriate landscape of final, tragic immersion in the landscape, the church and its cemetery half-buried in the sandy cliff at the end of the isolated bay. While, as I have suggested, such 'composite' constructions of place contrast with the 'insider aesthetics' explored in the final chapter of the book, such symbolic use of location nevertheless exemplifies the sense of deep involvement with, affect by and emplacement in landscape that often attends Cornwall on screen. When Laura tells Gilbert of Florence's engagement to A. J. on a dark evening, a cut to crashing waves on a beach mirrors the power and depth of his emotions in a familiar and clichéd use of landscape as pathetic fallacy in film. This, however, is also a location as yet unseen in the film, a new view that produces a dramatic and unsettling break from the repetition of a limited number of locations that have made us familiar with the dramatic space to this point in the film. As Gilbert walks the cliff, there is a cut to Florence and A. J. on horseback riding through towering rocks, between which is visible a tiny triangle of bright sky and then, as they ride across the beach, to his optical point of view from above from a canted, overhead angle, a shadow cutting dramatically across the image. This is a series of shots which in their diversion from the spaces and uses of landscape so far established in the film, are unsettling and anticipatory. Mimicking, presumably, Gilbert's movement, the camera creeps slowly forward to peer over the cliff edge and down at the couple who are sketching among the rocks, again providing an unfamiliar angle and relationship to space which is aesthetically aligned with Florence's later brush with death at the cliff edge. At the same time, these are horizonless images picturing the characters, and positioning the viewer, deep within the regional landscape in a familiar moving image grammar which indicates the overpowering nature of place which consumes both protagonists and viewer.

After Florence commits suicide and the opening close-up of her face and breath is recontextualized, a cross-fade on her face takes us on a significantly different journey from that which began the film. This time, a slow, sweeping pan of the cliffs and sea comes full circle, the shot ending on and dollying into the curtain blowing at the open window of the hut, where we see her dead on the floor, the camera rising up and away to leave her alone. In this moment, the classic panoramic shot of the view film, of the tourist gaze, becomes aligned with horror and death, in an insubordinate redeployment of the moving image grammar of Cornwall that speaks back to the self-conscious citation of the visual cultural history of the region with which the film began. The transition to the next scene occurs through a dissolve to a series of shots in which a stone hedge cuts diagonally across the screen, wind-twisted trees lean inland away from the sea and tamarisk stands leafless and bleak at the very edge of the cliff. These are all shots and locations seen for the first time at this moment, shots which suggest a puncturing of the fantasy of 'Summer in February' which has underpinned

GWR publicity, of the long history of screen Cornwall and, on the surface at least, of the Cornwall painted by the Lamorna artists.

Romantic film dramas of Cornwall have hovered around the anxious conjunction of war and women, and the audiovisual articulation of a powerfully immersive regional landscape, focused on a composite picturing of the coastal edge, has been key to their dramatic affect. It is interesting to note, though, that any notion of regional identity as significant in and of itself, outside of the centre–periphery dynamic and the symbolic use of landscape as affective setting, is largely absent. In these fictions, Cornwall is typically pictured as a remote paradise of possibility and precariousness and, in the context of war, as metonymically 'British' as opposed to 'other'. Cornwall appears much more clearly as a place with a distinctive history, culture and identity—as a region which is 'other'—in fictions adapted from novels of Cornwall written 'from within', most notably in the BBC adaptations of Winston Graham's *Poldark* and Daphne du Maurier's *Jamaica Inn*. At the same time, these picturings of region operate securely within the interrelated modes of romance, mystery and horror and describe a powerful, imaginary, romantic and affective space in tension with historically and regionally specific articulations of place.

Poldark: Cliff and Mine

The BBC has twice adapted Winston Graham's *Poldark* novels, the epic story of a Cornish mine-owning family which opens in the eighteenth century: first in the 1970s and more recently, to great media attention, in 2015, with a season released each year to date. Looking across the screen history of Cornwall, it is evident that the figure of the (ruined) mine at the cliff edge emerges in the place-myth after the publication of Graham's novels, beginning in 1946, which itself comes after the brief reinvigoration of the region's mines to support the war effort, and is reinforced by the publication, in 1967 and 1968, of H. G. Ordish's pictorial surveys of Cornish engine houses. The ruined mine stack and engine house have, since the 1970s adaptation of *Poldark*, become perhaps the key trope of Cornwall's place-myth, visible on bumper stickers, key rings, postcards and even in the marketing of Cornish Tea and, with the enormous success of the contemporary adaptation, within which it is a prominent and repeated image, its primacy has been reconfirmed. What are we to make, then, of the dominance of this romanticized sign of Britain's first post-industrial landscape? Here, I consider the ways in which the recent adaptation has inflected and developed '*Poldark* Cornwall'.

I have previously suggested the significance of two key aspects of the first television serialization of *Poldark*: first, the immersed yet distanced tourist gaze, taken up by viewers who wrote to me about their memories of the programme and which was located primarily in the television-specific elements of the serialized text—the opening and closing title sequences. Second, I identified the television construction of a place-myth drawing upon existing representations in fine art, but also emphasizing the conjunction of the ruined and romantic regional landscape with the strangeness of a barbaric peripheral rurality (Moseley 2013a). The affective power of the sublime Cornish landscape, the emphasis on crashing waves, towering cliffs and a Romantic score, was made very clear in correspondence I received in response to an appeal for fans of the programme to write to me, published in regional newspapers the *Cornish Guardian* and *West Briton* (Middleton 2011). Many, almost exclusively female, fans of the programme told me of a passion for Cornwall which the programme's picturing of its landscape had ignited, one which had frequently led to relocation and which was often connected in their recollections to their personal quest for a romantic love affair which would match that of Ross (Robin Ellis) and Demelza (Angharad Rees). Indeed, one couple wrote to me of their forthcoming renewal of vows at the 'Poldark' mine near Helston, which was to take place in period costumes reproduced from the first adaptation, deep underground, to be followed by a reception in 'Demelza's parlour'. Such examples of literal desire for immersion in the romanticized landscape are hyperbolic instances of the taking up of an audiovisual strategy of suture and address described throughout this book, and which demonstrates the effective and affective power of the moving image construction of place-myth dependent upon a picturing of landscape: Ross and Demelza's relationship, in the novels as well as in the adaptations, is not an idealized romance and the landscape which seems, quite literally, to have had the power to move people, was largely limited to framing and puncturing moments in the 1970s adaptation, rather than being thoroughly integrated as narrative setting or spectacular, 'slow television' or landscape porn which has been theorized as attention-grabbing (Lefebvre 2006a; Wheatley 2011).

The connection between romantic hero and romantic landscape was present in the 1970s text with much popular press attention given to Robin Ellis as 'heartthrob' Ross Poldark, but the connection between body and region was, in that instance, much more powerfully articulated in the conventional figuring of the landscape in relation to the female body, through the establishment of a binary between Elizabeth (elaborately coiffed, associated with the genteel interior) and Demelza, wild-haired and associated with the outdoors. While this is maintained in the 2015 adaptation, with Demelza (Eleanor Tomlinson) repeatedly pictured at the edge of the cliff, her red hair blowing in the wind, it is in relation to the body of Ross Poldark (Aidan Turner), that the attentive gaze at the romantic landscape is focalized. Publicity images for the serial emphasized the connection between regionalized place and the eroticized (and regionalized) male body. In official publicity, Turner posed as Poldark on a cliff edge, his flowing dark hair blown by the wind, against a CGI-painterly seascape recalling traditional Romantic oil paintings by artists such as Constable and Turner.

Here, the palette, as well as the touch of the elements indicated by the sideways flight of his hair, which blows in the same direction as the surf and the clouds, connects regional body with regional landscape. As Gemma Goodman and I have explored in detail this conjunction, and its relationship to the gaze, in both *Poldark* and *Outlander* (Goodman and Moseley 2015, forthcoming 2018; see also Goodman 2012), it is enough here to draw attention to the shift of attention to the male body which inherits, works and is connected intimately to the regional landscape, not least as the object of an admiring and acquisitive gaze, though the relationship of that body to the landscape is one of ownership not property, emblematized in the repeated prospect view of the title sequence and publicity material. Such a gaze is irrevocably political in relation to a landscape understood as internal colony (Hechter 1975), in a period of ongoing local and global territorial conflict, including the call for Cornish devolution. This context produces a frisson which forces a place-specific political reinterpretation of, for example, Wheatley's analysis of Demelza's watching of Ross swimming naked in the cove from among the grass on the clifftop, and at his glistening naked torso as he scythes. The latter formed an unofficial publicity image for the 2015 series, appearing endlessly in the popular press and on social media (Wheatley 2016: 215) and inspiring numerous parodic and resistant memes. This is 'landscape porn' in all its senses, including the whiff of exploitation attending the spectacularization of both body and place for commercial gain. 'Prepare to be swept away by the brooding, rugged allure of the new *Poldark*,' warned the continuity announcer at the start of the 2015 adaptation, neatly aligning the landscape with the desirable male body evident in press and publicity well before the first episode was broadcast.

The most recent adaptation of *Poldark* has certainly reiterated and reinforced the hysterical insistence on the edge of Cornwall. Indeed, the text has been so hyperbolic in this respect that the continuity announcer for the second series introduced it with the words 'And now, it's back to that clifftop, in *Poldark.*' At moments of emotional intensity, the main characters are repeatedly pictured through swooping, sweeping aerial pans at the very edge of a clifftop promontory, looking out to sea, and an aerial shot of Ross galloping across the same stretch of cliff, seemingly regardless of his origin and destination, is recurrent. The frequent repetition of this shot cannot be understood as a locating device, one which helps the viewer understand the spatial relationship between places; rather, it functions as the articulation, through excess, of a romantic, imagined space which responds to and participates in the construction of place-myth and which, in the process, continues the emptying out of the interior territory. This manoeuvre is part of the text's transformation from historical novel to romantic drama and in this respect it is significant that when Ross rides to Trenwith and 'rapes' Elizabeth, this is not his path. Rather, he travels through dark, misty woods, reinforcing the sense that the cliff edge as it has been articulated across the serial is a romantic and symbolic, rather than functional, space, and one which would be at odds with this troubling turn in the narrative. *Poldark* (2015–) certainly inscribes a tourist gaze in Urry's sense (2002) and operates predominantly as view (Gunning 1997) in relation to the spectacular edge: the second episode, for example, as Ross and Demelza work with the community to rebuild and reopen Wheal Leisure, which has fallen into disrepair, ends in a sunset cliff-edge picnic alongside the mine, complete with pasties and wind-blown hair—an intensely romantic tourist image of Cornwall of a kind which is ubiquitous across the series (Figure 11).

The elaborately constructed, composite title sequence of the 2015 adaptation is an affective condensation of these ideas set to a dramatic, romantic score in which vibrato violins suggest a Celtic theme over a tensely repetitive piano melody of quadruplets. The opening, a descent of two sustained violin notes in a minor key, sets the mood and is echoed in a camera movement down from stormy, sunset clouds over the sea as the main, soaring melody begins. This virtual downwards 'track' takes in the silhouette of Ross Poldark on horseback at a cliff-edge promontory and descends to a cave into which the sun pours through a dark aperture. The camera appears to pan left to the white water of waves crashing over rocks which dissolve to swirling clouds of water and the view, now, is of the water (or clouds) from below, and we are fully immersed in this dreamlike landscape, before a dissolve to a calmer green seascape with a ship in the bay, billowing clouds of water providing the sky. A further use of composite imagery layers a clifftop into the foreground, across which Ross gallops from left to right (the iconic shot of the series) as the camera seems, once more, to track down to the fire and sparks of the mine beneath the ground. A final dissolve brings us to Ross, silhouetted against a dramatic and moonlit cloudy seascape, the impression hanging over from the previous image of sparks shooting up from the ground below his feet as if he were forged out of the earth: a regionalized body. This sequence uses dissolves,

Figure 11   Tourist Cornwall in *Poldark* (BBC, 2015)

time-lapse, slow motion, digital layering and fades (of both images and typography) to produce an impression of merging spaces, ephemerality and the passing of time, and yet, at the same time, the painterly aesthetic fixes this dynamic, dramatic landscape as image. The overwhelming effect of the sequence, repeated, of course, at the beginning of each episode of the serial, is elemental, one of immersion in water, earth and air, of the relationship between outside (the pan across the cliff) and in (the track down below) and, above all, of an insistence on the Romantic edge.

As in the 1970s adaptation, mine engine houses and stacks are at the cliff edge, not inland, and are always already ruined, despite the fact that, in the narrative, they have been in disuse for only a few years. At the same time, in the 2015 adaptation, CGI is evidently used to place working mines, with smoke and attendant activity, in the background of a number of shots. This recreation of the living, historical mining landscape in conjunction with the contradictory ongoing presence of the post-industrial ruined remnants of the industry is indicative of the power of the ruined clifftop mine in the place-myth, and in this 'view' programme, but also of the political significance of ruins, in which 'symbols of social deprivation and economic decline become over time symbols of regional and national pride' (Orange 2008: 83). As Hell and Schönle suggest, ruins 'reveal an ambivalent sense of time, at once the awareness of an insuperable break from the past that constitutes the modern age and the sense that some valuable trace has endured and needs to be cherished' (2010: 5). 'The ruin is a ruin precisely because it seems to have lost its function or meaning in the present, while retaining a suggestive, unstable semantic potential. The ruin has blurred edges in more ways than one' (6). In *Poldark*, the presence of the ruined mine building at the cliff edge, in conjunction with its (digitally reconstructed) working past in the same frame, is precisely the articulation of this dialectic between past and present, loss and continuity, and the filming locations, already among the most photographed views in Cornwall as Orange points out (2008: 86), are part of a regional landscape which in 2006 was designated as a World Heritage Site. While the clay area of Cornwall has also been more recently promoted as a heritage site, the post-industrial china-clay mining landscape has not been appropriable for the tourist gaze in the same way, either in person or on screen, despite attempts by the tourist industry to position the white hills and shores of the now azure water-filled clay pits in relation to a discourse of spectacular 'beach' Cornwall.[22] As Orange argues, it is critical, in terms of their potential to be appropriated by the tourist industry in relation to the place-myth of romance and mystery, that (some, but by no means all of) the ruins of the Cornish mining industry exist 'within a rural and a heavily romanticised and mythologised landscape' (93). As Goodman has documented, the exploitation of Cornwall's landscape of (R)omantic ruination in *Poldark*, but also in *Doc Martin* (ITV, 2004–), has impacted significantly on tourism in the region (2016: 173–75). There has been a great deal of writing about the Romantic ruin in the landscape and, recently, of the post-industrial ruin in particular. Peterson has considered the effect and affect of the ruinous landscape in her work on the early travel film, pointing out that:

> [i]n the late eighteenth century, qualities associated with ruinousness and decay became picturesque: rough terrain, old buildings, winding

roads, wild foliage, bedraggled cattle, and, most notoriously, beggars and peasants, figures representing the rural poor. Ruins were appreciated for the way they served as emblems of the past, their decay in the present serving only to mark their evocation of a romanticized past (2013: 187).

Such picturesque romanticization means that real social conditions 'are transmuted into aesthetic pleasantries, [and] ethnicity and social class become exotic' (188). In the adaptation of Graham's *Poldark* novels for television, and the moving image texts' dependence on and development of the Cornish place-myth, a history of mining and poverty in Cornwall becomes the object of the tourist gaze, within which the post-industrial ruin becomes a Romantic sign of the past (still present) in the landscape, alongside the use of technology to 'bring the industrial past to life'. In this respect, 'the aestheticisation of dereliction' in which the clifftop mine building is 'ruin porn' (DeSilvey and Edensor 2012: 470) functions similarly to the prehistoric standing stones and Celtic stone crosses which mark the regional landscape: as an affective, material point of potential connection with a romanticized regional past. Indeed, the absence of the ruined Cornish mine from Edensor's work on the industrial ruin is indicative in this respect (2005). While Boym's essay 'Ruinophilia' (2011) attends specifically to the twenty-first-century fascination with the ruination of twentieth-century modernity, her comment that 'the fascination for ruins is not merely intellectual, but also sensual', and that '[r]uins give us a shock of vanishing materiality', remains helpful here, not least because the 2015 *Poldark* owes so much to the 'ruinous' aesthetic of its twentieth-century precedent text.

In contrast to Boym's suggestion of a prospective reflective nostalgia provoked by the ruination of twentieth-century modernity, the 'ruin porn' of *Poldark* is restorative, and dreams of 'imaginary pasts'. The conjunction of the Romantic post-industrial ruin with a CGI restoration of that industrial past in *Poldark* registers precisely such a dream of an imaginary past: it brings together a contemporary tourist gaze at the regional landscape and a nostalgic fixing of that landscape in the romanticized past in the same frame. Huyssen's discussion of the connection between nostalgia and the ruin is anchored in 'the irreversibility of time' (2006: 7) but, in the composite CGI image, time is, precisely, reversed and simultaneously preserved, a contradiction that speaks to the positioning of this adaptation as historical romance. Huyssen carefully distinguishes the nostalgic twenty-first-century cult of post-industrial ruins from the Romantic eighteenth-century interest in the ruin as picturesque, related to the rise of industrial modernity before the genocide of the mid-twentieth century. The cipher of the ruined engine house seems, to me, to sit somewhere between these two moments, available for romanticization in a way in which the ruins of twentieth-century modernity are not. Made from the land (granite) and bearing a material and visual relationship to the traces of much older civilizations which surround it (standing stones and Celtic crosses), the ruined mine building is a trace of the earliest moments of industrial modernity, a trace which also reaches back in time in continuity with much earlier moments of great human endeavour in the landscape. In this way, in *Poldark*, the Romantic, ruined clifftop mine simultaneously speaks antiquity and modernity, romantic, picturesque past and (in dialogue with the CGI working mine which shares its frame) modern, industrial present. As we have seen, the moving image place-myth of Cornwall has repeatedly fixed the territory in the past, in tradition and in relation to a nostalgic rhetoric of loss. The huge, international success of *Poldark* has enlivened and perpetuated that myth in its combination of nostalgic tourist gaze and landscape porn.[23]

Moor: The Unknown Interior

We have seen the way in which picturing the unsettled modern woman at the coastal edge has the propensity, occasionally, to tip over into horror, but it is in screen adaptations of du Maurier's 1936 novel *Jamaica Inn* that the potential threat lurking within the Romantic landscape—a landscape as likely to inspire and express horror and dis-ease as art, poetry and passion—is most evident. As Goodman has argued, the marketing of 'Du Maurier's Cornwall' has been and remains central to the tourist industry (2016: 171), and there have been numerous film and television adaptations of her story of smuggling, wrecking and murder (for example Hitchcock, 1939 and HTV, 1983). In the 2014 television adaptation, unusually for screen picturings of Cornwall, the landscape of the regional interior is given a life of its own, functioning neither simply as narrative setting nor as spectacular landscape, but, more ambivalently, as an agent of the drama in and of itself (Lefebvre 2006a). The agency of the interior landscape—specifically of Bodmin Moor—is not straightforwardly benign;[24] through a consideration of the unsettling and unknowable nature of the regional interior in screen fictions of Cornwall, we travel fully and finally into the mysterious and horrific Cornwall that continues to haunt its seemingly more settled imaginings.

'*Jamaica Inn* will draw you into its mysterious story in just a moment,' warned the BBC1 continuity announcer before the first episode of the three-part 2014 adaptation. The reception of the serial was less than positive, with much of the companion screen discussion, on Twitter for example, centring on the inability of viewers to follow the dialogue. The debate over the (mis)representation of the Cornish accent raged so fiercely that the *Guardian* asked the Cornish comedian and cultural commentator Kernow King to write a response piece (King 2014). Whether the intelligibility of some of the dialogue in this iteration of *Jamaica Inn* resulted from performance style (Sean Harris, who played Joss Merlyn, was particularly criticized), poor attention to the nuance of dialect, lack of quality control or issues around recording, transmission and reception technologies, the attendant brouhaha was emblematic of the way that the interior of the region remains to some extent unknown, unknowable, and beyond screen representation. In that opening announcement, the consuming potential of the remote and unknown moorland interior was also clearly signalled. The possibility—and threat—of being 'drawn in' by *Jamaica Inn* relates not just to the heuristic appeal of the mystery narrative, but also to the landscape in which it is set. The 2014 adaptation is packed with imagery of immersion, from the dark mud which soaks into and creeps up Mary Yellan's (Jessica Brown Findlay) skirts, weighing them down and hampering her movement through the landscape, to the repeated scenes of near drowning in which the camera—and we as viewers—are positioned at or below the surface of the sea to capture as closely as possible the sense of being unwillingly immersed in water, and struggling for the surface. The camera lens is splashed with water when it rains. The moor itself is presented as an active and consuming participant, an entity which can disorientate the traveller from outside with its undifferentiated expanse, lack of landmarks and sudden mists, and which might literally draw you down into the depths of a bog, hidden in plain sight.

Cornwall, then, is a landscape that can bewitch and, quite literally, capture the onlooker. Frequently, the camera is angled upwards or positioned low to the ground as if an unknown presence, with whom we are aligned, lies hidden in the grass through which the camera peers as Mary walks across the moor. We watch from between the granite rock formations of a tor as a coach passes, tiny against the expanse of the moor below; the horizon is always near the top of the frame. In this way, the drama positions the viewer in a very similar way to other romantic dramas of the region, securely within the Cornish landscape in an approximation of an emplaced, 'insider' view, differentiated from the more conventional panoramic tourist gaze from an elevated point. This is not to suggest that such an emplaced view is any less of a tourist gaze, in terms of moving image as virtual travel, than the mobile panorama, just that these dramas of place use affective strategies of audiovisual immersion to produce a look which seems to cross Caughie's categories of dramatic look and documentary gaze (2000). We often share Mary's curious optical point of view, whether via Steadicam as she follows her love interest Jem across the moor, or as she stands atop a moorland tor and the camera looks slowly around in the more classical gesture of a tourist gaze. She is positioned as both Cornish insider, at one with the moor but, at the same time, as the outsider to whom the vast entity of the moor is also unknown. The immersed tourist gaze embodied by Mary is both observational (documentary) and suturing (dramatic) in unsettling ways which underline the drama's Gothic mode. The curious, sometimes hidden act of looking can be aligned with Mary's optical point of view, but at other moments it seems to belong to the moor itself, personified, often through sound, as a great beast of uncertain intent. As Mary follows her Uncle Joss across the moor, hoping to discern his misdeeds, time-lapse photography of the mist moving across a peak is accompanied by a deep, hollow wail in the score, reminiscent of a coastal fog horn but at the same time animalistic and horrifying.

The interrelation of narrative, remote landscape and threat signalled initially in the continuity announcement are reinforced in the opening sequence, in which Mary's voice tells us that in the autumn of 1821 she headed 'to the ends of the earth ... to Bodmin Moor', and she is seen dragging her trunk up a muddy track, accompanied by the unsettling sound of a repetitive, picked autoharp which is eventually filled out by a wistful, legato string melody. The choice of instrumentation carries the echo of the sounds of Appalachia and the American Deep South, immediately connecting the interior of the extreme south-west of Britain with narratives of that other 'internal colony', narratives of dangerous, horrific remote 'redneck' rurality. The Gothic elements of *Jamaica Inn*, signalled initially in the eerie extreme slow motion of the coach past the camera, the hair which has escaped Mary's bonnet suspended in mid-air, and the saturated dark palette of the programme's interior scenes, also have specific coastal and moorland landscape forms. The use of an extremely desaturated image in the scenes of wrecking shot at Holywell Bay emphasize limpid greys of mist and sea and pallid, wet sand, against which the dark cliffs and jagged rocks in the bay stand out menacingly. Similarly, the moor is vast and undifferentiated, grey cloud hanging low over its scrub and peaks, and is frequently framed in ways which recall the iconography of the Wild West frontier from classic American Western films. The desolate, inhospitable wilderness landscape framed through a rough-hewn wooden gate or doorway, ragged cloth hanging limply, the 'settlers' looking out at arrivals and departures, juxtaposes the lawlessness of the wilderness with the law

Figure 12   Bodmin Moor as Wild West in *Jamaica Inn* (BBC, 2014)

of 'civilization' (Figure 12). As in the classic Western, there is ambiguity here, too, about the rightness of the forces of law and civilization; the Vicar Davey (Ben Daniels) is in fact the evil force behind the wreckings and murders Mary witnesses, rather than a power for good as he initially appears, and the moral polarities which have been understood to underpin the Western narrative are here more unsettled than ever in relation to the regional moorland interior.

In many ways, *Jamaica Inn* is a classic Gothic drama like du Maurier's *Rebecca*, in which the space of the 'home' is fraught with fear (see Doane 1987; Wheatley 2006). As Mary comments, retrospectively, 'there's nothing so dangerous as a headstrong girl who knows her own mind' and, in classic Gothic terms, it is indeed her desire to explore, investigate and act which places her at risk from Joss, the wreckers and Davey. This sense of dis-ease extends, in *Jamaica Inn*, to the landscape and particularly to the moor, which Mary must cross to reach the (apparent) safety of the church and the rectory. The moor plays an ambiguous role in the drama, expressed visually and narratively through Mary's relationship with it. While she struggles to navigate it at times, gets stuck in it and is watched from within it, at other moments the moor offers protection, for instance providing hiding in plain sight for the wreckers as they evade the Revenue. While Davey takes Mary to a granite tor with the intention of sacrificing her in a pagan ritual that connects the landscape directly to ideas of pre-Christian horror, at the same time the rocks enable her to hide, and Davey falls from them to his death. While the mud of the moor filthies Mary's skirts, it also makes her, visually, one with it as she strides off into the landscape and, repeatedly, the vast expanse of Bodmin Moor functions as a sublime source of solace. The use of time-lapse photography makes clouds and mist race over the moor at a preternatural speed as she stands in it, looking up at the sky, closing her eyes, breathing in the landscape. Time-lapse is used, too, in low-angle, high-contrast shots of the inn itself, making it loom in a sinister way which is heightened by the use of the autoharp and an odd, electronic buzz which is often audible low in the drama's soundscape. In *Jamaica Inn*, an aesthetics of immersion operates at the sonic as well as the visual level: the howling wind is almost perpetually audible from within the inn and the strange soundscape is ever present, sometimes at a very low level, uncomfortably inescapable.

Perhaps the most interesting expression of the ambiguous potential of the moorland landscape comes in Mary's cross-dressing in Jem's clothes when they visit the Launceston Christmas market. While on one level this is merely a practical disguise, at the same time it is an act imbued with a radical sexual charge. It is in this dress that Jem kisses her for the first time, telling her 'I like it' and pulling her hair loose. While his arrest disrupts their plan to make love that night, the moor is clearly figured as a liminal wilderness of possibility extending to questions of selfhood and sexual identity (just as it is for Demelza in *Poldark* and Claire (Catriona Balfe) in *Outlander*, in the far northern Celtic periphery of Britain). Crossing the moor can signal an act of remaking of self and, in this way, the moorland interior as a space of fluidity and change, signalled by the rapidly changing sky captured in time-lapse, can operate in a similar way to the coastal edge. The unknown moorland interior, though, is imbued with material threats—of getting lost, of sinking, of unexpected mists—which in *Jamaica Inn* are visualized through an aesthetics of vastness, immersion and perpetual change. It is these characteristics of landscape that make the Cornish moor an especially resonant setting for narratives of mystery and horror.

Mystery, hauntings and horror have been integral to the Cornish place-myth. Books of traditional folk tales and stories of shipwrecks, piracy and smuggling, which reiterate the connection of landscape with mystery, magic and danger, are displayed on revolving stands in every gift shop alongside those on recipes and place names, articulating a specificity of culture which includes the ghostly and the murderous alongside traditional dishes and the Cornish language. Daphne du Maurier's stories are known for their use of the Cornish landscape as a romantic, Gothic location and children's stories such as Enid Blyton's *Famous Five* series have depended upon the same sense of a darkness underlying the bright hues of tourist, seaside Cornwall. This is an ancient association with place, part of a regional cultural tradition, from traditional tales such as 'The Mermaid of Zennor', the Giants of St Agnes and St Michael's Mount, Cornish Piskies, Knockers and Spriggens, to prehistoric heritage sites such as the many standing stones associated with magical rites which mark the Cornish moorland, as well as the Witchcraft Museum in Boscastle, and the widely acknowledged ongoing presence of pagan religions and rites across Cornwall. The tradition of folk magic and mysticism, in particular, is still regularly adapted, especially for contemporary children's literature and fairy tales, in works such as *The Islanders* (Dunmore and Cobb 2011), *The Ferry Birds* (Dunmore and Cobb 2012) and *The Sea Monster* (Wormell 2006), as well as in retellings of ancient myths such as 'The Mermaid of Zennor'.

This aspect of the place-myth has made Cornwall an appropriate setting for both new and adapted screen fictions in the modes of mystery and horror.[25] From children's adventure films of magic, smuggling and piracy (for example, *Knights of the Round Table* [1953] and numerous film and television adaptations of Robert Louis Stevenson's *Treasure Island* [1883], such as the UK/US co-production of 1950) which depend upon the idea of Cornwall's association with mystery and danger, to the adult detective drama *Wycliffe* and the extreme horror of Peckinpah's British Western *Straw Dogs*, Cornwall's identification as a place where strange, unsettling and dangerous things might happen is ancient and traditional, but also part of its ongoing construction as a territory of backwards rurality, of 'West Barbary' (Deacon 1997). This has been discernible in the picturing of Cornwall in newsreels since the earliest years of the moving image and which has been unpicked and interrogated in the satirical sitcom *Wild West* (BBC, 2002–04) and through the examples of regional creative practice discussed in Chapter 5. Cliff, mine and moor have been central to this construction, in which a fine line divides the romantic from the horrific; both are somatic genres of feeling (Williams 1991), and in the final part of this chapter my interest is in exploring the ways in which landscape and place-myth are revealed as critical to the success of their affect. Craig and Fitzgerald demonstrate that the clay country, a part of the unknown and unknowable interior region largely invisible in on-screen Cornwall, has been used as a site for the filming of literal 'otherness', a location which has stood in for other planets and times in science-fiction drama in the 1970s (1999: 93). In the romantic fictions examined here it is precisely 'Cornwall as Cornwall' that is pictured as strange and terrifying.

Cornwall's 'otherness' was often intimated in newsreel and cinemagazine pieces where the ostensible subject was regional custom. These are some of the very few items to feature the interior territory of the region, rather than the coastal edge, as in the trope's continuation in *Straw Dogs* and *Wycliffe*, and it is here that the strangeness of local tradition and superstition are typically pictured. The ancient pagan springtime traditions of the Furry (often anglicized to 'Flora') Dance at Helston and the 'Obby 'Oss at Padstow were the topic of numerous newsreel and cinemagazine items across the history of the forms. *Helston's Ancient Furry Dance* (1921), *On with the Furry Dance!* (1925), *And They Sang As They Danced Along* (1926, 1929, 1930 and 1933), *Furry Clock* (1941) and the colour *Furry Dance* (1955) are archetypal 'view' films in Gunning's sense (1997), presenting both a tourist gaze on picturesque scenes as well as documenting a process. *On with the Furry Dance!*, for instance, is a clear observation of a regional curiosity, described as a 'Weird in and out the Houses "Hop" at Helston'. This 43 second, four-shot film uses pans and tilts to follow the procession of dancing couples up the hill and in and out of the house, and the dancers look to camera in every shot, seemingly directed to do so, thus returning the gaze of the camera in a way which does, as Peterson (2006) suggests, challenge the power relations inherent in this kind of view film. Some items on the Padstow 'Obby 'Oss rite, such as *Summer is Y Comen In* (1930) and *The Padstow 'Hobby Hoss'* (1932), signal the Cornish strongly as 'weird rural folk' (and are often catalogued by Pathé as 'entertainment and humour' as well as 'culture and lifestyle').

By contrast, those traditions which draw on ancient Druidic, Celtic or Christian customs, such as *All Soul's Day* (1910–19), where flowers are cast to sea to remember the souls of drowned sailors, *Cornish Gorsedd— Ancient Rites* (1946) and *People in Camera* (1946), which shows the Gorsedd parade at the ancient Plen an Gwari ('playing place')[26] of Perran Round, are taken more seriously and, in this immediate post-war moment, are presented as 'a living example of the endurance and strength of our traditional ceremonies'. These items connect Celtic Cornwall to Wales and incorporate it *within*, rather than *other* than Britain, in a celebration of the 'us' of the national and what we might, potentially, have lost, as I have argued in relation to the screen fictions of Cornwall in this period. The later *Cross Pilgrimage* (1965), on the other hand, shows a group of scouts helping to take an enormous cross through the countryside to Looe and strongly tends towards the 'comical Cornish' tradition evident across newsreel and cinemagazine history. *New Surf Boat* (1968), for instance, tells the story of Cornish lifeguards collecting a new Australian surf boat and attempting to take it home to Perranporth from London by Tube. Humour is also foregrounded in items on regional sports such as Cornish wrestling and hurling (as in the accelerated footage of *Battle of St Columb* of 1948), and *Sheaf Pitching Record* (*News in a Nutshell*, 1935) which also shows a game of football being played on stilts at a Camborne rugby pitch. Other newsreels focus directly on the presentation of regional 'oddities' and effectively position Cornwall in relation to the ancient and mystical. *Veryan* (1938) is a scenic about regional superstition in a village where the cottages are round and topped with a cross, supposedly so that the devil has nowhere to hide. 'Nowadays, the old man just comes home from work and doesn't even bother to look up!' says the narrator. The same custom is noted in *Old Superstitions* (1961), which also shows identically dressed little girls baptizing their dolls in a hole in a stone at the base of an old cross in order to keep evil away. 'But it's not only the little ones who believe in the little people, and the whole catalogue of magic,' says the narrator, over shots of granite standing stones at Madron, one with a hole through which mothers in the olden days would push their children in order to cure rickets. A clearly set up shot of a woman re-enacting this tradition to cure her arthritis is one of many such scenes in newsreel accounts of the region which position Cornwall securely as 'internal colony' (Hechter 1975). *Caught by the Camera 28* (1935) documents the ritual blowing of a horn as the Cornish Riviera Express leaves Penzance; *Horse Sense* (1950) shows the equine stout-drinking regular at the Marazion Hotel, and *Girl Water Diviner* (1954) is rather extreme footage of a Cornish girl who locates water by means of her violently twitching body. Such films are, of course, not unique to newsreel representation of Cornwall, but are typical of representations of rurality more generally; nevertheless, they participate in the construction of a place-image which positions the region, in its wider place-myth, as oddly other than the English centre.

A number of films and television programmes for children have used the backdrop of Cornwall and its association with strangeness, mystery, piracy and smuggling, for adventure narratives. Among these, those made under the auspices of the Children's Film and Television Foundation have been the most interesting and imaginative.[27] In particular, *Haunters of the Deep* (Bogle, 1984) uses the settings of cliff, mine and moor and traditional Cornish folk tales to construct a children's adventure narrative that is a classic example of the Foundation's productions. When the US company Aminco Mining begins to explore the old Strangles Head Mine and finds a rich seam of tin, the mine's deadly reputation proves founded when a collapse traps the investigating miners hundreds of feet below the sea ('That mine's run by devils, not you,' old Tregellis, a former mine captain, warns them). Contacted by the ghost of a child miner who perished in 1911, local boy Josh, accompanied by the daughter of Aminco's CEO, Becky, must interpret the ghost's clues to save the men. The children are curious, independent and resourceful, and while Tregellis helps them by translating the ghost's clues from the Cornish, and finding the forgotten escape route, an old injury prevents his participation. The children must go it alone to rescue the men, Becky's father and Josh's brother among them. *Haunters of the Deep* is a ghostly adventure story dependent upon location shooting on the Penwith peninsula, on classic Cornish myths and fables, as well as the place-image of Cornwall as simultaneously picturesque, mysterious and dangerous. The film is replete with beautiful shots of the Atlantic Ocean crashing against the rocks, panning and tracking shots as Josh bikes around the cliff, and dramatic shots of the misty ruins of mine stacks and engine houses which were undoubtedly influenced by the enormous popularity and success of the then-recent BBC adaptation of *Poldark*. It is the mythical Cornish Spriggens, the ghosts of miners who previously perished, whose taps and moans warn the miners of imminent disaster and lead them to safety.

The film's attention to its Cornish setting is not merely picturesque, however. The writers paid attention to regional politics, with the screenplay and imagery making important points about the impact of the decline of mining, the value of local knowledge, the widespread emigration of Cornish miners and the plunder of the land by external forces. One might interpret the mine collapse as the natural world's response to such exploitation: sound design produces the Cornish ground as animate, the sighing and tapping in the mine often indistinguishable from the sounds of the wind, waves and gulls. The special effects—the mist, editing and superimposed faces of perished miners—produce a powerful, picturesque supernatural adventure, a cautionary tale of Cornwall which, at the same time, was attentive to regional politics and history. *Malachi's Cove* (Herbert, 1973), an adaptation of Anthony Trollope's novel, was a film for older children almost entirely dependent for its affect upon a sense of deep audiovisual immersion in the regional landscape. Set in North Cornwall in the 1880s, the film tells the story of teenage Mally Trenglos (Veronica Quilligan) who, following the drowning of her parents, lives with and cares for her disabled grandfather Malachi (Donald Pleasence). Mally makes money by collecting the seaweed which washes up in their cove and selling it for fertilizer, and the narrative dramatizes her conflict with the nearby villagers, upon whose failure to respond she blames her parents' death, and her feud with one boy, Barty (Dai Bradley), who insists on 'stealing' the seaweed on which she depends for a living. This is a costume film which plays on the image of Cornwall as archaic, and reproduces imagery and shots familiar from the earliest actualities of the region (gnarled fishermen weave crab pots, narrow, winding, cobbled lanes between granite cottages) and elements of the familiar grammar such as the high or off-screen horizon. At the same time, however, *Malachi's Cove* is also an unusual, deeply impressionistic and atmospheric film. Optical point-of-view shots are used frequently around Mally, and her memories are typically prompted by a shot of a gull riding the breeze overhead, in tandem with the almost deafening gull cries and wave crashes which dominate the soundscape and blend with the score throughout. This overwhelming use of sound is particularly effective in combination with close-up shots of crashing waves in her memories of her parents' drowning, and in the near drowning of Barty in the film's present, and articulate a profound emotional connectedness to place which is echoed in her repeated claim of ownership of the cove to which her family built the path.

Central to the affect of *Summer in February* was an initial romanticization of the Cornish landscape, the subsequent revelation of that interpretation as mistaken, and the recontextualization of the site as one of horror. This device is evident elsewhere in screen fictions of Cornwall, and the articulation of its landscape in relation to fear and horror is often dependent upon an undercutting of its initial romanticization. While this is common to the horror genre, it is given particular resonance by the powerful and long-standing association of Cornwall with romantic fantasy in its place-myth, established in this chapter. In the BBC's first adaptation of *Poldark*, the title sequence for episodes thirteen to sixteen, for instance, operated in precisely this way. While reading on first viewing as a simple, picturesque long and wide shot of a clifftop at sunset, repeat viewing with the episodic development of the narrative leads to a reinterpretation of the romantic clifftop in which the distant and indistinct figures atop the cliff are understood as villages throwing a traitor to his death on the rocks below.

Such reversal of expectation around the meaning of the landscape image is critical to the way in which romantic representations of Cornwall have hovered between romance and horror. *The Uninvited* (Allen, 1944), adapted from a novel by the Irish writer Dorothy Macardle (1942), tells the story of brother and sister Rick (Ray Milland) and Pamela Fitzgerald (Ruth Hussey), who buy a beautiful house on a Cornish cliff, only to discover that it is haunted. Stella Meredith (Gail Russell), the young woman from whom they buy the house, is reluctant to sell her mother's house, where she grew up. Her father was an artist, and painted a portrait of Stella's mother, Mary, who died in a fall from the cliff; the image hangs in their current drawing room. The house hides a murderous, mysterious past, and in the course of the narrative the siblings investigate and reveal the truth: the Spanish nanny, thought to have killed Stella's mother in a jealous rage was, in fact, Stella's real mother and was fighting for the return of her baby. The source text is set in Devon, and the relocation of the story to Cornwall for the screen is significant. It indicates both the power of the regional place-myth in the audiovisual register (and its suggestiveness in relation to the conjunction of mystery and romance) and at the same time confirms the distinction, which this book sets out to demonstrate, between the place-myths collected under the wider 'region' of 'the South West'. The film comes after the success of Hitchcock's adaptation of du Maurier's Gothic woman's text *Rebecca* (1940) and is contemporary with *Love Story* and *While I Live*, the wartime women's films discussed above. The trailer emphasized the connection between place-myth and genre capitalized upon and developed into horror in this adaptation, describing the film's setting as 'A house of terror on the haunted cliffs of Cornwall' and its appeal as precisely the conjunction of romance and horror which I explore here: 'the breathless beauty of a haunting love!' The film opens with a slow-motion pan left across cliffs and the sea, moving down and over the waves crashing on rocks at the base of the cliffs. The use of slow motion in conjunction with the very conventional 'tourist' device of the panoramic sweep around the coastal landscape produces a strange temporality, marked by the slight blurring of the image as the waves crash, and an odd, vaguely supernatural atmosphere. Over this shot, a voice-over narration (which does not originate in the novel) calls attention to the mysterious nature of the landscape, linking it to the wider Celtic peripheries of the UK and suggesting an odd relationship of heightened awareness between local (rural, peripheral) people and place, a place which is 'terribly out of the way' and inherently unsettling.

As the narration ends, the camera has completed its pan to the left and has come to rest, framing the clifftop. The shot dissolves to a house on the cliff; a blasted tree stands stark before it. A further dissolve to a closer view of the house makes visible a couple climbing up the cliff towards it. The narration continues, 'Well, my sister Pamela and I knew nothing about such matters. Not then, we didn't. We had the disadvantage of being Londoners, just down for a fortnight's rest. That tenth day of May 1937, was the last day of our holiday.' This opening establishes the now-familiar centre–periphery binary in the premise of visitors from London on a retreat in Cornwall ('how I do hate living in a London flat!'), and at the same time suggests the strange otherness of the local people, who have an intimate, affective and emplaced 'insider' relationship to the regional landscape which is not shared by the incomers. As the narration ends, a dissolve produces a shot from the cliff edge as a dog barks and comes up into view, followed by the couple. The foreboding narration has been replaced by gentle, romantic string music and the coastal wind visibly blows clothes, hair, the dog's fur. The romantic, elemental setting is disrupted again, here, by the sibling rather than coupled relationship of the main characters, who wish to buy and live in the house together. Here, it is he who is the artist who wishes for a peaceful place to compose and, as they explore the house, we share their delight at the views of the coast visible through the windows. We also note, though, the strong shadows on the walls which are a classically noir or Gothic unsettling device, one which undercuts the sense that this house will represent a return to the innocence of childhood freedom (it has a banister to slide down, and a private beach).

The viewer is constantly reminded of the house's proximity to the cliff edge in shots which frame the view through every window, and the disturbing sounds of howling and wailing made by the wind at night, and which die away with the dawn breeze. As Rick investigates the sounds by candlelight, shots of the waves crashing below and of the house on the clifftop are accompanied by the 'magical' sound of a harp, a mischievous piano tremolo and a brass sting. The strange happenings in the house are associated by local people with Stella's father who had an 'artistic temperament', and his affair with his model, 'a foreign girl', 'a Spanish gypsy and an awful bad lot' who died at the house. The dangerous conjunction of foreignness, creativity and sexuality at the edge of the Cornish cliff have led to murder, haunting and possession with something shaped like a woman, only 'like a mist, a crawling mist', lurking at the studio door, once more intimately connecting elemental aspects of the regional landscape with the supernatural. The cliff edge as a site of both romance and horror is prominent, again, as on two occasions Rick prevents Stella from falling to her death there, as her mother did. The film gives no logical explanation for the mysterious events and sounds, and the sense of the regional landscape and the elements as supernatural forces remains in place at the end of the film, un-debunked. Stella, for instance, maintains that she felt pulled towards the cliff edge: 'The sea sounded loud and beautiful ... I just ran in that direction.'

The Uninvited has an oddly comic tone at times, ending as Rick jokes that he's 'had a narrow escape ...[the ghost] might have been my mother-in-law!' in a combination of horror and comedy which frequently attends rural horror and which is exploited in texts offering a different picturing of Cornwall, as discussed in Chapter 5. This tonal and interpretative ambiguity was also essential to the disturbing affect of *Straw Dogs*, with its jolly, melancholy and threatening score, its childishly playful and borderline abusive central 'romantic' relationship, its trike-riding, party-nose wearing, hysterically giggling antagonists, probably one of the most controversial films in the history of (W)estern cinema largely due to the ambiguous tone of its pivotal rape scenes. Filmed on the remote West Penwith peninsula of Cornwall, soon after Peckinpah's critically praised *The Wild Bunch* (1969), *Straw Dogs* has a long history of difficulties with the censors in both the USA and UK as a result of two sequences of extreme violence: a double rape in the middle of the film, and a concluding section in which a large number of characters meet gruesome deaths at the hands of David Sumner (Dustin Hoffman). The film was only finally granted a DVD release in 2002 (Simkin 2016: 66). There is a remarkably slim critical literature on the film given its reputation and, as Charles Barr commented in his early and insightful analysis of the contemporary responses to *Straw Dogs* by British film critics, fervent emotional responses of various kinds to the film's scenes of violence seemed to inhibit more careful analysis of the film's aesthetic strategies and achievements (Barr 1972). Gibson has written about *Straw Dogs* in relation to its representation of 'Celtic' Cornwall through the frame of Hechter's 1975 theory of internal colonialism, noting that the film relocates the source novel by Gordon M. Williams, *The Siege of Trencher's Farm* (1969), from Devon to Cornwall, and reading the significance of horrific representations of Celticity in *Straw Dogs* and *The Wicker Man* (Hardy, 1973)—a film which relocates its source novel from Cornwall to Scotland—in the context of late 1960s and early 1970s Britain (2013: 144). Gibson argues that, ultimately, these films present the colonizer as the most dangerous character, and not the colonized Celts of Cornwall and Scotland (150), but unlike Barr, who notes that the film identifies its setting broadly as 'The West Country of England', she reads the location of *Straw Dogs* as Cornwall directly from its filming locations. While sources such as the Internet Movie Database and Craig and Fitzgerald (1999) have made it known that the locations used in the film were Tor Noon, Morvah, St Buryan and Lamorna in West Penwith, to an insider, the landscape is immediately identifiable as Cornwall. Indeed, it matters a great deal, if one reads the film beyond the paradigmatic critical isolation of its scenes of brutality, that this is evidently Cornwall, for this is a regional and thus a politicized landscape. In this respect, Barr's suggestion that critics' focus on a perceived failure of realism in relation to the regional setting of *Straw Dogs* was irrelevant feels more troubling. It is precisely through the representation of this regional landscape that the film achieves much of its effect, as the analysis which follows demonstrates.

There is the odd comment in critical writing on the film, which draws attention to setting as place. Damien Love is one of the few writers to have noted its significance, pointing out that '[t]he film's clothes, cars and conversations mark the time as the present day, but the Neanderthal landscapes and primitive behaviour suggest something old and cold. *Straw Dogs* is the law of the jungle, writ on a monumental scale by a man revelling in its terrible truth',[28] confirming *Straw Dogs* as a continuation of the articulation of Cornwall as 'West Barbary' (Deacon 1997). Similarly, Kent notes the 'ethnic "heart of darkness" among the Cornish' asserted by the film, at the start of a decade which was seen as the golden age of Cornish nationalism (2003: 120), and argues that 'the film can therefore be read against the grain, and seen as a touchstone of that cultural conflict which was to dominate Cornish cultural and political life towards the end of the twentieth century' (121). Sragow points out that the David Sumner character in the source novel is obsessed with film Westerns, framing his relocation to the West Country through a fantasy of encounter with a British 'southwestern' frontier (2012), as does Barr (1972: 23). As I note throughout the book, it is difficult not to associate Cornwall and some kind of composite of the American Wild West/Deep South as a new 'frontier', given its picturing across screen history in ways which beg for the comparison to be made, from *A Tragedy of the Cornish Coast* to the 'Western' compositions in *Jamaica Inn* discussed above. The relocation of the narrative in the recent remake of *Straw Dogs* (Lurie, 2011) from Cornwall to the Deep South of the USA cements the connection.

In a rare moment of close attention to the precise way in which the film presents regional place, Sragow notes how Peckinpah:

> conveys the perverse, ingrown vitality of the town in the opening credit shots. Like a gothic impressionist, he paints hazy, scampering figures—a hive—slowly coming into focus. As he sharpens his gaze, we see that this insect-like scurrying is made up of kids at play in the village graveyard, forming circles of life that caper around gravestones (2012: 73).

Indeed, these opening images are critical in establishing a powerful mood and picture of regionality in *Straw Dogs*, a discourse of landscape and place based upon the dialectic between Deacon's 'West Barbary' and 'Delectable Duchy', a discourse of reversal upon which, I argue, the film largely depends for its affect (1997). The centrality of this discourse is emphasized in the design of the Fremantle DVD menu, where the romantic yet melancholy string and woodwind score is repeatedly interrupted by the sound of a gunshot smashing glass, as a shot of them driving with the bright Cornish landscape visible behind them in the convertible is simultaneously destroyed by glass being shattered by a gunshot. The first shot of the film is a low-angle, low-contrast, black-and-white view of an ancient, inscribed gravestone covered in lichen and, in the background, what appears to be a statue but which will be reinterpreted, in the course of the title sequence, as a young boy seated 'inappropriately' atop a tomb. The low angle of the shot makes this figure visible in the frame, but also establishes a couple of thematic and stylistic tropes in the film: the dissonant behaviour of local people and a play between extreme high- and low-angle shots of place. Both are critical to the opening sequence of the film, both the images which run behind the titles and the longer sequence which takes the viewer, with the central couple of the film, Amy and David Sumner, from the village of Wakely to their isolated house up on the moor, and establish a mood which Barr describes as 'nervous, visceral' and which carries through to the final shot (1972: 18). The following shot is a bird's-eye view—the image described by Sragow—of rapid movement around fixed objects. Our process of interpretation of this shot continues as the image and sound gradually come into visual and auditory focus but also into colour, and shifts from the possibilities of insect-life (Sragow's 'hive'), to people circling around standing stones and chanting, to the eventual confirmation of children playing and singing around gravestones, viewed from the top of the church tower.

These possible reinterpretations, and the way in which we are led through them, are suggestive and significant, for they establish an atmosphere of uncertainty in relation to both place and character. Are the stones natural, neolithic, pagan, Celtic, Christian? Is the activity around them biological, ritualistic, religious, disrespectful, playful? Gradually, the repetitive chime of instrumentation bleeding into the score develops into the ringing of church bells and confirms the interpretation made possible by the simultaneous shift to colour and clarity of focus. Barr identifies the use of a telephoto lens as producing an impression of reality dependent upon 'the sense that the scene is there, going on already, and that we overlook and overhear it' (1972: 21). In conjunction with the aerial shot, we have the impression of being simultaneously a distant (and unnoticed) observer of events taking place and, at the same time, uncomfortably, and dangerously, close to them. Barr describes this as an 'eavesdropping' effect which makes us 'distant-yet-close', our involvement 'enhanced by the nervous way the camera has to respond, at this distance/focal length, to the characters' movements' (22). There are numerous moments of unseen watching in the film, and our positioning as simultaneously distant/hidden and yet close is an aesthetic strategy that I have identified as characteristic of the audiovisual grammar of Cornwall. This is evident, for example, in *Jamaica Inn* and in both adaptations of *Poldark*, and has been critical to the production of an affective feeling of relationship to landscape, of emplacement. Here, that emplacement is used, as in the titles of *Poldark* (BBC, 1975), to unsettling effect/affect, as we are positioned as a helpless onlooker, powerless to do anything but observe and reflect on what we witness. In the opening scenes in the village, the children watch David and Amy's meeting with Charlie Venner (Del Henney), en masse, from the elevated churchyard wall, a positioning which the viewer will (almost) share as the village paedophile Henry Niles (David Warner) is observed playing ball with the teenage Janice Hedden (Sally Thomsett) from further along the wall. The same viewpoint is shortly after associated with Amy's other rapist Norman Scutt (Ken Hutchison), as he observes their arrival home from the garage roof where he is working. Similarly, in *Malachi's Cove*, the frequent use of the telephoto lens to 'spy' on Mally down in the cove from an elevated vantage point produces a similarly unsettling effect. While this is a historically specific stylistic device, fashionable in late 1960s and early 1970s cinema and television, its effect is significantly heightened in its use in filming the Cornish landscape, given its particular associations of anxiety and dis-ease.

The village is viewed initially in a bird's-eye view from the church tower, a place of brownish-grey granite buildings and walls which appear, through heightened perspective, to lean inwards and encroach on the square at its centre. The Sumners' home, Trencher's Farm, is presented in the same palette, a remote granite farmhouse high up on the moor above the village, frequently viewed from an extreme low angle which makes it appear to loom menacingly over the moorland landscape like the granite tors of *Poldark* and *Jamaica Inn*. The palette and the sense of claustrophobia characterizing the village exterior is echoed in the cramped interior *mise en scène* of the farmhouse, crowded with antique weapons and agricultural objects, and the crowded audiovisual space of the church hall during the 'social'. It is only in the couple's unnerving initial drive between the village and the farm, and the few shots that follow as they arrive at the house, that we glimpse the other Cornwall, the bright emerald and sapphire 'tourist' Cornwall of summertime and holidays. As Amy drives erratically along the narrow country lanes with their imposing high hedges, bright jazz and lively classical music plays on the radio and we are afforded spectacular views of the sunny, bright coastal landscape, the moor and the sea gleaming in the distance behind them from the convertible, the blue sky and verdant, sunlit countryside ahead of them visible through the windscreen as they tear along.

These and other momentary 'views', however, work mainly to emphasize the isolation of the farm from the village and the bright coastline, and the absence of any other dwelling. The classic picturing of Cornwall is further disturbingly undercut as David puts on his glasses and we have a brief, low-angle shot from his point of view, of cows silhouetted above the hedge, the sun glaring disorientingly behind them. The regional landscape is frequently a threatening element in the frame: when the local men are collected from the farm in an ancient truck, a shot of the driver, hanging out of the window, is framed menacingly by the dark, leafless, wind-blasted trees characteristic of Cornwall behind him. Landscape again dominates the *mise en scène* in a sequence of parallel editing between scenes of Venner and Scutt raping Amy, and David, sitting alone on the moor where they, and Chris Cawsey (Jim Norton) have lured and left him to 'shoot'. The flattening of space produced by the telephoto lens (Barr 1972: 22) emphasizes the composition of shots in which David is framed or obscured by stark, bare branches. In the final violent siege at the farm, the darkness of the moorland night is exacerbated by thick fog, and distorting brass notes in the score recall the warning tones of a foghorn, despite the physical distance of the farm from the coast. In this way, the elemental nature of the regional landscape is emphasized, and an intimate connection is suggested between place and the violent action of the narrative. While David and Amy's relationship is characterized by a childlike vindictiveness, there is a clear suggestion that its dysfunction pre-existed their move to Cornwall; it is as though the place itself has been the catalyst to the disintegration charted in the film. While critics have remained focused on the two key scenes of brutality for which *Straw Dogs* is infamous, I argue that this focus obscures a significant discourse around regional landscape upon which the film in fact depends for much of its effect/affect. The critical neglect of the overall aesthetic of *Straw Dogs*, resulting from overdetermination of the film in relation to the history of its censorship, is a particular instance of a wider neglect of the importance of landscape, and its articulation and interpretation, in the moving image.

Straw Dogs depends upon an idea at the heart of many constructions of peripheral rurality and a central place-image within the wider place-myth of Cornwall: a static and at times frighteningly isolated backwater, filled with odd, and occasionally terrifying, local people. While the 'oddness' of Cornwall in screen fictions is often initially presented as a comic device (for example through stereotypes such as those in *Doc Martin*), or for satirical and resistant effect in *Wild West*, the fine line across which the comic can tip into the horrific has been repeatedly walked in moving image representations of the region. *Wycliffe*, for instance, returns endlessly to this stereotype in its crime narratives, for example in episodes in which characters associated with pagan religion and ritual are revealed as perpetrators. While the local people of *Straw Dogs*, and in particular the character of Cawsey, the hysterically cackling 'rat man', exemplify this fine line between comedy and horror, such picturings of Cornwall as strange, archaic and frightening, especially in relation to its pagan heritage and inheritance, have been a feature of moving images of the region since the earliest moments, and continue to recur.

Into the Clay: *Stocker's Copper* (1972)

Screen fictions of Cornwall have tended to hover simultaneously at the generic limen of romance/mystery/horror and at the liminal site of the clifftop, coastal edge. This precarious positioning has been generative for film and television dramas of Cornwall, which have returned persistently to questions of identity (personal, sexual, creative, social and national), refracted through the provocative lens of regional landscape, particularly around the crisis point of World War II. The Cornish coast figures repeatedly on screen as a site of both possibility and anxiety, while its interior, where it is pictured in the moving image, remains, on the whole, threateningly unknowable.[29] There is one key screen picturing of Cornwall's interior that stands apart from the mainstream films and programmes discussed thus far: *Stocker's Copper*, a 1972 single television play in the BBC's *Play for Today* strand, a later incarnation of the *Wednesday Play* of the 1960s. The dramas written for and broadcast in these strands have been understood and debated in relation to a 'Golden Age' of British television drama, as a site of political engagement and formal experimentation.

Given this context, it is unsurprising that *Stocker's Copper*, written by Tom Clarke and directed by Jack Gold (perhaps best known for *The Naked Civil Servant* [1975]), should stand out as offering a distinctive challenge to existing screen Cornwalls.[30] The 'Copper' of the title is a Welsh policeman, Herbert Griffith (Gareth Thomas), one of many dispatched to Cornwall in 1913 to support mine owners in the clay area of mid-Cornwall during a strike by workers for better pay and conditions. Griffith is billeted with the Stocker family, the patriarch of which, Manuel (Bryan Marshall), is a striking miner. The drama rapidly establishes a troubling play between Caughie's documentary gaze and dramatic looks (2000) at the same time as it invokes and challenges the tourist gaze and narrative which characterizes screen Cornwall. As the programme opens, a steam train races through the frame, and shots of dozens of identical, aligned black boots, truncheons and heads, resolutely focused inwards, are contrasted with the curious gaze out of the window of one officer—the eponymous 'Copper'—at the moment when the train whistle shatters the insistent, rhythmic rattle of the train over the tracks and the silence of the carriage. In this way, the 'outsider' look at the landscape is immediately marked as both unsettling and discordant, in a direct contrast to the orchestral scoring which usually accompanies such a moment in the journey into Cornwall. We are aligned with Griffith's optical point of view, given in a shot–reverse shot sequence, in a pan across the dramatic white peaks of the 'Cornish Alps', the conical waste heaps resulting from the process of china-clay mining (as in *China Clay* [1964]). The repeated pan across the landscape is a familiar trope of the tourist gaze, but here the dramatic industrial interior landscape is its object, rather than the blue and green of the coast, and the accompanying sound is the insistent rattle of the train which brings the police to Cornwall, effectively aligning the incomer with a brutalizing, outside force.

The coast is never seen in *Stocker's Copper*, which instead presents the clay landscape, bathed in sunshine, as Cornwall. A shot of a dark figure atop a white peak is accompanied by the sound of a traditional Cornish silver band, the train's whistle blowing and a zoom backwards from the peak to show a miner and a smoking stack from a low angle, in stark composition against the sky. This is a rare screen Cornwall, particularly in terms of a grammar of place typically associated with a spectacular-izing tourist gaze at the 'view'; this challenge is made evident by Griffith's double take at a palm tree against the sky, and his gaze at a GWR poster of the Cornish coast at the station. At the same time, the landscape shots that typically act as scene transitions are reconfigured in *Stocker's Copper*, and movement between scenes is marked by two shots: first, of the beam in the engine house, rising and falling and accompanied by the sound of the steam engine, and the second, a low-angle shot of a smoking stack against the sky. Here, the dramatic industrial interior of Cornwall replaces the coastal pan or long shot, insisting on industrial landscape as place-image, and on the relation of labour to landscape, as we see the striking miners, the band and the banners approaching the mine from the hill through the opening beyond the beam.

The relationship between individual, community, labour and landscape is central to *Stocker's Copper*; the use of a telephoto zoom repeatedly contextualizes the individual in relation to an industrialized landscape. This is the Cornwall of mining and Methodism (Deacon and Payton 1993), and the minister's speech draws attention to the mine owner's exploitation of the workers, and to the landscape as 'stolen property'. When Stocker and his wife Alice (Jane Lapotaire) are then pictured in the classic 'prospect' pose, looking out over the Alps and the flooded pits, rather than the sea, the question of proprietorial relations to landscape in terms of both tourism and industry is brought into focus. 'It's like a Sunday,' says Stocker. A sunny day outside of that is 'bosses' weather', which they cannot usually enjoy.

The soundscape, which makes use of male choir and silver bands local to the filming sites, is integral to the play's challenge to existing screen Cornwall. These traditional musical forms, which have been appropriated as part of Cornwall's tourist address, feature in *Stocker's Copper* as a form of protest (in repeated marches to the mine) and are echoed in the instrumentation of the discordant, unsettling composed score, which accompanies, for example, attempts to convince miners to join the action. Alongside this striking redeployment of 'tourist Cornwall' for political purposes, the use of footage echoing archive newsreel footage of clay-working reminds us repeatedly of the play's relation to industrial history, taking us out of the narrative and returning us, repeatedly, to a more documentary gaze. Through the dramatic look, *Stocker's Copper* gradually establishes a personal connection between Stocker and Griffith, via the vegetable garden, cider and tobacco, and talk of the commonalities between Wales and Cornwall, making it clear that Griffith supports the strike in legal and personal terms. When the call comes to charge the miners, however, he participates in the brutal fight that leaves many dead or injured, saying 'it's nothing personal'. In this way, the play insists on the power of the centre to override human connection and connection between these 'internal colonies', plays with the potential in the dynamic of looks to disrupt conventional romantic narratives of Cornwall, and refuses to allow a settled inscription of the viewer into dramatic space, instead holding us between positions to enable a critical stance towards the representation of regional place. As the men sit in the landscape, comparing the 'black' landscape of Wales to the 'painted colours' of Cornwall, the industrial landscape of inland Cornwall is incorporated into the discourse of beautiful Cornwall as seen by the outsider, in a radical refusal of the 'emptying out' that I have argued is characteristic of Cornwall in the moving image.

Even in the exceptional instance of *Stocker's Copper*, dramatic Cornwall, overall, comes into view as an unsettled and affective space, seemingly resistant to the impulse to contain, restrict and shape characteristics of early actuality forms. While dramas of Cornwall do frequently mobilize an outsider, tourist gaze at the landscape, a trope that has been part of an audiovisual grammar of place since the very outset, Cornwall is simultaneously constructed as a place which invites the outsider in, though that invitation holds risk and the region's interior territory is difficult to navigate. Screen fictions of Cornwall are typified by an immersive and affective aesthetic that positions the viewer deeply within the audiovisual landscape. The sense of being 'inside of place', upon which that affect depends, is produced through a number of devices evident across the history of Cornwall's audiovisual grammar, including high or off-screen horizons, panning point-of-view shots and the use of auditory close-up. It is my contention, however, that it is often difficult to extract this 'aesthetic of the inside' from the production of Cornwall as a space of internal colony, signalled by the use of the prospect view and the tourist gaze. In the next chapter, the landscape documentary of Cornwall is explored as a form in which such prospect imagery, as well as the deeply proprietorial composition of the documentary moving image of Cornwall and its paratexts, reinforces region as internal colony, as a frontier wilderness to be conquered.

4

The 'Real' Cornwall

In this chapter we return to moving image 'actualities' of Cornwall—those taking the landscape and the place itself, ostensibly outside of the region's status as a holiday destination, as their subject. Cornwall has been a repeated destination for British holiday programmes, and for cookery shows such as *Floyd on Fish* (BBC, 1985) and *Rick Stein's Taste of the Sea* (BBC, 1995) as well as, more recently, the enormously popular daytime genre of property and relocation programming with series such as *Escape to the Country* (2002–), as well as prime-time iterations such as *Location, Location, Location* (Channel 4, 2000–) and *Relocation, Relocation* (Channel 4, 2002–11). The more 'everyday' Cornwall of television cookery and property programming is largely sidestepped here, but this decision does not indicate its lack of significance in relation to the ongoing screen construction of region. Indeed, it is perhaps in this genre that its repeated iteration as a site of escape, refuge and consumption, and as object of a 'tourist gaze' in relation to urban Britain, has been most insistently reiterated. Whether through the purchase of a second home, a retirement property or a desire to 'downsize', real-estate programming has continued to produce Cornwall as a picturesque and purchasable retreat from the urgency of modern city life, reinforcing a centre–periphery discourse which structures all screen narratives of Cornwall. In aesthetic terms, however, they are relatively uniform in their focus on the pans and aerial shots of the coast, which articulate a long-established grammar of Cornwall.

Instead, I consider 'event' articulations of Cornwall in actuality forms that aim for a view of Cornwall beyond escape and consumption. Here, the mainstream presentation of the 'real' Cornwall clearly emerges as shaped by the same audiovisual discourses which were established in the earliest forms of travelogue, newsreel and fiction film: Cornwall has been overwhelmingly produced, through the screening of (particular, restricted versions of) its landscape, as a site of emotional affectivity. This overdetermination has, with a couple of notable exceptions, meant the excision of other potential narratives of region, including those of industry, labour and modernity, confirming and perpetuating its future as a site of emotional release, tourism and consumption.

Wheatley has considered the recent explosion of landscape genres and rural imagery on British television, linking its new spectacularity to developments in high-definition (HD) filming and reception technologies, and revealing a much longer history (2016: 122–49). She shows the new ways in which television has operated as 'view' in relation to this, examining, for example, the design and positioning of HD televisions—in frames, on the wall—as 'art' (126). She writes about the use of 'spectacular montage' and, citing Brunsdon's work on empty spaces and the 'hesitation' in the cinematic image (2007a), she considers those moments where the camera 'lingers … meanders and rambles' over landscape in relation to the production of a space of contemplation for the television viewer (2016: 131–32). This theorization of a more general 'slow' representation of landscape on British television is helpful in locating the specificity of an audiovisual grammar of Cornwall. The syntax I identify in *Picturing Cornwall* is only occasionally slow, for example in moments where time-lapse is used (though even here there is rapidity in the texture of the long take), in the long-held close-up associated with emotionality, or in the moment where the woman is caught, and held, at the very edge. At other times, the pace is extremely rapid and the shot mobile, for example in the travelling aerial shot which traces the coastline, in quick cutting between increasingly close moving images of water and rocks, or the immersive shot from within a boat or the water.

In these instances, the desired effect is more kinaesthetic than contemplative, less a wondrous moment of contemplation of the 'noble sublime' theorized by Kant and more akin to the encounter with terrifying sublimity (1960). This distinction is critical, for it concerns the specificity of place-image and, in this case, the conjunction of aesthetic pleasure and potential horror at the heart of 'Cornwall'. The spectacularization of the regional landscape is evident in a number of subgenres of landscape documentary important in the continuing mainstream construction of Cornwall: the 'art' documentary, usually focused on St Ives; the television wilderness challenge, in which people are pitted against the regional landscape in a battle to survive; and the social documentary. Here, a vocabulary and syntax of place are explored as they have developed in documentaries of Cornwall, with discussion of newsreel and cinemagazine representations historicizing more recent screen Cornwalls. My concern is to make the case for a politicized understanding of the presentation of regional landscape on television, beyond dramatic fiction, and to consider the persisting picturing of Cornwall as internal colony.

Cornwall as Art

We have seen that Cornwall has been produced as a distinctive tourist destination, one that is distant, different and not quite the British seaside of the national cultural imagination. Romantic fictions of Cornwall have both constructed and depended upon this picturing of Cornwall as separate and uncommon, and one of the key ways in which this distinction has been crystallized is through the region's association with art and artists—painters, musicians, writers—and the sense that Cornwall is a place that inspires creativity. The region has been constantly made and remade through painting, sculpture, literature and music, and in particular the coastal sites of Newlyn, Lamorna and St Ives (which, since 1993, has been home to the Tate gallery) have place-images which remain powerfully determined by their long-standing status as 'artists' colonies'—places which have attracted groups of (largely incomer) artists because of their beauty and the quality of their light. While 'art' has been a key thematic and visual trope of romantic fictions of Cornwall, it has also been an important aspect of the screen documentation of the region, from the earliest moments of moving image representation to more recent television.

While Cornwall is associated with art throughout the history of its representation in the newsreel, for example in the *Eve's Film Review* item *Brighter Signs!* (1931) in which a woman paints a city sign for Truro, or in pieces from the mid-1950s which look at female sculptors at Mevagissey,[1] it is in the period of modernism associated with St Ives, from the 1930s to the late 1960s, that it features most markedly, with sculptor Barbara Hepworth as a focus. *Artists' Colony* (1948) begins with a still, picturesque view of St Ives, one of the 'smaller, more artistic cultural outposts of the metropolis' (Walton 2012: 6). This shifts to a high-angle panning shot of the harbour from the hill, in which the camera follows the curve of the bay from the houses, around to the left and up to reveal the bay and the sea and panning back across the town, cutting to a leftwards pan across the beach and boats, and then across the beach to the sea. This camera movement describes space in a graphic, linear way which contains and defines place at the edge and in relation to the sea, as the narrator comments that it is '[s]mall wonder that a town so quaint and picturesque, has a permanent colony of artists who, attracted by its mellow peacefulness, have made their home down here'. Shots of men and women artists painting *en plein air* are themselves constructed like picturesque landscape paintings with Turneresque skies. Cornwall, here, *is* art: containable and reproducible, barely different from *Scenes in the Cornish Riviera* (1904). An artist who could easily be taken for a fisherman by his dress and presentation is shown in a close-up profile shot; the lack of clarity around his identity efficiently expresses the erasure of labour in an identification of it with leisure typical of moving images of Cornwall, and in more recent media discourse, too, where the fisherman 'look' appears as just that—a purchasable and reproducible style of 'rugged' outdoor masculinity.[2]

The conjunction of picturesque views of St Ives and the Cornish landscape with modernist abstraction would reach its apotheosis with *Figures in a Landscape* (Shaw Ashton, 1953), one of the first films to be backed by the British Film Institute's Experimental Film Fund and described by Korossi as '[a]n imaginative Technicolor documentary … a collaborative artwork in its own right. It spearheaded an alternative British art cinema that ultimately became the focus of the Experimental Film Fund (1952–99)' (Korossi 2015). The film dramatically, and sometimes contrapuntally, juxtaposes Hepworth's sculpture with the landscape which inspired it, while the poet and writer of mystery stories Cecil Day Lewis gives a highly mannered reading of words by the archaeologist and writer Jacquetta Hawkes, which characterize the regional landscape again, as art, in terms of both sculptural form and emotional affect. The score was written by Priaulx Rainier, a South African-British composer whose athematic and increasingly abstract, chromatic music was greatly influenced by the African music of her childhood. Rainier spent considerable time working in St Ives from the late 1940s, becoming good friends with Hepworth and her husband, the modernist painter Ben Nicholson, and her music in this score responded directly to the Cornish landscape, as did her much later orchestral suite *Aequora Lunae*, dedicated to Hepworth (Routh [1972] 2018).

The film is a modernist work about modernist work and is extremely self-reflexive throughout. The opening black screen and titles provide a simple foil for the score, which layers woodwind instruments with a hollow, percussive, almost abstract use of glockenspiel, to produce a wavering, exploratory and spare accompaniment which carries moments of drama, through silence or sforzando. The emphasis on wood and reed in the music is a constant, denotative reminder of the landscape underpinning the film. The titles run over a canvas sized with visible brush strokes; while the visibility of the materiality of artistic production key to modernism is referenced here, the emphasis is on the figurative reproduction of the world through art. This occurs in the wording of the titles 'Figures in a Landscape—Cornwall and the Sculptures of Barbara Hepworth', the referentiality of the score and the gradual fading up of an image of tiny waves rolling onto a shore which replaces the canvas and directly references the representational relation between the observable world and abstract art which the film will explore. The film's initial presentation of the landscape, as with *Gallivant* (Kötting, 1996), indicates the typical mainstream audio-visual grammar of this region by its divergence from it. As the image begins to cut between different shots of the landscape, to larger waves, to waves crashing onto rocks, coming into colour, the music ebbs and flows with the rhythm of the tide. The next series of shots brings us gradually but certainly into the space of the landscape: a shot of towering cliffs shows the other side of the bay, or a different one. A cut back to the opposite side of the bay, or to another, situates us on a cliff opposite the view. A cut back to the other side looks down at the beach.

This sequence contrasts strongly with the syntax typical, for example, of *Poldark* (BBC, 1975), of a long shot of the coast, moving to a medium shot of waves crashing against the cliff, and down further still to a closer shot of water swirling over the rocks, a progression which indicates the emplacement of the visitor on the cliff and their gaze down to the sea. *Figures in a Landscape* has a different, more unsettling concern, to emphasize directionality and the graphic impact of the landscape when viewed from different perspectives, its materiality, the contrast between solidity and status in the frame, and the perpetual movement of water against the softness and changeability of the sand. The following sequence, over which the narration begins, reinforces this film's rather different picturing of the region through sound and image. While its emphasis is on the coast, and it moves from one edge of the land to the other, it includes and incorporates the interior as part of its articulation of region, rather than simply describing its edge in a panning or travelling gesture. From a shot of the open sea, the camera pans slowly inwards to show the opposite view of the coast, continuing to pan inwards across the rocks, their pale bottom exposed by the lowering tide, as narration replaces the music: 'Cornwall, a horn of rock, its point thrust out into the sea. Smooth or ribbed with waves, pale, deep blue or angry dark, the sea lies round about it and from three sides sends up its mirroring light.' The pan continues across the cliffs, which dissolve into clifftop heathland and moor as Day Lewis continues, 'Here at Penwith, the moors narrowing to Land's End, from the sea coast to the north, it is not far across the rusty moors, where the rocks break through the bracken, not far to where the sea lies to the south.'

A further dissolve takes the pan across the cliffs on the other side of the peninsula and to an opposing wide, sandy beach onto which gentle waves roll from the right; this series of three shots gives the impression of a narrow strip of land where, while the edge is foremost, the interior is important too. As the pan reaches the sea ('never far'), it continues around the horizon, giving the impression of a 360 degree panorama, before cutting to a shot through a rock archway on a sandy beach with a pool of water at its base. Coming to rest on this bold form, pausing on a high-contrast graphic, almost abstract composition of the image, the narration begins to personify the landscape in allusion to the connection between the natural formation of the landscape by the elements and by the hand of the sculptor: 'It shapes the rocks, sometimes fingering them gently, sometimes forging them with long, thundering blows, hollowing those caves where waves revolve in darkness.' As a rising, exploratory clarinet starts up again, the film cuts to a layered shot of hollowed-out rocks and cliffs beyond and pauses on it, the lone clarinet wandering the image as our eye does. The film and narration proceed through a series of images of dramatic rock formations (the 'elephant's trunk' at Bossiney, the rocks at Land's End, a granite tor, Brown Willy and Rough Tor, the moors) produced by the action of wind and water that have been 'whittling their images. They're at it now—and have been at it a million, million years beyond the reach of clocks.'

While this narration emphasizes the ancient nature of the landscape, it also acknowledges change and development across time. Its immediate juxtaposition of the ancient, evolving landscape with one of Hepworth's carved forms, though, seems to fix it as image, picture it as art, as a colonized landscape, as something to be gazed at. This happens both through the words which compare the sculptor to nature, and the images which provide a 'view' of Hepworth's work, set against the landscape view which, we are to understand, inspired it. A close-up shows a smooth wooden sculpture with holes in it, set on a plinth on a moorland peak, the sea in the distance, and the clarinet begins again over the held shot as the narrator makes the connection explicit over more images of sculptural rock formations, juxtaposed with Hepworth's pieces: 'Forms, rising in the minds of man he carves into images, carvings that draw power from land and sea.' As the opening sequence and the title of the film suggest, then, these sculptures are not purely abstract, but bear a representational relationship to the landscape. This is the conceit pursued by the rest of the film, which combines images of landscape and sculpture, either by cutting between them or by complex dolly shots such as one which moves out through a hole in a sculpture, then out through the hole in one of the Men-an-Tol stones, contextualizing both in the wider landscape. At the same time, the voice-over and musical narration tells mystical stories, both pagan and Christian, of these earlier stone sculptures in the landscape, and the wandering woodwind music fades in and out around it like the sea around the rocks, sometimes overlapping gently, sometimes crashing powerfully into the image.

Filming through holes in the rock, or the spaces between rocks and buildings, is a strategy of regional representation visible across the history of moving images of Cornwall, from *Scenes in the Cornish Riviera* to *West Country Journey* (Sharples, 1953), *Poldark* and *Summer in February* (Menaul, 2013). This trope is always potentially an immersive one, positioning the viewer deeply within the landscape to offer the impression of an emplaced experience. In *Figures in a Landscape* it also offers changed perspective, both immersion and emergence, positioning the viewer inside the landscape in an experiential way. Sometimes, we peer at forms through foliage, our relationship to the space unexpectedly changed, as in the example of the Men-an-Tol dolly shot. In a similar way, camera movement and score are sometimes used contrapuntally; a pan left, from a standing stone to a stark white Hepworth piece, with the stone circle behind it, for example, is accompanied by a startling glockenspiel sforzando. The smooth, continuous camera movement encourages us to perceive both continuity between forms and between forms and the landscape, but the sonic cue prompts us simultaneously to recognize the aesthetic and formal disjunctions between them.

The film uses the now iconic image of the ruined mine at the cliff edge in a series of juxtapositions. 'Now men came as miners, bringing machines,' says Day Lewis, as the film cuts to a shot of a ruined engine house and stack. 'They built stone chimneys, and houses for their engines. They sank shafts and dark tunnels down through the rock.' On a cut to a different angle of the ruin, he continues, 'seasons and centuries claimed them for landscape' and a shot of a solitary engine house in the landscape is held as the narration gives way to the haunting, hollow sounds of oboe and glockenspiel. A cut to ruins at the cliffside pans left to reveal a tall wooden Hepworth piece on a clifftop in the foreground. While the ruins on the distant cliff refer to the romanticization of Cornwall's de-industrialization, the change in optical perspective produced by the pan and the juxtaposition of the crumbling grey granite with the smooth, shiny mahogany verticality of the modern sculpture ask us, in contrast, to focus on ideas of power, solidity and warmth that the colour and form recall. The romantic place-image is challenged by means of this extraordinary contrast, which speaks of the region's industrial heritage, echoed by the hollow knocking of the score.

The focus on the edge is not an insistent or determining one here, however, for *Figures in a Landscape* spends as much time at the region's interior, making use of the graphic contrast of the china-clay 'Alps' and Bodmin Moor. Where the coastal edge is emphasized, the film's concern, taken from the artworks, is on questions of development and change.

The contrast of the man-made form (both ancient and modern) with the natural environment, and thus the representation of region in *Figures in a Landscape*, despite travelling some of the same territory, is often very different as a result of the Modernist interest in industrial forms. The camera pans across a coastal view with an island lighthouse in the distance and then down, revealing a smooth white Hepworth piece juxtaposed on the shore in foreground. An asymmetric, curved vertical plane and a ball on a white plinth sit on the rough, aged rock, echoing the lighthouse as the clarinet wanders and the glockenspiel punctuates, suggesting the continuity of the landscape, the features which stand out within it and its typical grammar, in its very musicality. Here is a different syntax of region from that which traces the romantic periphery (it is not a grammar because it has not been repeated and become systematic), one which picks up on contrast and conflict in texture, colour and form in the act of producing place, rather than smoothing and shaping by camera movement and legato score.

The film finishes at St Ives and, in ending here, virtually gives up its deconstructive, disjunctive aesthetic, which is seemingly held in check by the historical picturesque possibilities of the town. More customary, sometimes symmetrical, shots of the town, beach and fishing boats are followed by shots of the sculptor working on her pieces with St Ives as backdrop. The score livens, the glockenspiel echoing the sounds made by Hepworth's hammer and chisel and, as we watch her work, the music is fully replaced by ambient sound. In this sequence, the sculptor is often tiny and presented as wholly immersed in the complex, high-angle, layered image. The frame is crowded by leaves in the foreground or at the frame edges, their movement in the wind and the play of their shadows on the sculptural forms a constant reminder of the film's concern with the symbiotic relationship between landscape and art, the artist herself becoming part of the picturesque view of place. In the same way, her studio and garden, now part of Tate St Ives, have latterly and literally been absorbed into the art tourism of Cornwall. Both Hepworth and her own look at St Ives are viewed through the spaces in her sculptures, which form a modern frame for a view which has been 'picturesque' since the outset of the moving image. The final few shots of the film show pieces on plinths against the white wall of a gallery, dollying in and panning across to look at details of form, emphasizing the play of light and the transformations effected by the shifted perspective.

This is still a tourist gaze, but a gaze dependent on a different kind of cultural capital, one quite literally picturing Cornwall through the lens of modern art. St Ives retains its association with British Modernism, and

Cornwall still draws a particular kind of middle-class, educated tourist on these terms, and here the troubled relationship between centre and periphery is most keenly felt. Their gaze at the landscape is guided, as in *Figures in a Landscape*, through the production of the internal colony as 'to be looked at', but St Ives is looked at through Nicholson, Hepworth and Alfred Wallis, Porthleven and St Just through Lanyon, rather than through the differently romantic gaze of more conventional tourist imagery.[3] By the 1960s, Hepworth was the subject of entire newsreel items, as in *Barbara Hepworth Sculptress* (1960–69), which made the centre–periphery dynamic evident. This film moves from shots of Hepworth working in her garden at St Ives to an exhibition space in London; it operates as a view film which, like the Cornish 'flower film', follows the raw material through the process of transformation and into consumable, profitable product made from the periphery for the benefit of the centre.

The BBC arts documentary *Summoned by Bells: John Betjeman Remembers his Childhood* (1976) also frames Cornwall through artistic production; narrated in prose and poetry, the programme combines contemporary and archive moving images and photography. Again, Cornwall is both backdrop and muse, but here it is also a site of memory. Critically, it is introduced to the viewer, thus, as picture. Betjeman stands before Frank Bramley's enormous and affective painting 'A Hopeless Dawn' in the Tate in London, and tells us that this work was 'the first to inspire' him to try to write about his inspiration by the landscape. It matters, for me, that it was a painterly representation of Cornwall—and a tragically romantic Newlyn picturing at that—which inspired Betjeman, as much as his experiential relationship of the landscape itself. Cornwall may be as affective through its picturing as its presence, it seems. Certainly, the history of representing Cornwall in images as well as in words, and the question of relationships between place and representation, are raised in this opening moment. Almost immediately, the journey to Cornwall's edge by train which has been so formative in constructing the region's place-myth, and particularly its early moving image representation, is vividly evoked: archive footage of an early nineteenth-century railway station, of a steam train travelling right, and footage inside a dining car, is accompanied by cheerful brass 'seaside' music. An intertitle recalling early film (though emphasized with the sound of a steam whistle) tells us: 'From 1908 the Betjeman family holidayed annually in Cornwall.' A long shot of a gorse-lined cliff path, the sea in the distance, a grown-over railway line perhaps, is accompanied by the sound of a steam whistle and a train chuffing as in voice-over Betjeman reads from his poem 'Cornwall in Childhood': 'Teatime shows the small fields waiting ...' ([1955] 2006: 418). Betjeman's poetic recollection of his childhood in relation to the landscape is juxtaposed with his gait as an elderly man, as we watch him make his way across the beach, with the help of a stick, to the water's edge.

The sequences in Cornwall combine Betjeman in Cornwall in the present—by the sea, on the cliff—with cut-in shots which suggest his point of view: of the landscape, the sea, children playing on the beach. These are juxtaposed with old family photographs, to signal the process of personal memory prompting and recollecting, as he looks down from the cliff at a little boy with red fishing nets climbing across the rocks. We are thus invited to witness and participate in his apparently nostalgic journey back to the Cornwall of his childhood, presented first as a place of reassurance and escape: 'And back across the years I swing to safety, with old friends again' to 'safe Cornish holidays before the storm' of World War I. Betjeman's recollections of adolescent times in Cornwall are less unequivocal: the freedom of exploring Cornish churches by bicycle, guided by the sound of their bells, is interrupted and displaced by memories from his troubled relationship with his father. Later, at St Enedoc, Betjeman remembers that 'in search of mystical experience, [he] knelt in darkness' there, and the fine line between mysticism and Christianity at the heart of the Cornish place-myth functions here as an unsettling, rather than romantic, underscore of mood. While the walk to the edge of the sea structures the Cornish segment of this programme, and the final images are the more familiar cliffs and waves of the regional moving image grammar, their meaning, coming as they do after a sequence in which a familiar, comforting place-myth has been interrupted by the disquiet which can unexpectedly attend memory, is less than settled.

In contrast, more recent arts programmes *A Picture of Britain: The Mystical West* (BBC, 2005) and *The Art of Cornwall* (BBC, 2010) present a more general view of the region's historical relationship to art, operating more like travelogues of Cornwall for the middle-class armchair viewer. *A Picture of Britain* was an episodic documentary series presented by David Dimbleby, who travelled around Britain in his Land Rover to trace the various transformations of place into art—literature, music, painting and sculpture. The Cornwall episode looks at the wider 'West' of Britain proclaiming at the very beginning that '[a] place with a hint of the pagan just below the surface … this is Britain's mystical West'. Before the border between Devon and Cornwall is finally crossed, the oddness of the West has been effectively established through attention to the magical landscape paintings of David Inshaw, to Glastonbury, Edward Burne-Jones and Arthurian legend, Welsh bards, British Welsh artist Richard Wilson and crop circles (because 'strange things happen in the mystical West'). In Cornwall, the programme focuses on the writer Daphne du Maurier and on the art of St Ives. Dimbleby's commentary highlights Cornwall's strangeness as a powerful influence on du Maurier; she found there a 'sense of continuity, of the past and the present, merging, but always this sense of the ancient. Of this being a very old country.' Cornwall is mysterious and thrilling; he reads from *The Birds* and then visits Pridmouth Beach in relation to *Rebecca*, two du Maurier novels directed for Hollywood by Alfred Hitchcock. As Dimbleby walks on the beach, the camera follows for a while right at his feet as they hit the sand, in an unsettling change from the usual mid shot of the presenter. 'These things disturb me,' he says, 'and there is a kind of eeriness to this place, that she captured in that book.' The music in this sequence features high-pitched violin notes and a melancholy repetitive piano melody and, after he walks out of shot, we are left alone with a distorting wide-angle shot to look out at the beach.

The final destination—of both the episode and the series—is St Ives, which he approaches by driving across the moor, motivating a long, high-angle shot of the town and its bays from the hill. The presentation of St Ives in this programme is through a vocabulary remarkably similar to that of *Artists' Colony*; as Dimbleby walks along the breakwater in the harbour, the town's association with art—and as a peripheral outpost of and escape from the English centre—is noted: 'St Ives is famous now as an artists' colony, but even one hundred years ago it was teeming with painters, many of the professionals from London, jaded with living life there and wanting to come down here to this beautiful seaside and this magical light.' The artist chosen to represent St Ives is a local, Alfred Wallis, a retired fisherman whose paintings were 'discovered' and championed by Ben Nicholson. The moving images through which the segment on Wallis is presented attempt to reproduce the particular viewpoint articulated in his work, taken up by his Modernist celebrants as a graphic simplification and 'naive' distortion of space. The bay behind Dimbleby is shot in an extreme wide angle, capturing an extended and enclosing view similar to the circling panning shot which mirrors the onlooker's gaze around the open coastal space. Wallis's paintings often position the viewer inside place in this way, refusing an omniscient view from outside in favour of an immersive positioning from which the world crowds inwards at changing angles. Dimbleby goes out on a fishing boat, and shots through binoculars of him watching the fishermen work are alternated with Wallis's paintings of fishing boats. This is a clear juxtaposition of two ways of seeing region: on the one hand, the surveying tourist gaze at the labouring local through a lens and, on the other, an immersed, experiential perspective from within place. The camera moves across the painting's surface, tracking and panning up and down in a wave-like motion and, in conjunction with the sound of a boat cutting through the water from a close point of audition, the programme attempts to position the viewer kinaesthetically with the artist and to bring the painting to life. Dimbleby tells us that:

> Wallis painted simply, like a child, with ships painted on driftwood or cardboard, to bring alive his memories of his life at sea. Wallis captured the spirit of Cornwall as vividly as the professional painters who had come to live in the town ... [his] painting showed the instinctive response to landscape that they were trying to achieve.

A Picture of Britain presents a familiar narrative of Wallis's work: instinctive and primitive in comparison with the work of the artists who came to St Ives and 'discovered' his 'naive genius'. I think Wallis is more usefully understood, however, like Peter Lanyon, the other Cornish artist associated with British Modernism, as an artist who articulated an insider view of place (Relph 1976), one which comes from long-term experience. As a sequence of shots takes us from a painting by Wallis of cottages in St Ives, to the new Tate, and paintings by some of the most famous artists influenced by him (Nicholson, Wood, Hepworth, Heron), Dimbleby tells us that Wallis, in contrast, 'died in poverty, his last days spent in the workhouse'. Clearly articulated across this sequence is the juxtaposition of the outsider view associated with tourism, colonialism and profit (as these artists benefited from the 'influence' or rather acquisition of this local painter's style), and the immersed, experiential viewpoint of the insider, Wallis, which communicates the experience of region from within.

The Art of Cornwall also focuses on St Ives as the centre of British Modernism, ending on the work of the Cornish artists Peter Lanyon and Patrick Heron. The programme passes quickly over the late nineteenth-century Newlyn School as a fantasy of romantic Victoriana (ignoring Lamorna completely) and moves straight to the more highbrow story of Christopher Wood and Nicholson's encounter with Wallis, the arrival in St Ives, during World War II, of Nicholson and Hepworth (who escaped wartime London to Carbis Bay with their children) and of key European avant-gardists, such as Naum Gabo, who followed them there. The story of Wood and Nicholson's 'discovery' of Wallis while visiting from London mirrors the documentary's set-up, in which the Cambridge art historian Dr James Fox recounts his own discovery, as an undergraduate, of the Cornish modernists at the university's tiny Kettle's Yard gallery. The documentary claims to present an 'unknown' history of Cornish art, an odd take given the number of international exhibitions and pages of scholarship that have been devoted to St Ives. This triple discovery narrative, however, powerfully reinforces the centre–periphery dynamic of the story of bringing Modernism to Cornwall from London and Europe, and of the programme itself, which switches back and forth between London and Cornwall, where Fox is repeatedly pictured in the classic colonial prospect pose at the very top of cliff and tor.

The Cornwall of this documentary is a place of dizzyingly high cliffs, crashing waves, intense colours and dramatic rock formations. A familiar vocabulary is used to provide a simultaneously sublime and immersed experience of region: aerial shots trace and emphasize the edge; a camera peers through and around rock formations and ancient standing stones. The score is less classical than typical romantic representations, but the postcard views it accompanies, of ruined cliff-edge mines, the ancient mysticism signalled by standing stones and picturesque framings of St Ives, dominate much of the visual and verbal register of the programme. Cornwall, for example, 'cast its spell' on Gabo against his will, transforming his work. Nicholson chose a studio with no view and used jazz to block out the sounds of the coast, only for it to emerge in his work anyway. While the description of Lanyon's attempts to render 'the Cornwall only a native could understand' gives the presenter the opportunity to cling to the edges of cliffs and take a glider over the Penwith peninsula, providing further dramatic and spectacular views of place, the discussion of the work itself is insightful. Close-ups of mooring lines across a beach are juxtaposed with Hepworth's and Gabo's three-dimensional forms, Terry Frost's 'Walk along the Quay' (1950) is retraced and explained, and Lanyon's 'St Just', a painted memorial to the Levant Mine disaster of 1919, is explored in detail as a piece which represents 'the Cornwall of work, of tragedy … that no-one but Lanyon had the bravery to paint'. Cornwall is overwhelmingly spectacular here, in Lefebvre's sense (2006a); indeed, it literally appears as art, as both artwork and spectacular view, a tourist destination of distinction. The history of picturing of St Ives, in particular, has always been accompanied by the suggestion that a particular kind of classed cultural capital is required of the tourist in order to make a visit rewarding. Art and the artist, pictured in and picturing Cornwall, are persistent tropes of region and in the moving images discussed here: art and the artist become part of a consumable 'view' of region, simultaneously incorporated within the regional landscape, and reproducing of it.

Cornwall as Sublime Periphery

Cornwall's near-island status is frequently invoked, particularly in relation to discussion of its claims to independence. Accordingly, items on shipping, storms at sea and shipwrecks dominate extant newsreel of Cornwall, particularly in the early pre-sound period, itself an indication of the emphasis on the region as coastal and peripheral in its place-myth, and many items focus on its extremity and associated dangers. *Around Britain—Cornwall—Floods* (1948) anticipates the focus, sixty years later, on the Boscastle flood in *A Seaside Parish* (BBC, 2004); *The Beacon!* (1931) a Pathé Pictorial newsreel item featuring the most southerly lighthouse at Lizard Point, notes the solitary work of the romanticised figure of the lighthouse-keeper who keeps watch over the treacherous sea and cliffs. In reporting on the modern lighthouse, 'not the ancient braziers of years gone by, which too often were used to lure poor sailors to their doom', this film makes reference to the old practice of wrecking, invoking the association of Cornwall with wildness, mystery and tragedy and, in the rather late use of an iris in and out, fixes the region in a cruel, archaic past. A *Stepping Out* item on *Devon and Cornwall* (1939) took the filmgoer to the 'mysterious, deserted village' of Port Quin, which 'once flourished in fish, but the sea demanded its toll, and one tragic night it was transformed into an eerie playground for ghosts'. The camera pans at a high angle across the deserted village, taking in a solitary female tourist through whom our view is inscribed; at the same time, the inclusion of the female outsider at the edge of the region is a trope traceable across the entire history of representation of Cornwall.

Cornwall has featured repeatedly in *Coast* (BBC, 2005–), a documentary series exploring the British shoreline. Wheatley takes this programme as a key example of the growth of spectacular landscape programming on British television (2016), and Thompson has written of the way in which *Coast* can be seen as having shifted from understanding the British shoreline as a 'defensible natural boundary line' to a riskily 'permeable location of exchange and migration' in its construction of national discourses (2010b: 429). The programme has been discussed, then, in relation to its generic identity, its aesthetics, and its place in the history of British television, but the parameters of its discussion have remained resolutely national. *Coast* has presented itself as a series bringing hidden histories of the British periphery to light, so what might be gained by thinking about *Coast*'s representation of a specific region, the periphery of a periphery that is Cornwall? Episode four of the second series of *Coast* (2006) covers Cornwall and the Isles of Scilly, and the opening narration (made from the now-familiar moment of the crossing of the River Tamar at Plymouth) describes Cornwall as Britain's most coastal county, almost cut off from the mainland apart from four miles of land without which 'it would be pretty much an island'. The first images are also familiar: sweeping helicopter shots across the bridge and along the railway at Saltash cutting, on a brass sforzando, to a close-up of waves crashing on rocks, white foam and turquoise water, drawing up and out from this to a swirling aerial shot of waves around a rock in the sea and a travelling helicopter shot over the beaches at St Ives. The narration presents Cornwall, alongside this archetypal picturing, as *the* holiday destination for five million British holidaymakers per year: 'if all you take home are your holiday snaps, you're missing the bigger picture. We're not going to.' The suggestion is that a side of Cornwall not usually seen will be revealed for the viewer, through diving over wrecks at the Manacles, 'the Cornish light that has lured artists to St Ives over the centuries', a beautiful beach which is not 'natural' and an exploration of the Isles of Scilly by an archaeologist which will refigure them as 'The Isles of the Dead'.

While the claim here is that the mainstream place-myth of Cornwall will be resisted and challenged, beginning with the opening instruction to 'forget the bucket and spade', in fact the programme largely reinforces it. As we have seen, the 'bucket and spade' British holiday has been one place-image of Cornwall, but not an especially determining part of its place-myth. Equally, if not more powerful, have been shipwrecks and fishing, the lure of the possibility of an immersed perspective and an inside view of place, art and St Ives, mining (post-*Poldark*) and ancient mysticism: these remain the place-images referenced in *Coast*'s 'bigger picture'. The Cornish rocks are described as 'like the old historic heart of a town; this is where you find residents that have lived here forever', invoking the familiar insider–outsider discourse which underpins Cornwall's intermedial production and, further, the programme immediately invokes Cornwall as simultaneously home and away: 'This is a county which is isolated, yet on our doorstep; it seems foreign, and yet familiar,' describing it as Britain's Wild West, and going so far as to make the connection that 'in 1859, the year that Billy the Kid was born, Brunel ... was opening up the gateway to Cornwall with this magnificent bridge across the Tamar'. This reference to Cornwall as Wild West, as a frontier wilderness to be explored and settled, is a familiar one in the place-myth, the title of a parodic sitcom of Cornwall and a repeated refrain in this episode, supported by both image and score. A helicopter shot brings the viewer out from behind a granite tor on a clifftop to sweep round a rocky coast above azure water, taking us from a position of immersion to one of absolute mastery over the landscape. The music changes with this shot to a theme reminiscent of the scoring of classic Hollywood Westerns, a galloping string and brass melody. 'So sit back and enjoy,' instructs the narrator. 'I'm off to explore the Wild West of Cornwall.' In this moment, the armchair tourist is invited to participate in a gaze clearly established in relation to a dominant moving image genre of place, community, difference and colonization.

The picture of Cornwall produced across this episode of *Coast* is more complex than most and demonstrates how powerful place-myth can be in the face of resistance and critique. At the same time, its repeated use of 'spectacular montage' (Wheatley 2011: 244) points up the specificity of moving image grammars of place. While the presenter's narration and voice-over insist upon a different picturing of Cornwall, a revelation beyond the familiar place-images which typically picture it, the devices used remain bound by the history of its moving image representation, not least because they are spectacular and picturesque, kinaesthetic and comforting. They also offer an incontrovertible tourist gaze at Cornwall situated by the episode in a hundred-year history of the moving image, even as it attempts to resist it. Archive footage from *Scenes in the Cornish Riviera* is intercut with contemporary swooping helicopter shots around the coast and over headlands, like a roller-coaster ride which takes the ground from under us, as the narrator confirms the visual register with the verbal: 'On the way to Looe, it's classic Cornwall, all the way.' At Looe, footage from the 1904 film is used again, followed by images from a 1960s tourist brochure as a haunting version of 'Cockles and Mussels' plays and the narrator tells us that '[i]t's always been the quintessential picture postcard on the grand tour of Cornwall, and it still is today'. The point of the Looe sequence is to highlight the difficulties faced by the Cornish fishing industry, as well as to emphasize the quality of the catch here as supported by television chef Rick Stein. Even as the presenter claims that 'romantic idyll it may be, but there's more to Looe than tourist brochure banter', he is seen snapping the view—one which echoes the earliest images of Cornwall, to the sound of a shutter click and a frozen image. The emphasis here is on continuity with the existing place-myth, rather than on contradiction or development of it.

Throughout the episode pains are taken to point away from insularity and towards Cornwall's international connectedness. Sequences about the Telstar event in 1962 which 'puts Cornwall in a unique place in the history of modern communication', at Porthcurno, which focus on Marconi's undersea network connecting the world via telegraph, telephone and fibre-optic cables, and at Falmouth, which was '[a]n international communications centre—two hundred years ago, Falmouth was *the* place to be ... more cosmopolitan than London, in the eighteenth century', emphasize this. In these moments, Cornwall's peripheral status, and the emphasis on the periphery of the periphery which has determined its place-image are, as Thompson has argued of *Coast* in general, mobilized in ways which acknowledge it as 'a permeable location of exchange and migration' (2010b: 429). Porthcurno, for example, is described here as having been a major Nazi target during World War II. While the Cornish coast has often been figured as a risky, liminal space in romantic fiction, this is a significant departure in the documentary image. Rare moments like this, however, sit within hegemonic and overdetermined visual, verbal and sonic registers, which drain them of potency. The lead-in to discussion of Telstar positions the Lizard as a remote place of 'unrestricted panoramic views', home of the rare chough[4] on the Cornish coat of arms which has recently recolonized from Brittany, effectively marking the peninsula as both mythical and Celtic. At Falmouth, rigged packet ships are replaced, via CGI, into an image of today's harbour, literally pasting the picturesque past onto the present place, where the local paper is still called *The Falmouth Packet*. The approach to Porthcurno is made via sweeping helicopter shot across the cliff and a 'Western' score, to an 'enticing little cove ... turquoise waters, pale, powdery sand, a holidaymaker's dream. Appearances can be deceptive.' They are not deceptive, however, because the main 'appearance' here is precisely that of the familiar object of a tourist gaze; while the verbal register attempts to challenge a popular place-myth, it is constantly reinforced at an audiovisual level. The beach at Carlyon Bay is approached similarly, via directional helicopter shots skimming the coast, right to left, carrying us along like the journey around Cornwall in the early railway films which trace the edge of the territory; a Google Earth map shows precisely this route along the coast. The alternative story of the beach is that it is not 'natural', created from the waste products of the inland china-clay mining industry, washed down to the coast. This is an unusual inclusion of Cornwall's inland mining industry but, of course, it is pictured in relation to the coast and role it has played in creating it, rather than in and of itself. Spectacular aerial shots of the clay pits and accelerated film of the many products in which it is used are accompanied by silent film-style piano music; picturesque colour archive footage of a clay industry horse and cart includes a pan across 'The Cornish Alps' which subject it, unusually, to a tourist gaze.[5]

The main part of the episode is even more securely hegemonic in its mobilization of place-myth, despite its claim to be showing a 'different side' of Cornwall. We remain at the sublime periphery, a dangerous coastline 'littered with thousands of wrecks'. The programme offers the armchair tourist an immersed gaze, literally below the surface, as the cameras follow a dive over the Manacles; the wrecks are described as 'prime real estate' for marine life, referencing the 'posh coffee shop effect' which indicates that a neighbourhood is being gentrified. This is unfortunate phrasing in relation to a place which suffers dramatically from second-home ownership levels which have led to local people being priced out of coastal living, given that this is not a topic addressed in the programme; it only reads as a political commentary on the region's changing economy from an 'inside' perspective on place. The Isles of Scilly appear here, as they do in the early travelogues discussed in Chapter 2: gorgeous white beaches and turquoise water, revealed in helicopter shots and slow, level pans which are quite different in pace and effect from the vocabulary of mainland Cornwall and make you think that 'you could be in the Caribbean'. The unknown aspect of the islands revolves around the mystery of the high concentration of Bronze Age burial chambers they are home to. Their precise origins are unknown, and the programme presents this as a vaguely Gothic mystery in perfect harmony with Cornwall's place-myth as a site of spirituality and horror.

Coast's particular moving image articulation of Cornwall is based largely upon spectacular helicopter shots swooping rapidly between cliffs and across beaches, appearing around tors and headlands to reveal beaches and picturesque villages, and skimming the coastline. These images simultaneously offer the impression of immersion within an enormous landscape, omniscient description of and mastery over it, and an exciting element of surprise for the tourist viewer. Steimatsky has theorized the use of aerial landscape photography in relation to Italian Fascism, linking it not only to modernity and modernism, but simultaneously to Fascism's inclination towards a 'controlling, unifying perception poised to crystallize reality as an aesthetic object' (2008: 13) and to colonialism:

> [t]he encompassing, inspiring, abstract beauty of the aerial view in that historical moment cannot be quite detached from the aggressive, militarist and imperialist uses of such images: the superior possession of vision and knowledge that aerial reconnaissance affords often prepared for the actual—not formal or metaphorical—controlling or levelling of the terrain by aerial bombardment. The aerial view has come to embody the perfect aestheticization of Fascist aggression (16).

While Steimatsky's example is historically, nationally and politically specific, the idea that aerial shots produce a 'unifying and universalising, possessive vision of the regional landscape' (18) is suggestive for *Picturing Cornwall*. As 'internal colony', Cornwall has been endlessly pictured through sweeping aerial photography since at least 1919, the object of a controlling tourist gaze. Often in *Coast* these travelling shots are cut together in order to contrast directional movement: for example, a moving aerial shot over a rocky promontory which shows the variation in water colour at the edge, green grass and yellow lichen on headland rocks, and produces a movement across the screen upwards diagonally from left to right. A cut on this movement reveals another helicopter shot, this time travelling past a ruined engine house on a cliff in an opposing diagonal movement across the screen, from right to left. The next cut is to a contrasting helicopter shot, in the same direction, which hugs the coastal rocks close to the water, unexpectedly revealing a white beach behind a headland. Such a series of shots certainly offers the viewer an opportunity for contemplation, as Wheatley has suggested of the landscape programme in general and *Coast* in particular (2011), but does not, I argue, represent a hesitation or pause in the image, and is anything but slow. The speed of travel and use of directional contrast, through the editing together of shots which are around two seconds each in length, produces an unsettling kinaesthetic effect as well as an impression of wandering and diversity which is reinforced by a romantic, repetitive and non-linear Nymanesque piano score. At the same time, the images thoroughly reinforce the existing place-myth and a directional sense of travel is maintained, recalling the movement around the coast determined by the path of the railway in early travelogues of Cornwall. Edited into and contained within these rapid aerial travelling shots is the occasional slower and less dizzying moment, in which the helicopter hovers away from villages nestling in the cliffs in a panning motion which, through the use of a zoom, appears to move inward at the same time like a Hitchcockian dolly out/zoom in, a gesture which simultaneously suggests protective enclosure and a surveillant, possessive gaze. My purpose, in using this sequence to interrogate Wheatley's analysis of the aesthetics of the landscape programme, is to demonstrate the potential for particularity within a more general rhetoric. The grammar I have described here is specific to region and suggests that a particular vocabulary and ordering of camera movements might contain a complex set of ideas in relation to the politics of region, here, around a possessive gaze and the simultaneous production of a place positioned as internal colony as both spectacular and vulnerable, protected and controlled.

The final images of the episode are interesting. While the presenter walks to the end of a clifftop promontory and stands in a classic prospect view, the programme has set this up as an outward-looking gesture, one speaking connectedness as well as emphasizing mastery and control:

> I've not been the regular bucket-and-spade tourist, but I've seen another side of this county that's not often explored. So next time you're sitting on a beach in Cornwall, just think, round that corner, there's a global cultural centre. That harbour houses internationally renowned fish. And you might just hear the lapping of waves, but under your beach towel 36 million calls may be connected ... Cornwall

is England's most coastal county, and maybe that's why so much of its history is outward-looking, with an eye to the far horizon. It's certainly a place that belongs far more to the sea, than to the land.

Coast, in this episode, presents Cornwall as outward-looking and connected, its coast less of a national boundary and more of a porous and changeable limen, as Thompson has suggested (2010b). It acknowledges that outsider and insider views of a place may be at odds: 'Let's face it, unless you live here, it takes a long time to get to Cornwall, which is why there's often the view that it's isolated and remote. But that depends on your point of view.' Nevertheless, the very premise of the programme restricts Cornwall to its coastal edge and denies its interior territory, other than in its relationship to the periphery. *Coast*'s aesthetic of Google Earth imagery and 'spectacular montage' (Wheatley 2011) is both characteristic of genre and specific to region, a continuation of a moving image grammar which, as we have seen, has a long history. Indeed, the incorporation of archive footage from that history, a literal ingestion and regurgitation of the region's place-myth, plays a significant part in that perpetuation of both place-myth and its moving image aesthetic.

Cornwall as Frontier Wilderness

America's West, a frontier land, a wilderness to be tamed and colonized, has been the subject of an enormous scholarship across literature, film and television. The southern states of the USA have also functioned as a marginal space, possibly the final national frontier, more distant, more difficult to rationalize, even, than outer space. Constructions of Cornwall on screen have produced it simultaneously as Britain's chaotic Wild West and its abject South, a peripheral territory, strange, backward and other, yet ripe for possession and the object of a controlling, organizing, imperial gaze. These connections were cleverly drawn upon in the satirical comedy series *Wild West* (BBC, 2002–04), discussed in Chapter 5, but have also been at the centre of programming in which Cornwall figures as a wild and chaotic landscape to be taken on and conquered. Cornwall's construction as remote wilderness, as well as its popularity as a setting for romantic screen fictions, has made it readily available as the backdrop for factual entertainment formats in which people are pitted against the regional landscape and must both struggle and become intimate with it in order to 'survive'—a classic 'frontier' narrative.

In 2011, BBC2's *All Roads Lead Home* was a three-part series in which three celebrities (comedian Sue Perkins and actors Stephen Mangan and

Alison Steadman) were taught natural navigation skills and then dropped somewhere in a region close to their hearts in order to use their new-found knowledge to find their way to a given spot. In the first episode, Sue Perkins took her companions to Cornwall. The pre-credit sequence of this first episode blends together shots from their journey across Cornwall from Bodmin Moor to the coast as they get lost, hug trees and encounter standing stones: the Merry Maidens of Penwith are shown here with one stone looming large in the foreground, a star filter, a low horizon and a big sky which shout 'ancient mysticism'. Perkins describes Cornwall as 'the place I call home', over a hilltop shot down to the small harbour and turquoise water of Mousehole. The titles are digitally manipulated images, in blurry black and white, in which a map is torn up and technology crushed, finally revealing them on moorland hilltop. Over aerial shots of the landscape and time-lapse images, the voice-over explains natural navigation. This programme is about becoming connected—and insider to—the regional landscape, learning it intimately using 'the techniques our ancestors used', including the sun, the prevailing wind, lichen and dung (shown, later, in a vignetted shot). Immediately, Cornwall is ancient wilderness, a territory to be conquered in a primal battle between (wo)man and nature.

The programme begins, predictably, with the journey by train across the Tamar and into Cornwall, and the grammar of region is immediately apparent in the sequence of shots, their types and subjects: an aerial shot travels over and in towards a wide beach with rolling waves and the camera pans up to reveal the sky above cliffs; following a cut to an aerial shot of a cliffside engine house, a cut to an aerial shot which pulls up and away from the rail and road bridges over the Tamar reveals the railway track with a train crossing the bridge to Saltash in Cornwall. Cornwall is quickly established here as a coastal territory, one with a watery border to be breached. A drawn map of Cornwall includes fishing boats with the flag of St Piran, the Celtic sea and the English Channel as well as key place names which will be important in their journey from Bodmin Moor to Cape Cornwall. A further cut returns to the train crossing the bridge into Cornwall, emphasizing the mythic status of this moment and its representation, which endlessly reiterates its separation from the nation. Over this, we hear the conversation of the participants on the train, as Stephen Mangan asks Sue, 'Are we crossing into Cornwall right now?' 'We are,' she replies. 'Oh, wow!' exclaims Alison Steadman. We see them gazing out of the train window as they cross the Tamar, and the hysterical repetition of shots of the crossing both anticipated and insisted upon this moment, as Perkins tells them: 'This is the transitionary point—your life gets better from this point.' Cornwall is figured as escape here, but it is also spectacularized in its mysterious difference. As with the earliest moving images in *Scenes in the Cornish Riviera*, the moment of crossing the Tamar by train is drawn out as they question her on what makes Cornwall so special: she can't explain why it pulls her in and makes her happy, and a cut to a point-of-view shot through the train window zooms in towards the Cornish landscape in an echo of the phantom ride into the region of more than one hundred years before.

The mythical moment of crossing is extended further, as gentle but pacy electronic music echoes the rhythm of a train crossing points and a closer aerial shot of the bridge shows the Brunel sign and emphasizes the colour of the water as the train enters and crosses the bridge. Perkins's voice-over describes her 'whirlwind romance' with Cornwall: 'I came here on holiday (cut to personal snaps of her sitting on a beach, then on top of hay bale) five years ago … and six months later, I moved down permanently.' A shot of her on a cliff path, with Cape Cornwall in background, zooms into her face as she explains, 'I'm hoping that this trip will show me a side to my new home that I haven't seen before, and help explain Cornwall's irresistible pull.' While the voice-over suggests that we might see a new picturing of Cornwall, that it might be demystified by the programme, a cut back to the train still crossing the bridge from above, in which the camera pans round the landscape in an enclosing motion, insists almost hysterically on the symbolic and emotional significance of crossing into the region: 'I just sort of can feel all the stress melting away as I cross the Tamar.' Perkins articulates a classic narrative of escape and self-discovery, one repeatedly articulated in romantic fictions of Cornwall picturing women, quite literally, on the edge. Her face is shown in close-up as she continues her story: '… and, erm—I'm properly myself, I think. There's not so much of that [as she makes the movement of a chattering mouth with her hand in front of the camera, which she is addressing directly at this point] which I'm sure will be a real relief.' Alison Steadman shares that she once went to Cornwall when she was seventeen and can't wait to return. Cornwall is tied here, as in more evidently fictional representations, to life narratives, memory, and periods of transition and change: in an encounter with it, one might find escape, peace and authentic selfhood.

All Roads Lead Home does show Cornwall within the edge, from the empty wilderness of Bodmin Moor to the tea plantation at Tregothnan (a significant and unusual instance of Cornish industry which is not entirely dependent upon tourism), though their picturing is heavily determined by the hegemonic place-myth. Bodmin is gnarly, wind-blown trees, standing stones and 'The Beast of Bodmin'. Helicopter shots trace stone circles and skim across moorland to the Cheesewring granite tor as they reach its summit: their achievement represents both physical and visual mastery of the apparently unreadable space of the moor, articulated in the circling aerial shots which celebrate it and in their own commentary as they take up the classic prospect position: 'That's quite a view … that's Cornwall, you can see for miles … you can see 360 degrees.' 'All the way to England,' Sue points out, emphasizing Cornwall's separate identity, yet later Tregothnan is described as 'the home of English tea'. There is emphasis on the strangeness and magicality of Cornwall's ancient rurality throughout the programme: the boats moored in a foggy Falmouth harbour are filmed in time-lapse, creating eerie movement across the screen and glowing lights. Mangan has learned that 'as a city boy, [he's] nothing to fear from the country, yet …': the possibility is always there, and the following sequences are reminiscent of the much earlier newsreels of 'strange Cornwall', and even *Straw Dogs* (Peckinpah, 1971). The 'Obby 'Oss rites at Padstow are shown and Perkins says, 'Don't speak too soon, there are some strange goings on down the road at the village of St Buryan.' This 'other side' of Cornwall is ongoing paganism and white witches: the playing of repetitive accordion, drum and whistle music accompanies dancing with a horse's skull, and close-ups show the reactions of the three celebrities as they move through the dancers. Sue Perkins comments, 'Oh dear … it's a bit like Alice Cooper, isn't it?' She pulls some worried faces: 'Yes, it's satanic Morris dancing.' While Perkins's well-known comedy persona frames the folk tradition as odd comedic spectacle, it is left, as in early view films, as just that: there is neither intertitle nor explanatory voice-over, simply a 'view' of local custom, not unlike the 1925 'weird in and out the houses hop' film of the Furry Dance.

The only contextualization of this scene situates it more firmly within the mystical strangeness of the region. A cut takes us from the dance to a shot of a granite tor, with the sun emerging from the clouds behind it—a typical shot used to signify the magical, and sometimes threatening, conjunction of elemental power and regional landscape. As Perkins tells the viewer that 'nowadays, these witches call themselves "wise women"', there is a cut to the stone circle of Boscawen from the very edge of one of the stones in close-up at the right-hand edge of frame; the viewer is positioned as if inside the space, peering warily around the stone. An aerial shot of the stones circles it just as Perkins and the two witches do. Here, Perkins tells them her story, of crying when she had to leave Cornwall, and of her profound emotional connection to the region. The scene at the circle is shown through a sequence of shots which often include a stone blocking the frame and positioning the viewer inside the space, the image made an unsettlingly acidic yellow and green in post-production.

The discussion is about the different pace of life in peripheral Cornwall, compared with 'up country, in foreign parts', over a tracking shot across a granite standing stone past which the sun peers; flares appear across the beam of sunlight, signalling mysticism in relation to the ancient landscape. There is no 'mystery' to Perkins's love for Cornwall, though: its appeal is simply articulated, here, in a conventional dualism of rural and urban space, where there is no time to 'smell the roses' or think about the journey rather than the destination. The image of enclosure is completed at the end of the sequence, in a filtered image of the stone circle and the dramatic sky. The camera circles them as they walk round its edge, producing a triple encircling of the space in the centre in a gesture which, in the grammar of this region, can signal isolated or demarcated space, but also serves as a containing gesture.

'Only one thing could make me more mellow,' says Perkins. 'That's right—a flute melody.' As appropriate woodwind music plays over a final image of the ancient stone circle, the edge in her knowing comment on the programme's construction is lost in the close matching of the flute melody with the image of the ancient landscape which has been presented as closely related to pagan tradition and strange rites. Perkins's comedic persona continues to undermine any serious attention to regional issues: a visit to the grave of Dolly Pentreath, thought to be the last woman to speak the Cornish language before its recent revival, is followed by a scene in which the celebrities chat to a man in the pub at Paul who speaks Cornish for them. The camera pans across their focused, confused faces to emphasize the strangeness of what we are hearing, and Perkins comments 'That sounds like me when I'm drunk.' Her comic repartee functions here to undermine and diminish the issue being addressed, which has since become a matter of significant import since the Government rescinded Cornish language funding in 2016. While this moment would likely have been deemed problematic in relation to Gaelic or Welsh, Cornish, with its lack of official 'national' status and the power of the 'weird locals' place-image, is apparently fair game. The village of Paul sits on the hill above Mousehole, the village which Perkins says made her decide 'to give up British citizenship and become Cornish'; this is a joke, of course, and any potential political undertone in the comment is neutralized by the comic scene which preceded it. The visit to Mousehole, which they approach through a green tunnel of trees ('a hidden route, probably used by smugglers'), eventually affords them, and us, the perfect tourist gaze down at the harbour. They have found the coast, and the view, but the path has come to an abrupt end and they are lost, stuck at the edge, with no way down to the picturesque paradise below. They find their way down eventually, but this moment of pause at the edge is significant in its frustration of their, and our, instant access to the desired object of their appreciative gaze. Their journey is presented as an epic one—another frequent regional narrative as I have suggested, in which the remote beach or fishing village is the reward for a difficult journey. Despite occasional cuts to a map which shows the general direction their walk should take, the Cornish landscape is shown as chaotic, full of obstacles and dead ends, the picturesque goal frustratingly just out of reach. This is a wilderness, where the ultimate goal is to find the coastal frontier, at Mousehole and, finally, at Cape Cornwall. Spectacular aerial shots of Mousehole, skimming over the rocks and pools exposed by the tide and in towards the harbour, emphasize the clear turquoise water and are accompanied by Perkins's commentary. She draws a direct and intimate connection between her identity and the territory: 'Cornwall is remote. It seems like a totally different country to England, and with a rebellious, free spirit.' Cornwall is escape, freedom and selfhood.

The final destination is Cape Cornwall, a remote spot on the West Penwith coast. An extended time-lapse sequence of dawn over the sea suggests a timeless landscape where the only change that occurs comes with the shifting of the light. Their journey, from St Just to Cape Cornwall reinforces this—they will navigate via lichen analysis and the visual recap of their lesson (grey and green face north, yellow and red, south) is shown in a vignetted image, which, as in the newsreels of the 1920s and 1930s, conveys a sense of archaicism. It signals not just something that happened a few weeks past, but rather ancient knowledge of an ancient land: Cornwall is a place out of time. While Stephen Mangan's episode on the west coast of Ireland draws on similar notions of ancient Celticness, the presentation of regionality is quite different and helpfully demonstrates the specificity, the grammar, of moving image representations of Cornwall. While Mangan's connection to place through ancestry is made clear and is meaningful, it does not carry the same charge, the same archaic sense of emotional connectedness with regional landscape expressed in the final moment of personal epiphany, and realization of selfhood, pictured at Cape Cornwall.

The programme suggests the connection between the sublime view from the edge and unexpected emotional outpouring: as they approach the spectacular panoramic coastal view at Cape Cornwall, we hear 'now that's a view' and there is a cut to a close-up profile shot of Alison Steadman wiping away tears. The camera pans away from her face, around the view from the peninsula, and back to her face. She says, 'Sorry, I've just got really emotional. It's just that there's no people here, not that that's a good thing, but it's just the whole sea, the rocks … it's incredible.' We share her profound and unexpected emotional response to being at the edge of the territory via her visual and auditory experience of the landscape, her optical, panning point of view of the cape and the sounds of gulls and waves. 'It's just to be with nature, quietly,' and on a cut back to her we see that Sue is next to her, '… and just to see everything just … happening … in a completely natural way. It's just so uplifting and moving [she gulps tears back] and it's so beautiful, just wonderful.' Perkins shares her own response to Cornwall: 'I was so coiled [she clenches her fist], so coiled, and the moment you allow yourself to release a bit, and just take a bit of it in, it's so deeply profound I won't even bother putting words to it.' The Cornish coast, here, is a space of emotional possibility, realization and (potentially excessive) transformation and release—'it's really beautiful … it's almost too much'—and, as we have seen, the trope of the emotional woman at the sublime edge of Cornwall is one which can be traced throughout the visual cultural history of Cornwall.

The final images reiterate the familiar grammar, the camera panning around the bay of Cape Cornwall, cutting down to waves crashing against the rocks and then to a helicopter shot which skims over the sea, rocks and in towards the coast once more, with the sweeping score and the ambient sounds of gulls and waves providing continuity over the changing images. A helicopter shot shows them sitting at the peak of the cape, and moves away from them as the camera pans away too, producing a spiralling effect which seems to articulate their response to the scale of the coastline: 'the end goal … was quite a shock'. Stephen Mangan's final words to camera are a refusal of modernity and technology and produce Cornwall, once more, as a land outside of progress and development: 'On a day like today, in a place like this, it's really nice not to be listening to an automated voice from a GPS, or trying to fold up a map and work out where you are. It's quite nice just to be out here.' The refusal of technological advance and the restorative power of the return to nature suggested here is directly contradicted by the accompanying cut to a helicopter shot which circles the cape, showing new parts of the view with each second, but Alison Steadman's voice confirms and reinforces it, as she is framed in mid shot against the sea and sky: 'Everything's so convenient now, with cars and planes and satnav and all the rest of it … it's just been a wonderful experience to realize that every single thing in nature means something and is a sign for us, and if we can only appreciate that, it just makes life all the richer.' Cornwall, in its role as Britain's Wild West, provides the possibility of a 'raw' and transformative encounter with the wilderness and the potential of escape from modernity. Sue Perkins has the final words, unintentionally describing the screen grammar of region which has developed around Cornwall, in its dominant juxtaposition of the panoramic travelling shot, the enclosing pan and the reiterative close-up: 'I just think it's really important that everyone on earth should have somewhere where they feel safe, and expansive and free, and most fully capable of realizing who they are and this place is, for me [as she gestures down at the ground with her hand and then looks directly to camera] here.' Freedom, safety and selfhood are available at the remote Cornish periphery, in the conjunction of spiralling sublimity and the reassurance of the grounding and protection provided by connection with the ancient landscape, articulated in the panoramic shot and repetition of the encircling camera.

Hugh's Three Hungry Boys (Channel 4, 2012) also pictures Cornwall as wilderness, but the challenge between man and nature takes the form of foraging. The programme is a clear development of the earlier 'travelling chef' genre of the British cookery programme, from the Galloping Gourmet, through Keith Floyd, Rick Stein (who is closely, and problematically, associated with the region) and Jamie Oliver.[6] In this case, it is Hugh Fearnley-Whittingstall, whose *River Cottage* books and programmes elaborated the genre from the male chef/'tourism-educative' programmes explored by Nikki Strange (1998), and reflect the vogue for 'back to the land', man-against-the-wilderness traditional masculinities, foraging and slow cookery movements which are highly gendered (see Moseley 2001; Bell and Hollows 2007). In this four-part programme, Hugh challenges three male university students to make the mythical journey west, to find their way from River Cottage in Devon to Land's End in Cornwall with no money, living only on foraged food. The programme shows its awareness of a growing concern with the environment, providing the students with a more eco-conscious form of travel in the form of 'Daisy', a modified 1980s milk float with rechargeable batteries. It also very clearly references the recent return to celebrating traditional modes of hunter-gatherer masculinity (iron man, hunting, fishing, shooting, spearing), but encourages the use of electronic communications technologies (iPads, Twitter).

The boys have very little success with foraging, but repeatedly trade manual labour for locally produced food; the programme hovers between local gastronomic tour (shellfish, tea, wine, wild plums) and travelogue (the post-break title looks like a written journal entry, a collage of lined paper, hand-drawn map, drawings and photo booth pictures, and the illustrations are almost Darwinian) but its main theme is masculinity in its encounter with the wilderness. The programme is littered with dialogue reinforcing hegemonic constructions of gender: Trevor fails with the spear gun and 'casts like a girl' and Thom finds that it's '[q]uite a satisfying manly feeling to win a sheep-shearing competition'. The moment when he finally catches a pollack off the rocks at Lizard is triumphant. The programme is a test of their ruggedness, a classic Western journey in which Cornwall is figured as the British equivalent of the mythical West whose resources are mined in the name of the discovery of youthful modern masculinity from up country. Marooned (voluntarily) on Asparagus Island (Kynance Cove, Lizard) the boys eat sea beet and rice, build a fire and sing songs like cinematic cowboys. The programme takes in 'strange' pagan festivals, shows the viewer how to construct and use a Dutch oven and prepare snails for consumption, and demonstrates how the ancient practice of harvesting salt for the sea continues, although by means of more modern technology than clay pans over gorse fires.

The final destination is Land's End, but they avoid the tourist site and pull up on the less populated cliffs above Sennen Cove: 'mate, that is a view and a half!' As they get out of Daisy to take in the view in its raw entirety, we can hear the wind through the microphone from a close point of audition that gives an impression of immersion. Arriving at Land's End itself causes great excitement, and we see the view through their window as they pull in front of the exit sign. The boys are determined to find their way right to the very edge: 'There's still land that way. I'm not happy with that. We have to perch right on the edge of Land's End!' This is a frontier story of rebellion and adventure and they decide to ignore the road signs and go for it, referencing the Hollywood road movie narrative with hysterical laughter, rock music and a foot braced against the dash: 'Right, go! Thelma and Louise-style!' The very edge is, once more, the ultimate destination: 'And that, boys, is as far as we can go!' Just as in *Westwood Ho!* (Rolfe, 1961), a shot of the benches, telescope and stones which mark the edge precedes the view as Daisy pulls into shot and stops. 'Ah, gents, check out that view!' They stand at the very edge, on the rocks preventing vehicles from rolling over the cliff, whooping and punching the air. 'Yes! Come on fellas, hug it out … We've done it … we've properly done it.' As in *Amish: The World's Squarest Teenagers* (Channel 4, 2010), in which young people finally encounter the sea and embrace liberation by surfing near Land's End, the encounter with the edge of Cornwall, as in *All Roads Lead Home*, holds the potential for an emotional moment of self-discovery. Here, it is in relation to masculinity, authenticity and return to the land; in 2012, the journey is made in an eco-friendly milk float, rather than a Volkswagen camper van.

Social Issues Documentary: Cornwall at Risk

Rarely has Cornwall been pictured as a site of serious economic or industrial concern, but there is a long history of newsreel documentation of the Cornish fishing and, to a lesser extent, farming industries for educational purposes. In these films, and in later television documentaries, Cornwall's 'traditional' identity is often wistfully presented, with the accompanying suggestion that the old ways are at risk of replacement by modern technology and methods; as Wheatley has acknowledged, landscape programming, more generally, can work to assert 'the unchanging nature of the British landscape and, by association, British national identity' (2016: 128). *They Bring You Fish* (1949)—'A Pathé-BIF Classroom Film' which recycles footage of Newlyn from *Fishing Village* (1946)—and *Pilchard Fishing Industry* (1949) explore traditional fishing methods and show the aproned housewives who then pack and can the fish. This film nods to the introduction of modern mechanized methods, but the emphasis is on picturesque tradition with shots of fishing boats with sun glinting through their sails, Penzance harbour, the coast, and close-ups of the weathered faces of Cornish fishermen. Tradition is also the focus of films such as *Crab Pots* (1949), about traditional crafts such as the continued practice of making crab pots from willow and hazel in Cornwall, rather than from steel. The 1955 colour film *Cornish Fishermen* looked at the fishing fleet out of Mevagissey and is resolutely within the tradition of the early picturesque newsreel and travelogue films of the Cornish fishing village. Here, Mevagissey is pictured 'nestling cosily in a granite coastline as tough as the heritage of its seafaring people'. The accompanying music, and gull cries, are reminiscent of Hubert Bath's 'Cornish Rhapsody', the score written for *Love Story* (Arliss, 1944), and the focus of the piece is on romance, danger and ongoing, unchanging, ancient tradition: 'Today, men like Bob Barron, the same hardy breed as their forefathers, go to sea in the same vessels, living the same life of hard hours: monotonous, heartbreaking but always satisfying, the life of a fisherman.' Similarly, the later *Look Out, Lobsters!* (1965) notes that lobster fishing in the region is still practised 'in ways that go back for centuries'.

While most newsreels of Cornish industry look at fishing, one or two newsreel items looked inland and to farming: *The Farm of Many Industries* (1935) showcased a co-operative endeavour at Stoke Climsland on the site of a former prisoner of war camp, which had been started by a local vicar in 1931 in an effort to ease local unemployment during the depression.[7] *Serpentine Rock* (1963) is an insistent return to the edge, and to Cornwall as a tourist destination where labour is erased and presented as hobbyist. A whistle, brass and string shanty is the soundscape for this film about serpentine rock-turner Arthur Williams; a shot of the cliff against the sky pans down to a man chipping it from the cliff face in his apron, then in close-up, while the narrator tells us that the serpentine is 'wrested from the savage coastline and transformed and sold to people all over the world who are too well acquainted with the concrete of cities'. Nevertheless, this living offers him 'a peaceful life ... a life that only demands a steady fall of rock'. The film ends with shots of him turning the serpentine in his workshop in Lizard village, as a woman admires the finished objects and the narrator mimics conversation between a couple about which souvenir to choose for whom. As Gunning has suggested, the 'view' film often looks at both picturesque and process, the product of which is presented for the pleasure of a middle-class consumer (1997).

Social documentaries presenting Cornwall as a traditional place at risk have tended to focus squarely on the coast and, in particular, on the tiny, traditional fishing village nestled between the towering cliffs. It is here that we have seen most clearly the development and articulation of a moving image grammar of place based upon the spectacular travelling panoramic shot of the coast. The apparent impossibility of viewing Cornwall outside of a rhetoric of tourism has a long-standing history; much earlier newsreel film of the Cornish fishing village often functioned as picturesque travelogue, even where the ostensible purpose of the item was fishing as regional industry, and here we have a clear antecedent for more recent television representations. *Wait for It! Polperro* (1937) is a classic construction of romantic Cornwall, within which it clearly inscribes and mimics the tourist gaze. The voice-over is accompanied by a legato harp and string score, and the film pans around the harbour, offering picturesque framings of the village's twisting lanes, paths and steps, fishermen and gulls. Polperro, the voice-over reminds us, is 'an ideal place for the game of hide and seek which the smugglers in the olden days played with the Kings' officers'.

This film offers remarkably similar footage to the scenes of the village in the first moving image footage of the region, *Scenes in the Cornish Riviera*. The camera pans left, from an aproned woman feeding scraps to the gulls, and across the harbour-side buildings as the narrator describes 'that artists' Mecca in south Cornwall', mimicking the gaze of the visitor to the harbour. The romantic score continues over shots of fishermen working on crab pots, as the narrator emphasizes the archaic and unchanging character of the region, exemplified by the fishing village: 'There, ancient fishermen carry on an ancient calling, amid the scenes and sounds of centuries.' Emphasis on the bygone and static nature of Cornwall has been a central and successful device in the promotion of the region as a holiday destination, the object of the romantic tourist gaze, as its persistence in present-day moving image documentary and fiction demonstrates. The region's successful tourist economy, then, can be understood as based in part on a picturing of Cornwall as a place of stasis, in which development and change (including the development of an economy beyond tourism) are both unlikely and unwelcome. Here, the political significance of moving image rhetoric of region is clear. *Fowey* (1938) also emphasizes 'charming, old-world' character and 'narrow, winding streets and ancient dwellings', constructing the town, in addition, as a foreign, primitive place: 'Fringed with palms and subtropical vegetation, the harbour might quite well belong to one of the South Sea Islands, except for the natives speak a different language, with a musical intonation that only a native Cornishman can master.' *For Men Must Work: Port Isaac* (1938) makes reference in its title both to Charles Kingsley's 1851 poem of Cornwall, 'The Three Fishers', apparently inspired by a visit to Port Isaac and later set to music and turned into a ballad by the composer John Hullah, and to Walter Langley's painting of 1883, made during his time in Newlyn, which is named after the full line, 'For men must work and women must weep.' The phrase refers to the tragic loss of the lives of fishermen, and the women who wait for them in vain, and the tragedy and romance of the literary and artistic references is played out across the film's imagery, score and narration. This film begins with an aerial coastal shot that starts on the headland and sea and pans in and around the harbour, while the narrator recites from Kingsley's poem:

> For men must work and women must weep,
> And there's little to earn and many to keep,
> Though the harbour bar be moaning.

While the narration reiterates the unchanging character of the Cornish fishing village which has 'defied the passing of time', the panning camera presents the view in a moving image which, contradictorily, will eventually, through its repetition, come to signal stasis and lack of movement. The densely punning narration ties together the mysterious past with contemporary romance for tourism: 'Like many other Cornish coves, Port Isaac was once a hotbed of smuggling, now the holiday coves come here to do their snuggling.' The voice-over narration is replaced by the score over a pan out from the village, around the cove and across the breakwater out to sea, in an encircling, enclosing and protective gesture towards the fishing village which will become part of the region's audiovisual grammar, alongside the pan, the aerial shot and the time-lapse sequence. 'But men must work,' continues the voice-over, 'and it's the sort of work that they and their families have been doing for many generations. Lobster fishing.' Much of the film emphasizes Cornwall as ancient and unchanging in this way, focusing on the '[n]arrow, rocky streets, so typical of Cornwall, [that] lead down to the sea. And the sea wall bears the scars of many an encounter. But there's life in the old dogs yet, and if you want to hear a good yarn, these are the lads to tell 'em.' These words are followed by a shot of old fishermen on a bench outside a pub. The patronizing tone of the narration makes a direct comparison between the rocky, scarred walls and Cornish landscape and the elderly fishermen being gazed at, who are thus produced as equally ancient, scarred and unchanging. However, in trying to reproduce the higgledy-piggledy organization of the village a montage of shots at canted angles produces graphic oppositions and an abstracted imagining of the archaic space. Inadvertently, this anticipates changing approaches to representing landscape in the visual arts, the graphic simplifications and dynamism of Modernism developing in St Ives in this period which would, as we have seen, become the subject of later newsreel and cinemagazine films of the region.

The Woman at the Edge

The spectacular conjunction of the sublime periphery and the picturesque Cornish fishing village was employed in an exploration of the modern church in rural Britain in the BBC's series *A Seaside Parish*, which focused on the ancient, tiny, north-coast harbour village of Boscastle. Following a new parish priest, the Reverend Christine Musser, and her struggle to be accepted by the community, the programme depended upon a nexus of associations and oppositions key to Cornwall's place-image. The key themes are spirituality, both pagan and Christian, and its relationship to landscape and selfhood; tradition and modernity, within which gender, in the figure of Christine, is a key, disruptive force; and community and the insider–outsider dynamic. Narrated in the breathy voice of Dervla Kirwan, an actress whose most famous television role was Assumpta Fitzgerald, the landlady of the pub in the Irish village of *Ballykissangel* (BBC, 1996–2001) (which acquires a new, young English priest), the programme positions Christine, a recently ordained Anglican priest who represents the modern Church and changing ideas about gender, as an outsider who threatens to disrupt the traditional way of life in Boscastle.

The story of *A Seaside Parish* is that of her gradual acceptance by a community repeatedly described as 'quaint', 'isolated' and 'fiercely traditional': 'a network of fields and farmhouses that have scarcely changed since Norman times'. Christine is both 'controversial' and 'determined to keep the spiritual life of her parish aflame', a problematic figure who holds the potential to reconcile the programme's key contradiction between tradition and modernity. The programme is serial, with the possibility of 'trouble' attached to the incomer frequently used as a dramatic cliffhanger between episodes, for example the consequences of her (clothed) participation in a charity calendar in which local men will pose semi-naked to raise desperately needed funds to repair the church at Forrabury.

The series' title sequence is complex in organization and dense with meaning, effectively establishing and reinforcing, through repetition, the picture it presents of Cornwall. Each image of the sequence is a composite of two, one on each side of the screen joined by an area of dissolve, rather than a line, suggesting merger not division. Each of the thirteen images which make up the sequence combine an image of place, be that crashing waves, local people or the harbour, with an image related to the church (sunbeams shining through stained-glass windows, the lighting of candles, Christine herself). While the images emphasize the close connection between the community and the church (for example, a shot of the village is combined with a stained-glass window of fishermen), the overall effect is to suggest Christine's uneven but gradual acceptance in Boscastle as part of both church and community: she appears on both sides of the image at different times. In the final image of the titles, light shines through a stained-glass window on the left, which blends with a windswept image of Christine in ecclesiastical dress looking out to sea at the cliff edge, on the right; here, the deep connection of spiritual selfhood and landscape are efficiently communicated, even though Christine remains precarious, and searching, at the edge (Figure 13).

Movement and change are emphasized in every image, whether through wind blowing hair around a face, a slight pan, the time-lapse movement of a sunbeam or the use of slow motion (which evoke a particular pace of life). The music accompanying this sequence also blends the archaic and the modern, suggesting continuity through change, with organ and strings blending together in a repetitive piece reminiscent of the compositions of Michael Nyman. The programme's repeated use of dissolves, slow pans and time-lapse film of the landscape as scene transitions further emphasizes the theme of persistence in the face of change, as well as suggesting a particular temporality of place: unhurried. Often, it is the particular combination of spirituality and landscape that is shown to persist, in shots of Celtic crosses or the church as the light and sky change around them. Here, the programme suggests, there is time to observe peacefully, to consider, and such reflective possibility is located, in particular, at the periphery. The Cornish coast is repeatedly articulated by the now entrenched sublime, swooping helicopter shot which repeatedly rears up over cliffs, homes in on and circles the tiny fishing village, omniscient and protective, followed by cuts to medium shots of cliffs and waves and to close-ups of waves which dissolve to picturesque shots of the harbour. Often, landscape

Figure 13　The troubling modern woman at the Cornish edge in *A Seaside Parish* (BBC, 2004)

sequences such as this carry profound emotional charge and weight, for instance when they are used to link the story of a grieving widow with Christine's reflection on the recent death of her own father, and her calling to the Church, as she stands at the clifftop, looking out to sea.

Christine's church on the headland at Forrabury is often filmed in a wide-angle panning shot which amplifies both the movement of the camera and its description of space within the frame, drawing attention to the isolation of the church, a single light shining in the darkness. Even shots of Christine's inland parishes pan quickly towards the coast or include it in the distance, repeatedly reminding the viewer of the importance of the coast in defining this place. While Boscastle's location makes it vulnerable, it also makes it potentially dangerous, and the programme hints at the possibility of horror in Cornwall's place-myth as it ends episode seven of the first series on a cliff-hanger announcement. The village is enjoying its annual Christmas Music Hall Show, but, the narrator tells us, over shots of the sun setting over the coast, 'from down by the sea on the darkening coastal path, there's been some startling news which has moved through the village like wildfire': someone has reported having seen a body floating offshore. The following week, the episode begins with the search: '[t]here is a concern that the coastguards must find the body, before a member of the public inadvertently stumbles across it'. While nothing is found, the potential horror which lurks in the regional place-myth lingers, adding another layer to the ongoing presence of witchcraft and ancient religion

Figure 14   Spiritual reflection at the edge in *A Seaside Parish* (BBC, 2004)

around Boscastle which has been previously established when we were told early on in the series that '[t]he influence of the old pre-Christian religions in this remote community, focused on Graham's witchcraft museum by the harbour, is probably larger than nearly anywhere else in Britain'.

In the second series of *A Seaside Parish*, Cornwall is pictured as environmentally vulnerable as a result of its precarious location at the junction of two rivers, which pour down through the village to the sea via the harbour. The filming covered the disastrous floods of 2004, and documented the enormous support for Boscastle from all over the world in their wake. As a result, Cornwall is briefly and unusually positioned as part of both a national and an international community, though one vulnerable and in need of aid. The main risk for Boscastle, though, is Christine herself, simultaneously the emotional centre of the programme and its disruptive force. The charity calendar causes a great deal of disquiet in the community, as does Christine's decision to reach out to members of the local pagan community in the hope of bringing spiritual communities together. Quite apart from the new ideas that she brings, Christine is also youthful, modern, liberal (she is married to an American man and both were previously divorced) and female; her troubling position is physically represented by repeatedly figuring her perched at the very edge of the cliff (Figure 14). This insistence on the figure of the woman at the edge is as significant in this programme's vocabulary of place as the helicopter shot, pan and time-lapse, and its use here, in a contemporary television documentary which pictures Cornwall at risk, cements it as a key element in the intermedial vocabulary of the

Cornish place-myth. Its relevance in *A Seaside Parish* is clarified when it is viewed in the long history of its mobilization in relation to the search for self, the modern woman and the significance of the limen, particularly in periods of conflict when questions of personal, national and international identity come to the fore, as we saw in the previous chapter. Christine is often pictured in this way, walking the edge of the coast and standing alone in reflection or spiritual quest at the top of the cliff.

The search for self at the edge of Cornwall is always inflected with spirituality, through the landscape's ancient relation to and marking with the monuments and symbols of ancient pagan and early Celtic Christian faith; this aspect of place-myth is amplified in *A Seaside Parish* by the programme's direct address to religion. The composition of, and transition between, images of Christine, her church and the nearby coastguard lookout on clifftop promontories reinforce the idea that she stands as a symbol of hope and light in a precarious and isolated position. In more prosaic moments, Christine and her daughters walk along the beach as they discuss the social issues which affect the region: the problems of second-home ownership and low-paid seasonal work; the scarcity of other young people produced by the need to leave Cornwall to find employment; the lack of reliable public transport in remote rural areas; and the survival of the community into the future. In these moments, the edge of the territory is already strongly infused with liminality, uncertainty and spiritual quest, and the landscape carries an emotional weight and significance, refusing categorization as either pure spectacle or narrative setting, operating even beyond Lefebvre's notion of 'impure landscape' (2006a).

The Fisherman's Apprentice

The acceptance of the outsider within the remote Cornish community is a central narrative, too, of the six-part documentary *The Fisherman's Apprentice* (BBC, 2012), in which the marine biologist Monty Halls goes to the small coastal village of Cadgwith, on the Lizard peninsula, to work for eight months as a fisherman. The purpose of the documentary is to explore the physical and economic hardships faced by twenty-first-century British fishermen, but the audiovisual rhetoric is so deeply inflected by the existing place-myth of Cornwall that a tourist gaze is embedded even in the interstitial material preceding the first episode of the series. The continuity announcer speaks over an image from the perspective of someone lying on the back seat of a moving car and looking up through a half-open sunroof at trees, blue skies and clouds as they pass. Immediately, a road trip, a summertime journey—maybe a holiday—is suggested: 'Fools and outsiders not suffered gladly now on BBC2. There are ropes to be learned in a new series. *The Fisherman's Apprentice*, with Monty Halls.' The trope of insider and outsider, and a potentially antagonistic relation between them, are also immediately established here, before the programme begins. In the pre-credit sequence, the conflict between traditional small-scale and trawler fishing is staged, and dramatic string music plays over a long shot of a small boat and fishermen at sea, then of boats being dragged up a pebble beach. 'While big boats prosper,' continues the voice-over, 'our small boats are in crisis,' and here there is a cut to a shot of waves crashing up what will become familiar, for the outsider-viewer, over six episodes, as Cadgwith beach. Taken from up on the small cliff which separates the cove's two beaches, in this shot the ancient hamlet, with its stone and thatch buildings, appears overwhelmed, under siege from the sea. 'Can they survive the threats to their future?' asks Halls, on a cut to a close-up of waves crashing onto the rocks at the base of cliff, taken from just above sea level. This sequence shows awareness of the difficult economic, political and environmental circumstances facing small-scale fishermen and makes use of a familiar image of the Cornish coast, the romantic but dangerous sea battering the cliffs, to underscore the suggestion of threat.

The remainder of this sequence shows participant-presenter Monty Halls in fishing and diving gear, at sea and working on the beach, as the voice-over sets up the premise of the programme: 'Marine biologist Monty Halls is going to explore the challenges facing our fishing industry but from the inside. For the next eight months he will live and work as a Cornish fisherman.' We then hear Halls's voice saying, 'It's a very, very different thing than anything I've ever done before,' over cramped close-ups of him working. 'He'll experience the physical demands of the most dangerous job in the UK,' says the narrator as we see him submerged in the sea, and then emerge, in close-up, accompanied by dramatic music. Halls says: 'You get that cold shock, and the cold shock's a killer,' and then we see him hauling a tub across the beach. 'Monty follows his catch from the sea to the plate, as he travels overseas to find out if there is a better way to support our fishermen.'

While this pre-credit sequence draws in the viewer by setting up suspense (about the fishing industry, about the personal challenges the presenter will face), it also establishes two key discourses sustained across the six episodes. First is the idea of the outsider (or, seen from the inside, the 'incomer') who arrives at the Cornish village and must strive to be accepted. The narrator says that Monty will experience things 'from the inside', and this is emphasized by shots which position him securely within the landscape, walking up the beach, shot at sea level with a high horizon, or in silhouette at the prow of a small boat as he heads out to sea from the protection of the cove. It is clear, though, that running alongside this story about Cornwall's fishing industry under threat is another narrative, one which underpins fictions of Cornwall and other peripheral 'internal colonies' from *Love Story* to *Doc Martin* (ITV, 2004–) and *Outlander* (Starz, 2014–) (Goodman and Moseley 2015, forthcoming 2018). This series will play out the fantasy of assimilation and incorporation so often accompanying colonial narratives, in which the real story is that of Monty's struggle to be accepted by the locals. By the final episode, his daughter has been born in Cornwall and the community toasts the arrival of the latest 'Cadgwith girl' in the pub.

Second, and related, is the narrative about the search for self, and again that self is related to a return to retro notions of authentic masculinity currently in vogue. Man will be pitted against natural wilderness—here the sea—in the search for an adventurous, tough and outdoorsy masculine self, one which is eminently saleable and consumable (as Ferrier [2016] demonstrated) in that it seems to offer access to an authentic identity and lifestyle associated with place. There is also an accompanying ecotourism discourse here, with Monty as an environmentally concerned tourist through whom the programme's picturing of Cornwall will be focalized. This is made clear in the credit sequence and the images leading into it, as well as in Monty's drive to and arrival in Cadgwith. The narrator's 'outsider' voice and the fishermen's 'insider' voices are both juxtaposed and harmonized. 'What will happen if we lose our traditional fishermen?' asks the narrator. A wide-angle shot taken from the road shows the Cadgwith fleet on the beach, with post-production filtering emphasizing their bright primary colours, and time-lapse photography drawing attention to the continuity of the boats and the place against the passing of clouds overhead. Over this shot, a Cornish-accented male voice appears to answer: 'If you took the fishing boats away, the pack of cards would fall very, very rapidly,' on a cut to a close-up of the fisherman we hear speaking. The fishermen work on nets and a high-angle shot shows the classic 'postcard' view of the cove as he continues, on a cut back to him: 'it is a fishing village, there is no point in it existing, if it's not a fishing village'. The Cadgwith fishermen participating in the filming (not everyone agreed) are shot against the inside of the old stone building where the gear is kept. While the background is slightly out of focus, but speaks appropriately of traditional fishing practices with nets, floats and other icons, the men's rugged, often bearded, weathered faces are in clearly focused close-up and medium shots, as they speak to camera in Cornish accents which contrast strongly with the received pronunciation of both Halls and the narrator.

The title sequence, when it finally arrives, begins with a helicopter shot sweeping in towards the cove from the sea as rousing orchestral music comes to a crescendo of brass, drums and strings. The title of the programme is layered over a watercolour wash map of clouds and photographs of fishing boats; Halls is in focus in the foreground of the image, with the participants we have met in the pre-credit sequence collaged behind him and the village, misty and watery, behind them. This image is a rich condensation of the key discourses set up in the opening sequences, familiar across the history of screen Cornwall. The Cornish fishing village, here, is fixed as art (in the painterly, postcard image) and myth (a faded, slightly blurry background); Halls, the outsider-insider, is both one of the group (he shares their uniform and their weathered appearance) and yet also hierarchically set apart from them, in the foreground. The image blends a focus on traditional regional industry with an organizing tourist gaze (Figure 15).

As the speaker insisted, it is the fishing industry that underpins the tourist place-image of Cadgwith, and other similar Cornish places. If the industry is lost, the village, one of the most picturesque in Cornwall, will not exist. They are bound together, and it is two-directional. Much of the local income depends upon the visitor economy, and tourism depends on the place-image of the fishing village. While the programme was about supporting local industry outside of tourism, it also acted effectively to boost the local tourist economy; participants in the programme report repeated instances of visitors to the village eager to talk to them, attracted to the Lizard as a result of the series.[8]

Monty's story begins, unsurprisingly, with a recollection of the childhood holidays to Cornwall where his love of the sea began. The region is closely connected, once more, to ideas of memory and identity as he speaks directly to the camera, positioned in the passenger seat of his 4x4, and folky guitar music plays. 'My relationship with the sea, I think, is fundamentally different to the relationship that the people I'm about to meet have with the sea.' We share Halls's journeying perspective from the beginning—a cut to the view through his windscreen from behind him shows Goonhilly Down as he nears his destination. 'I'm a conservationist, and the guys I'm off to work with are fishermen, and part of me thinks that those two worlds very much collide.' As he bumps his fists together on the steering wheel we see that his left wrist is strapped up, and he wears multiple leather bracelets, a GPS/orienteering watch and a crumpled linen shirt. There is stubble on his tanned face and gear inside and on top of the 4x4. 'I've almost been the opposition in a way, because obviously they're taking things from the sea, and I'm all about trying to conserve things within the sea, so this is

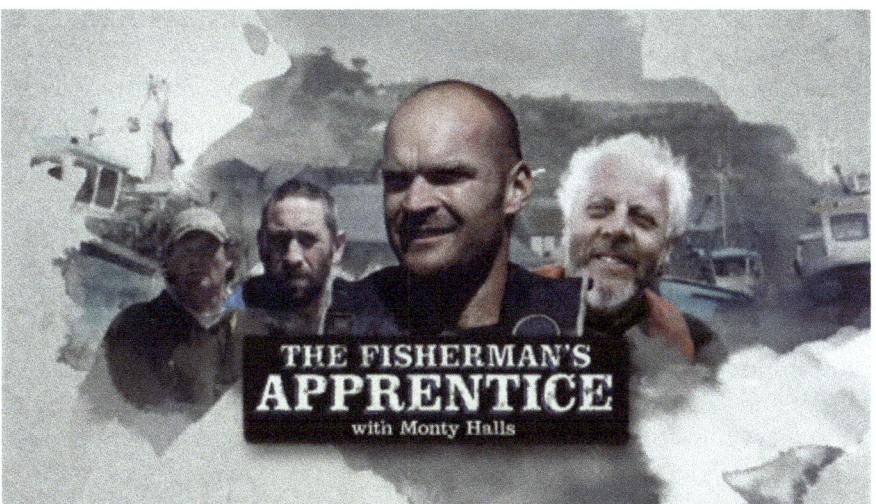

Figure 15   *The Fisherman's Apprentice* (BBC, 2012)

going to be a very interesting experience for me, I think, almost going over to the other side, in a way.' While our meeting with Halls establishes a fundamental conflict of the programme, one which underpins the outsider–insider dynamic (different worlds and viewpoints will 'collide'), his existing 'outdoor adventurer' masculinity is also established, though the deliberate focus on his appearance in these few shots seems to draw attention to it as a 'look', despite his known identity as a marine biologist, in contrast to the authenticity of the Cadgwith fishermen. Part of Monty's challenge will be to prove himself in his encounter with them.

Cadgwith, 'one of the last traditional fishing coves left in Britain', is introduced through a zoom into a map, a track across it and a tilt which brings us to sea level as if on a Google Earth digital enlargement, a device which Wheatley argues is a source of visual pleasure linked to the tourist gaze (2016: 135–37). The repetition of two notes of a chromatic piano scale is anticipatory, and as strings swell to fill out the music, a sudden cut positions us with a helicopter skimming over the fields to the village, revealing the sea at the left of the frame: 'Arriving in the village is like stepping into the past,' claims the narrator. 'Fewer than a hundred houses, many of them thatched, are crammed into a steep-sided valley.' As he says this, there is a cut to another helicopter shot from above the village, and slightly out to sea, as it moves out from and around the village in a sweeping encircling movement emphasizing its isolated and sheltered location on the coast. As the camera follows his arrival at the beach and boats, adjacent to the narrow lane through the village, and a hand-held camera follows him down the beach, the voice-over continues, 'Eight small boats work off the beach, as they have done since medieval times, and the skipper of one has agreed to take Monty in as his apprentice.' Nigel Legge will let Monty fish with his boat 'if he can prove himself worthy'. Monty will be learning the work of the small and declining UK fishing industry of 'hereditary fishermen, who have followed their fathers and grandfathers out onto the sea'. The score is often Celtic, even archaic in feel, a folky combination of pipes and guitars.

The voice-over narration makes repeated reference to the danger of fishing, 'by far the most dangerous civilian occupation in the UK. Making a mistake at sea could be fatal'; it also emphasizes the need for Monty to 'prove himself', to be accepted by the fishing community at Cadgwith. As Monty and Nigel put out to sea in his boat *Razorbill* for the first time, the camera films both from within the boat and at water level outside it in immersive shots which suggest an 'insider' view; the music is rousing, jaunty and reminiscent of a classic Western theme. The aesthetic of the programme offers an extremely privileged 'tourist view' of place, combining spectacular helicopter shots which sweep around the cliffs low to the water and high-angle shots of the village from above. Immersive images capture the lurching experience from inside the boat and on the water, the camera attached to the bow as it ploughs through the waves, or actually in it, attached to crab and lobster pots as they are dragged up to the surface. Though the 'view' of place and process presented here is simultaneously omniscient, prospective and 'from the inside', it nevertheless still adheres to Gunning's sense that the 'view' film, which re-emerges here in the contemporary landscape documentary, reproduces the process of looking (1997). Here, modern technology enables a kinaesthetic experience of regional landscape both from above and from within. The 'shooting from within' in *The Fisherman's Apprentice* seems related to its proclaimed project of allowing Monty, and the viewer, to experience regionality 'from the inside', as well as to produce an immersive, affective, kinaesthetic experience also characteristic of romantic screen fiction: this is a clear trope of the wider audiovisual grammar of Cornwall.

The first episode of *The Fisherman's Apprentice* is visually and thematically rich, establishing a moving image vocabulary of region elaborated across the rest of the series. The programme does a good job of raising awareness about the problems facing the British fishing industry (issues of sustainability, European quotas), and its aim is to educate the viewer about the resource, economy and environmental impact. Monty tries, and fails, to establish a local sustainable fish box scheme during his stay. Its other, equally insistent, story, however, is about place-image, outsider and insider perspectives and notions of authentic wilderness masculinity. The programme constantly refers to Monty's 'outsider' status and his need to prove himself to the cove's fishermen. While this involves overcoming seasickness, the ultimate test (of both his acceptance by the community and of his ability to occupy an appropriately 'wilderness' mode of masculinity) will be skippering Nigel's boat, *Razorbill*, alone at sea. A close-up shows Nigel's bloody hand: 'just a scratch' he says. 'A mere flesh wound,' adds Monty, mobilizing the vocabulary of war. While Nigel is able to locate himself accurately at sea, using cues given to him by the landscape (the natural navigation referenced in *All Roads Lead Home*), Monty does not yet have the intimate relationship to the landscape necessary to 'find' himself within it, and the end of the first episode is a helicopter shot which shows him alone and silhouetted in *Razorbill*, dwarfed against the open sea, man against nature. While becoming intimate with the landscape, seascape and the community will allow him to 'gain an insight into problems facing all the small-boat fishermen in the UK', it also has the effect of reproducing the stereotype of the isolated rural community as suspicious and inward-looking. The Cadgwith fisherman John Tonkin says to camera 'we don't see many newcomers here', and scenes of community gatherings on the beach often capture Monty set apart from the community through both the composition and focus of the shot.

The programme delights, typically, in local superstition, custom and craft; the fishermen fear the mention of rabbits ('underground racehorses with long ears'), taking pasties to sea or seeing a man of the cloth on the harbour before putting to sea. Gifting Monty a knife carved with his initial, he asks for 50 pence, 'an old tradition: you must put silver in someone's hand for the gift of a knife, or break the friendship'. Much is made, too, of Nigel Legge's diversified occupations. Alongside fishing, he runs tourist boat trips and produces artwork and crafts—making lobster pots by hand in the old way, and painting seascapes on stones, driftwood and tins. This picturing of the Cornish fisherman is familiar from early 'view' films of local custom and the Cornish fishing village. While *The Fisherman's Apprentice* is presented as an analytical social documentary, and it does achieve its aim in relation to the fishing industry, its representation of place is inextricably bound up with a tourist picturing of place as consumable and romantic. There is no concern here, for example, for the dynamics of the seasonal coastal economy based on tourism underpinning the common necessity to make ends meet from numerous jobs.

The establishment of a thematic place-image around the Cornish fishing village in *The Fisherman's Apprentice* is consolidated by the moving image rhetoric. Built upon a familiar vocabulary, it links together particular shots and camera movements in relation to landscape and mood to construct a powerful grammar of region. The three main devices used are the travelling helicopter shot, the sunrise or sunset time-lapse sequence and the close-up: of water on rocks, of flora, or of picturesque details of industry. It is not a coincidence that these kinds of image also form the basis of picture postcards of place. In addition, the series makes repeated use of underwater filming which is used to produce the impression of a more intimate, literally inside, view of place. The camera position is often immersive—low on the outside of the boat's bow, or inside the boat with Monty, for example, where the lens gets splashed with water, and the (surprisingly violent, to an outsider) rolling motion which causes his seasickness is captured kinaesthetically and presents an insider experience of small-boat fishing in stormy conditions. Monty dives over the pots so that Nigel, who has never seen his own pots underwater, gets an immersive view new even to him.

This use of the underwater shot to take not only the outsider (the viewer, Monty) but also the true 'insider' deeply inside the regional landscape reveals 'insideness' as a discourse, a construction. The suggestion has been that an 'insider' view of place might be a more realistic one, but in *The Fisherman's Apprentice* the voice of the insider is often used to support the hegemonic place-myth of Cornwall which maintains tourism as the main regional economy (rather than, for example, prompting investment in other regional industries such as fishing). Nigel Legge, who figures here as the archetypal Cornish fisherman, asks 'Can we afford to lose these sort of communities? I mean once they're gone, they'll never ever come back again. You couldn't replace it. These sort of places, even for the holiday trade, are just priceless. I mean, it's what people come for. The amount of people say to me when I'm doing boat trips, "Well Nige, just do one thing. Don't ever change it, just keep it as it is. You don't realize what you've got."' The use of a local, 'inside' voice and image to support notions of timelessness and resistance to change is a powerful device, as with the example of a shot of net maker Luke Stephens, with his weathered face, beard and traditional blue smock, as he describes Cadgwith as 'one of those little pockets that have been forgotten by time, I think', which seems to verify his words in its own indexicality. Deacon has argued that 'insider' views of Cornwall have often incorporated outsider views (1997) and, while the programme attempts to look at Cornwall from a different perspective, focalizing it through the experience of a participant-presenter who is attempting to become part of the community in order to offer a more 'authentic' inside view, the tourist politics of the image remain powerful and deterministic.

The repeated, rapidly moving helicopter shot which circles and encloses place is a gesture simultaneously isolating, protective and proprietorial, one which operates as a modern take on the sublime experience of landscape in literature and poetry, for example, as well as in early panorama shots. The time-lapse landscape sequence is also used repeatedly in *The Fisherman's Apprentice*, mainly as a transitional device between scenes, signalling temporality, the change from night to day or vice versa. Time-lapse scenes usually show the village in a wide-angle virtual silhouette, a few lights glowing, as time passes and the sky and sea change around it. The choice of a wide-angle lens extends and exaggerates the panoramic view across the village, and makes the edges of the frame appear to curve in, a further enclosing gesture emphasizing its smallness and vulnerability. The clouds speed overhead, the light changes as the sun sets or rises, and we hear the movement of the waves. Cadgwith, though, is stable and unmoving, huddled between the cliffs, unchanged and unchanging as it has been for centuries: timeless in an elemental setting. Glockenspiel notes in a 3/4 time signature support this interpretation, the waltz rhythm suggestive of repeated movement within a circumscribed space.

The oft-repeated close-up of waves crashing onto rocks can function in a similar way, suggesting stability and stasis through change as, for example, when the shot is used, accompanied by dramatic strings, as a response to the narrator's comment that '[t]he beach and its fleet are exposed to the full force of the sea'. While close-ups of the cove's fishing boats and gear sometimes frame picturesque details in interestingly 'arty' ways, with a focus on bright colours, a sharply focused foreground and blurry background—the winch, a coil of rope on a dinghy, a rope hook on wood, an orange float, the boat's name written in pen—the close-up shot is used in other ways which move beyond a simple 'postcard aesthetic'.

The landscape close-up is often used symbolically, to carry emotional weight. The programme emphasizes the tragedy of shipwreck in fishing fleets, a trope central to romanticized representations of Cornwall throughout the history of literature, painting and the moving image. The voice of net maker Luke Stephens is heard over a long shot of the cliffs and sea, a cut to the rocks, and then to a close-up of him speaking to camera, and trying to hold back tears as he speaks of his losses. A quiet two-note piano melody continues over a focused close-up of bright pink flowers before a blurry wall, waves rolling onto the beach, and a high-angle shot down onto waves on the rocks, as the narrator gives facts and figures about deaths at sea. This repeated play between shot types in the programme locates the speaker in relation to landscape, but also makes the landscape shots carry emotional weight through their juxtaposition with speech and music, and the way in which they function to stand in for the close-up of the distressed speaker once it becomes too intimate. This is what Lukinbeal has called the 'small metaphor' of screen landscapes (2005: 13).

While the programme attempts to challenge the romanticized place-image of the Cornish fishing village, its constant reiteration at the level of image and score euthanizes the political critique present in the voice-over and narrative. Moments of critique are either accompanied by or alternate with imagery that can only undermine them. A helicopter shot rises up and away from the village, accompanied by a slightly mournful piano melody, as the voice-over tells us that '[l]ife in Cornwall is not as idyllic as it looks. The decline of the fishing and mining industries has left it the poorest county in England.' This is meant to be a moment of counterpoint between image, score and narration, but the meaning attached to the spectacular helicopter shot of the Cornish coast is exceptionally powerful, reiterated and reinforced not just over the period of the programme but over a century of moving image rhetoric. As the voice-over continues to describe the increase in second-home ownership, tourism and the numbers of Cornish people leaving the region to find work, glorious helicopter shots skim across a beach, across, around and away from the picturesque village, speeding away to reveal its sheltered position in the context of the wider Lizard peninsula. Such images read so immediately as omniscient tourist spectacle that it is difficult to see how they could function to support the political impulse in the narration. The programme's verbal discourse is about sustainability, modernity and development. Monty argues at the end of the series that '[s]ome elements of Cadgwith have remained unchanged for centuries, but its fishermen have always moved with the times, embracing new technologies and new techniques', and the programme has been at pains to picture Cornwall's place in national and international contexts, as well as its regional identity.

The final moments of *The Fisherman's Apprentice* perfectly articulate the tension between word and image, as Monty ruminates on his experience: 'My overriding sensation, as I drive away and I look at Cadgwith in my rear view mirrors, is that this isn't some quaint representation of the past; it's a potential sustainable fishing model for the future. And we as a nation, and as local communities, must support our fleets, because otherwise they will disappear.' The images are contradictory, though, with a high-angle shot of the cove from the cliff and the credits rolling over an image of fishermen in caps, sitting on a bench against the old wall of the gear shed, drinking tea and smoking pipes, with close-ups of local characters in the pub and the iconic details of traditional small-boat fishing. These are tourist views of place, hardly different from those in *For Men Must Work*, and do little to support the argument that Cadgwith is the future, rather than a quaint picturing of the past. In *The Fisherman's Apprentice*, Cornwall remains, despite its declared intent, a timeless and picturesque haven and a frontier wilderness under threat, where man might pit himself against the elements and discover an authentic, masculine self.

Challenging Pictures of Place

Molly Dineen's documentary *The Lie of the Land* (Channel 4, 2007) also aims to educate the viewer about questions of sustainability and environment in rural Britain, but is a significant departure from such hegemonic representations of Cornish industry. The long-standing emphasis on Cornwall as a coastal place, as the periphery of a periphery, has meant that the industries of the interior, mining and agriculture, have received little to no attention in any moving image format; in this respect alone, *The Lie of the Land* stands out. The programme presents several examples, but the initial, and most stark, looks at beef and dairy production on Cornwall's remote Lizard peninsula, a place whose image has been overwhelmingly coastal. The programme's title is suggestive of the disingenuous nature of conventional landscape representation, as well as referencing topography, and the Channel 4 announcer warns the viewer to '[f]orget the greenery and fresh air' as the programme contains 'stark images of animal slaughter, which some people might find upsetting'. The film sets up its project to reveal a side of rural life not usually seen in terms of the country–city divide. The opening images show the marches in London against the 2004 ban on fox hunting, while the filmmaker's voice tells us that she '[f]ound [her]self on an unexpected journey … heading west, to get as far away from the city as possible … to somewhere where the people really depend on the countryside for their livelihoods'.

As in so many screen texts encountered in this book, it is the railway journey out of the city that takes us to Cornwall. The film will look at the amateur Cury hunt on the Lizard; immediately the video image is lower definition, shaky and hand-held: we are away from modernity and 'out in the wilds'. As the master of the hunt comments, pictured on horseback in front of a satellite dish on Goonhilly Down, 'It's like the modern and the old, en it? Something from the eighteenth century and something from the twenty-first.' The focus of the Cornish segment of the programme is the routine slaughter of male calves, the feeding of them to the hunt's hounds, and the revelation that 'every hunt in the country does this'. By the time this message is communicated, there has not been a single shot of the Cornish coast, despite the fact that the Cury hunt is located in one of the most coastal regions of the British Isles, on a peninsula of a peninsula. The sea is occasionally visible in the background as Dineen accompanies 'Knacker Man' John as he drives between farms, and at one point we see a rainy shot of Poldhu beach through the windscreen, from her perspective in the passenger seat of his old van, on which the window doesn't work. Just a part of his routine journey, the image is not a spectacular view but a dreary backdrop, one that, in the context of the other programmes explored here, reads as part of a politically motivated aesthetic.

The images of Cornwall in this documentary are, rather, medium and close-up shots of the people who care for the animals, of calves—'the waste products of the countryside'—being shot at close range, kicking after death in reflex and being dragged about, and of hounds tearing them apart in the 'flesh house'. The troubled regional economy is the atypical concern of this programme: John is paid £4 for the slaughter and disposal of a cow, £2 for a calf; he might occasionally be gifted a bag of fudge. 'What was wrong with that one?' asks Dineen, after we see him shoot a calf. 'Nothing. There's no value in him, he's a Guernsey cross ... there's no trade in 'em at the moment. One of the sad things about the countryside.' The brutality of the economy underpinning Cornwall's tourism-oriented place-images is foregrounded in this programme; there is no looking away from the Cornwall usually hidden from view as bodies are skinned by attaching them to an accelerating vehicle. Dineen hesitates to film the slaughter of a horse, and her reluctance points up the common double standard in non-rural attitudes to animals bred for meat, compared with those considered domesticated. We see the mare being shot, and in this moment the usually picturesque Cornish countryside—the gorse, the hedgerows—is more than a simple narrative backdrop, a meaningful and affective landscape, but here in relation to harsh reality rather than romanticized fictions of region.

Inside John's house the focus, perhaps predictably, is on a lack of modernity. Shots of the house show that it is as it might have been in the 1940s: there are open fires, faded family photographs and antiques. This is underscored later when Dineen accompanies him to his elderly mother's house, where she cooks lunch for him and his brother every day. The brothers are framed against antiquated wallpaper as they eat and debate the causes of the region's economic instability. The responsibility is laid squarely at the feet of the tourist, and the viewer: we don't eat veal because, squeamishly, we see it as cruel, but at the same time we demand meat: what we see in *The Lie of the Land* is the consequence: 'They want the land as a playground for the people in the towns,' the brothers tell Dineen, while elsewhere in Cornwall, a dairy farmer has to supplement his income with growing daffodils and running holiday lets: hypocritically, we import food, but are unconcerned with animal welfare abroad. The countryside which provides the tourist with picturesque 'views' is dependent on a farming industry which is under threat, partly due to urban hypocrisy: 'The countryside is only like it is because it's farmed ... if it isn't farmed, we'll end up with a very different-looking countryside.' While Cornwall, in *The Lie of the Land*, is shown to be archaic, outside of modernity and change, the programme does not descend into familiar stereotypes of strange, backward or bucolic rural locality. Instead, *The Lie of the Land* manages to offer a confrontational view of region, challenging the viewer to understand Cornwall's picturesque antiquity as the result of urban Britain's simultaneous removed queasiness about the realities of the countryside and demand for picturesque rurality.

Cornwall has always featured in British holiday programmes, available as a location for anything from the traditional bucket-and-spade holiday to the more distinctive 'glamping' in a yurt, or a foraging, art or yoga retreat. These increasingly fashionable forms of 'staycation' continue to produce the region as a space conducive to various kinds of retreatist alternative lifestyle, providing an easily consumable, mediated and temporary experience of 'place in the raw'. Helen Wheatley has argued that the older format of the holiday programme has declined as landscape programmes such as those explored in this chapter have developed on British television (2016: 138), and it is clear that the explicit 'tourist gaze' of the older formats continues in much of the contemporary programming which has supplanted it, including real-estate programming such as *Relocation Relocation*, proliferate in recent years, which imagine Cornwall and other Celtic peripheries as potential sites of permanent escape form hectic urban life, where one might downsize, simplify and either raise a family (differently) or retire. Such narratives are dependent upon the place-myth, explored in *Picturing Cornwall*, as a remote space of tradition and resistance to modernity and change.

ITV's *Cornwall with Caroline Quentin* (2012) demonstrates such developments so perfectly that it verges on parody: the series is a chaotic travelogue, repeatedly visiting the same kinds of site and business across episodes and producing a reiterative and restricted picturing of place. Episodes open with Quentin standing on a clifftop, looking out to sea in a striped top and yellow waterproof, before turning to address the camera. She will look at a range of Cornish businesses, from crab fishing to vintage tea parties, choices that reinforce the existing place-image around tourism and leisure. Visiting a lobster hatchery, which has made an enormous difference to the future sustainability of the local fishing industry and the marine environment, she tells the viewer that she 'can't imagine why anyone would need to raise money for lobsters'. Turning a basic economic problem into a tourist activity, she asks, 'Who's got the mayonnaise?' Out on a small fishing boat to watch the retrieval of crab pots, she describes the job as 'trawling for treasure' and, gazing out at the calm water and blue sky, comments that '[on] a day like today, [she] can see why' the fisherman does his job. In this moment, the physical labour of a 12 hour day and the economic hardship of small-scale fishing highlighted in *A Fisherman's Apprentice* is entirely elided, made hobbyist as in *Scilly Isles* (1963). Quentin later learns how to dress a crab then sits at a table outside in the sunshine to '[t]aste the fruits of [her] labours' while the fisherman and his wife bring her a crab salad, a glass of chilled wine and watch while she eats. So succinctly and satirically put in the first episode of *Wild West*, 'Cornwall is England's whore' in this moment: 'Don't sit around! Get out there and get me some more crab!' she jokes. A group of young women who run a vintage tea party business have various other jobs, farming pigs or making pasties: there is no sense of the tourist economy which underpins this, making it necessary to eke out a living from multiple occupations. Instead, the programme presents a twee 'Cath Kidston' picture of English rurality, with antique China, tea dresses and bunting. 'It's hard to tell the difference between work and pleasure with this lot!' she says. After a commercial break which also reinforces Cornish place-images, featuring fishing, Premier Inn (where, presumably, one might stop on the long journey south-west), holiday cottages and a 'Pasty Wars' episode of *Food Glorious Food* (2013), Quentin jokes that where tea was once smuggled in Cornwall, now it is grown. This opportunity to look at a growing industry outside of tourism is, of course, skimmed over. Each scene is separated by predominantly coastal landscape shots, lasting a beat longer than necessary, and which do operate here, as Wheatley suggests, as contemplative narrative pause (2011). Fishing villages are pictured in relation to a verticality which emphasizes the narrowness of the old buildings and the steepness of inclines, while the spatialization of the landscape in this programme once again alternates between the fishing village and the edge, underscored by an alliterative voice-over noting 'the craggy cliffs of Cornwall's north coast'.

It is not coincidental, I am sure, that I have occasionally mistakenly referred to this programme in teaching as '*Caroline Quentin's Cornwall*', for a powerful and deeply uncomfortable (internal) colonial discourse sits at the very surface of the text, as it does in the more recent *Joanna Lumley's Japan* (ITV, 2016), in which the presenter's patronizing manner is only reinforced by her existing television persona, overdetermined by her role as the superficial, condescending Patsy in *Absolutely Fabulous* (BBC, 1992–2012). The focus on a leisurely lifestyle and the denial of work and economics in *Cornwall with Caroline Quentin*, the presenter's repeated taking of the prospect stance, high on a cliff with the landscape spread out behind her (which is common to both the programme itself and its

Figure 16   *Cornwall with Caroline Quentin* (ITV, 2012)

paratexts), speaks not of uncertainty and possibility, as in the figure of the woman at the edge, but rather of proprietorial outsider occupation of space and an acquisitive tourist gaze at place (Figure 16).

Programmes such as this commodify Cornwall, presenting it as the source of an alternative, enviro-conscious lifestyle which can be procured and appropriated, given the right cultural and economic capital, in the form of a striped top or artist's smock, a yellow waterproof or a sail-loft second home. This conventional and persistent discourse of colonization emerges, in the context of neo-liberal, post-industrial Britain, in relation to Cornwall as 'internal colony' (Hechter 1975), and my use of this term is elucidated in comparison with Thompson's notion of the 'home hinterland' in the contemporary television 'geography' genre (2010a). For Thompson, the concept of the 'home hinterland' offers a way of thinking about the processes of estrangement and re-familiarization through which the viewer is taken in programmes which, though not travelogues, explore parts of the nation less often seen. While Thompson suggests that '[i]n the case of travel in the home hinterland, there is no easily assumed otherness, no obvious distance from what is being represented, and, indeed, the risk of over-familiarity' (61), the very clear othering and distancing of Cornwall in relation to the centre demonstrates the need for a more precise and politicized understanding of the picturing of regional place through landscape in the moving image. As we saw in the previous chapter, it has only been at moments of conflict and uncertainty that the Cornish hinterland has been integrated within a more inclusive picturing of national identity.

While occasionally works of artistic and social intent work to deconstruct and challenge the hegemonic place-myth of region, more often than not they participate in its fixing and reiteration, producing it as static, spectacular and to be looked at, so powerful and determining is the moving image grammar developed over the long twentieth century. Across mainstream actualities of Cornwall, including the earliest ones discussed in Chapter 2, we can see the development of this grammar of region that informs and structures the representation of place. Formed from a restricted vocabulary (particular shots or tropes), organized syntactically (from long shot to close-up; opening, closing or punctuating sequences) it speaks a familiar place-myth around sublime and picturesque views of place. The viewer is positioned as a virtual tourist who both gazes from outside, but is continually offered the possibility of a more intimate 'inside' view, a tension produced by an oscillation between impressions of kinaesthetic immersion and omniscient mastery. Within this grammar, the regional landscape is never simply freed from eventhood or narrative setting (Lefebvre 2006a), but is always charged with meaning, whether it bears the emotional weight of character epiphany or grief, expresses the precarious positioning of the modern woman or speaks (internal) colonial power through producing place as art or the reiteration of the prospect view.

In considering scholarship which makes a case for 'travel' as cross-cultural encounter and deterritorialization of culture, Loshitzky suggests that such attempts to deconstruct the ideas of centre and periphery which have been central to understanding travel and tourism in relation to empire may not be entirely positive (1996: 323). Arguing for the retention of a perspective that allows power dynamics to remain in focus, Loshitzky is concerned mainly with the role played by global television, and looks not at the operation of 'travel television' but at 'television that travels'. In this chapter, I have considered screen picturings of place best described as national, which continue to reiterate a set of long-standing thematic and visual discourses of place which produce Cornwall not simply as 'home hinterland' (Thompson 2010a) but also as internal colony, even where the intention is critique. The regional place-myth seems to be so powerful, its grammar so reiterative, that it is often impossible to fully sidestep it. The possibility of critique may be attenuated or even closed down in an encounter with the familiar and powerful rearticulation of place on television. It is vital, not least in this moment of territorial instability and change, that we retain approaches which can attend to and unpick the powerful relations of centre and periphery that remain so securely in place. With this in mind, the final chapter turns to moving images of Cornwall attempting to offer a different view.

5

A Different View

We have seen how Cornwall has been constructed through the travelogue, drama, newsreel and documentary. A moving image grammar of region has developed across these forms and across the long twentieth century, not simply a vocabulary, but a persistent narrativizing and spectacularizing arrangement of shots which have pictured Cornwall as place in particular ways: as traditional and unchanging, epic in scale but narrow in outlook, a place located at the very edge of a territory, its interior unknowable and, in the main, unpicturable. Screen Cornwall has, predominantly, had a bright, sunlit, traversable edge and a dark, mysterious and unnavigable interior. These have been images 'from outside', images bound up in more than a century of tourist gaze at Cornwall, a gaze which is implicated in the perpetuation of its picturing as available for consumption and reproduction, by particular groups, to the exclusion of others. Close analysis has shown the ways in which screen Cornwall participates in and perpetuates a narrow place-myth in which colonial relations of looking have loomed large. At the same time, this place-image has developed in dialogue with other visual representations of the region, in painting and photography, for example. While the majority of artists and filmmakers commonly associated with Cornwall have been 'outsiders' in one way or another, the production of Cornwall by image-makers from inside tells a different story of place. This final chapter turns to amateur film and to contemporary Cornish film practice, to think about the different views of place that have emerged from within.

Amateur Films of Cornwall: Newton Kennedy and Major Gill

The South West Film and Television Archive holds a mass of moving image material related to the wider 'South West' region, including the archives of the regional television companies Westward Television and Television South West (see Hall forthcoming 2018). It also has two holdings of amateur film of Cornwall from the interwar period: the Major Gill and

Newton Kennedy collections. Not much is known about the provenance of these films, and they hover around the category of 'orphan films' (Stone and Streible 2003: 125) with little available contextualizing material, making them difficult to interpret with any great certainty (Norris Nicholson 1997, 2008). The Royal Cornwall Museum (RCM) holds some of Gill's annotated lecture scripts, which tell us something about the context for which they were made and exhibited, and Sue Coney, who is researching Gill, tells me that she suspects 'his interest in photography stems from his family connection to the Branwells of Penzance who were also passionate early photographers'.[1] All we know about this donated collection is that it was shot in West Cornwall and the Isles of Scilly in the 1930s. On the whole, though, these films accord with Norris Nicholson's description of 'orphan':

> visual diaries, comprising numerous scenes from different occasions, simply edited together for convenience. These often lack titles, credits and pose many interpretative challenges, since little or nothing may be known about the people and places included in the footage, and even knowledge of the filmmaker's identity may have been lost over time (Norris Nicholson 2009: 115).

Zimmerman has written of the expansion of what counts as evidence in the new film history, and the inclusion of that which is 'suppressed or at the margins of official events and practices', asking how amateur films 'function as a counterpoint to public history' (2008a: 1). The question results from a turn away from grand narratives and towards 'history from below' (3) and, as with her other work in this field, Zimmerman presents a polemical position in which amateur film occupies an oppositional space in relation to mainstream, commercial moving images. Shand has also argued that the three paradigmatic approaches to amateur film have understood it as domestic, oppositional and evidential (2008: 38), noting that the resistant potential of amateur film has been gleaned largely from amateur film journals, rather than from the films themselves (42). Moving away from the 'home mode' within which amateur film has been largely figured, Shand suggests 'the community mode', which might also include:

> those who belonged to film societies and entered their group-made films into the annual film festivals that were held around the world, as well as travel filmmakers who toured with their films, and also more locally based civic filmmakers who rented town halls and other available exhibition spaces (53).

Among such 'civic filmmakers' was Major A. W. Gill of Truro.

The Gill and Newton Kennedy collections are not only 'amateur' films, but can also be framed as 'local films', a category of moving image which has been, as Fullerton has argued, 'until recently, a blind spot in film historiography: the production and exhibition of films which were shot in a given community and shown to local people who constituted the first (and perhaps only) audience for the film' (2005: 3). Johnson argues that local film is distinctive because 'it emphasizes and assumes local knowledge held by a public audience' (2010: 34), and Shand emphasizes the 'particular intimacy' of amateur filmmakers with local worlds, compared with the temporary and potentially exploitative position of professional filmmakers working 'on location', asking 'what, precisely, is the "local" inscription of place characteristic of amateur film production?' (2009: 156). Does the local film's emphasis and assumption of 'locality', then, produce views of place differentiated from the mainstream, 'outside' perspectives and grammar explored thus far? Czach (like Shand) argues that the dominant frame of 'national cinema' has contributed to a lack of attention to amateur cinema, with its frequent local or regional focus, suggesting that the amateur archive is 'the repository of images of the nation par excellence' (2014: 29). The regional, as a category, holds the potential to move beyond the frame of the national; might less homogenized views of what constitutes 'the nation', then, be found in amateur film?

I want to suggest that we approach amateur local film with a less automatic desire to find an 'oppositional' stance; instead, we might ask how they intersect, discursively, with mainstream films and television programmes. As Norris Nicholson has pointed out, amateur filmmakers:

> seem unlikely to have been isolated from real and fictive place identities mediated by other visual, written and academic sources including newsreels, documentary, promotional, educational, and commercial feature films (2009: 117)

suggesting that:

> [a]mateur movies and modern home videos tend to use a borrowed visual vocabulary and reproduce stereotypes. Early amateurs drew upon inherited conventions and replicated the imagery of picture calendars, greetings cards, advertisements and Boys' Own magazines. When amateurs confronted scenes for which there were few cinematic precedents, a fast growing visual code, provided by documentary reportage, Pathé newsreel and photo-journalism provided frames (1997: 208).

Amateur local film, then, as well as other regional forms of creative practice, might not necessarily simply 'mobilise an active historical process of reimagining and reinvention' (Zimmerman 2008b: 275) in which 'national allegories collapse into a range of differences, eruptions and discontinuities' (276), but might, rather, trace more complex and ambivalent paths. I set up this project in relation to Relph's (1976) framework of inside and outside relations to place, and within a revised understanding of Hechter's notion of 'internal colony' (1975), a framing which makes available an understanding of image-making from within in terms of the post-colonial. Can the colonized speak in a voice entirely outside of that of their colonizers?

I think we might approach both amateur film of Cornwall and contemporary practice from this post-colonial perspective, drawing on Bhabha's sense that the voice of the colonized is, in process, partial and ambivalent, and thus avoiding a construction of Cornish practice from within as homogenous, oppositional and autonomous. Bhabha's work articulates the contradictory positioning of the post-colonial subject, noting that:

> the image—as point of identification—marks the site of an ambivalence. Its representation is always spatially split—it makes present something that is absent—and temporally deferred—it is a representation of a time that is always elsewhere, a repetition ([1986] 1994: 118).

The mainstream (colonial) picturing, then, is always present as a point of reference against which the post-colonial subject makes images. How do amateur films of Cornwall—and recent Cornish films—speak both within and against dominant representations of regional place?

The SWFTA website notes that the Newton Kennedy films include scenes of fishermen at Cadgwith,[2] one of the most visited sites of screen Cornwall, from fiction films such as *Ladies in Lavender* (Dance, 2004) and *Summer in February* (Menaul, 2013) to television reality series such as *The Fisherman's Apprentice* (BBC, 2012). This tiny, picturesque fishing cove has been the heavily reiterated object of the tourist gaze in postcards, paintings and jigsaw puzzles, and the archetypal viewpoint is an elevated one, from the cliff to the east of the cove, capturing a spectacular and enveloping panoramic shot of the village. This classic, proprietary tourist gaze at place is reproduced across the moving image history of Cornwall, but the Newton Kennedy Collection proposes a different view of Cadgwith, while simultaneously acknowledging the wider representational trope. They do not proceed from a point of elevation or panorama taking in sea, coast and village; rather, they are predominantly shot down in the cove itself and show people working, unloading crabs from fishing boats on the beach as little girls peer in, trying to help. Gulls fight over crab scraps. Crab pots are not 'crafted', they are hauled in, baited and reloaded. Fish are gutted, or flap helplessly on the ground. A pan moves between the names of the boats on the beach, fostering recognition of place and affiliation for a local audience (Johnson 2010). Fullerton and King's notion of 'local view, distant scene' (2005) is helpful here (though this is not how they mobilize the distinction in their work on early Mexican films). These are local views filmed from within the scene, from an emplaced position. This is working, everyday, not picture-postcard Cadgwith, seen from an intimate, immersed perspective, rather than a panoramic view for tourist consumption (though of course, once archived and 'past', the films become available in this way).

In the Newton Kennedy film of Cadgwith, regional landscape is neither spectacular view nor narrative setting, but rather an integral part of a scene within which the filmmaker is emplaced. Occasional distant views capture everyday activities, the life of the place. At one point in the collection, there is a sudden change from black and white to colour that coincides with a typically picturesque, 'postcard' view of Cadgwith from the cliff.[3] A shot of the rocks that bifurcate the cove captures the intense turquoise of the shallow sea. It is surely no coincidence that colour was used for this moment of spectacular picturing of place, and this moment articulates familiarity with and recognition of the value of the elevated picturesque, panoramic view of place, Norris Nicholson's 'borrowed visual vocabulary' (1997: 208).[4] The dialogue between amateur and professional film is especially clear in the Newton Kennedy collection, which contains an entire 'flower film', what I have termed a 'genre of Cornwall'. Like a cinemagazine film, *Flowers from the Scilly Isles* has title and end cards, credits and intertitle-cards to introduce each scene and describe the familiar narrative of the flowers' journey from Cornwall to London.[5] Despite this evident attempt to produce a film in a professional genre, *Flowers from the Scilly Isles* has a clearly differentiated discursive form and perspective (and no voice-over narration).

The arrival at St Martin is shown from inside the boat and the film includes shots of agricultural preparation work, horses and ploughs, and men and boys carrying baskets. There are no establishing landscape shots, just images of labour. In the scenes titled 'Early Spring: Picking, box making and packing are in full swing', the picking is filmed from close to the action, with a high horizon. A brief shift to colour stock shows a little girl in a red coat and hat picking bright yellow daffodils alongside two older men, again, a choice made in acknowledgement of the associations of colour with spectacle (Wheatley 2016). In the greenhouse where the blooms are prepared for shipping to London, there are close-ups of hands working, people young and old, men and women, rather than the focus on the pretty Cornish 'maid' of the newsreels—a community working together. The same sequence is immediately repeated in spectacular colour, in aesthetic play with technological novelty to produce spectacle, rather than a focus on landscape, a clear indicator of the film's 'amateur' status. A pan across a house from a low-angle shot with a rocky field and Cornish hedge in the foreground clearly shows people corpsing at a window, watching their family being filmed. The inclusion of intimacies such as these distinguishes the local film from its professional counterpart, along with an attention to haptic materialities of place in the image—wind blowing clothes, hair, leaves and waves—which produce a sense of place, or of sensory emplacement beyond the visual, which is typically absent from the cinemagazine flower film. One of the Newton Kennedy films shows a professional film being shot on a beach, with black actors, and white girls dressed in grass skirts. Families sit around on the rocks and the cliffs, watching the spectacle, and here two looks coincide dialectically, calling up the typical tourist gaze at Cornwall, positioning it in a wider colonial perspective, but simultaneously inscribing a 'local' view, one which aims for recognition—of place, of individuals and groups—alongside the colonial spectacle on/of the beach. In this moment, the positioning of the local film, between professional and amateur, outside and inside, is brought into focus.

The Major Gill Collection is presented by the SWFTA archive website as follows: 'In the 1930s a Truro shopkeeper realised his beloved Cornwall was changing. He set out to record the life and times of the county as a moving record of the past for the future.'[6] It is thus understood by the archivists as local film interested in the capturing of regional specificity, one among many 'nations' recorded in archives of amateur film (Czach 2014), and here Cornwall is part of but also, as we shall see, distinct from the larger national frame. The transferred collection includes both complete, titled documentary films and 'visual diaries' (possibly footage not used in the former) and, while mainly in black and white, also includes some key sequences shot in colour. It is clear from looking at Gill's papers at the RCM that he made films to show in town and village halls, and at Truro's Museum Buildings, for the Royal Institution of Cornwall (13 October 1936), the Royal Cornwall Polytechnic Society, the London Cornish Association and for the Federation of Old Cornwall Societies meetings and other community gatherings. His scripts connect him to the tradition of the early cinema showman, who would project films and accompany them with a lecture, and, at the beginning of a typed script for his *The Spirit of Cornwall* film presentation,[7] he likened himself to:

> 'Copper Chris'. Fair. Penzance, Showman who lifted the curtain. I lift the curtain on my film before a CORNISH audience. ... But I don't wish

you to look on this film as a NEWS REEL. Certainly you will see many well-known Cornishmen in it, but each scene is typical of similar scenes, of Rites and Customs, work and play, mystery and tradition, which represent the spirit of Cornwall, handed down to us through countless generations, so many of which Customs are fast disappearing [capitalization original].⁸

Here he makes clear the ambivalent relationship of his films to the newsreel, emphasizing their intended 'localness'. While Gill's films show the kinds of tradition and custom, legend and myth that form an important part of Cornwall's place-myth as ancient and mysterious (as when in a moment of camera trickery, a suited man appears magically beneath the Men-an-Tol, peering up at it) and which are repeated newsreel and cinemagazine subjects (the springtime Hal-an-Tow,⁹ the Helston Furry Dance, the Padstow 'Obby 'Oss, the harvest Crying the Neck, Hurling at St Columb), they are presented differently, in the context of a wider history of place, of national and international connectivity. Cornish 'Wrastling', for example, is described as:

> a very ancient sport. The Cornish contingent at the battle of Agincourt, 1415, marched under a banner on which was depicted a pair of wrestlers in a 'hitch'. Cornish wrestlers competed at the 'Field of the Cloth of Gold' at Calais in 1521.¹⁰

As he says in the same introduction, 'My first idea was to make a film of ANCIENT CUSTOMS of Cornwall, but I found that that limited the scope of the film, so I gave it a wider basis and called it THE SPIRIT OF CORNWALL.' At the same time, Gill clearly subscribed to the Celtic revival (lecture scripts are often headed by the phrases 'KERNOW BYS VICKEN' (Cornwall for Ever) and 'BEDHEUGH BENYTHA KERNEWEK' (Remain Forever Cornish), and *Cornwall* ends on romanticizing shots of a beach at sunset, the flag of the Federation of Old Cornwall Societies featuring the chough and the phrase 'Tyrha Tavas' (Land and Language), and final titles 'Bedheugh Benytha Kernewek' and 'The End' over a shot of the beach. While the films clearly participate in the construction of the mainstream place-myth, then, they also do this from a position that also presents place as local 'from within' and constructs Cornwall as outward-looking as well as distinctive.

Within the 'visual diary' material is another flower film for which colour has been used to display the daffodils, as 'on one day four million golden blooms are sent to London'. The film is accelerated in an enhancement of the spectacle ('Speed up for the flower express!') as a girl turns to display the colours to the camera. Shots of individual blooms against a black background name specimens—a 'localized' discourse which is not a feature of professional iterations of this genre—and the film ends on 'A parcel for Betty', who poses for the camera with arms full of blooms. In Gill's films, family and friends are often used as 'actors' in the staging of local practices and traditions, positioning these films between the 'home' and 'community' modes proposed by Shand (2008). A complete documentary, *Cornish Crafts and Industries*, shows Cornish cream production, the slate works at Delabole in North Cornwall and fishing work at Cadgwith and Porthleven. Following the title 'Now let's go to Mevagissey to see boat building' is a view of the harbour, cliffs and sea, panning across the bay and reminiscent of early travelogue and newsreel films of place discussed in Chapter 2. A cut to a familiar and picturesque shot of the harbour with boats and gulls, again familiar from much earlier film views, is captioned 'While father and sons work, the "spirit of the yard" knits'—the 'spirit of the yard' being a pretty Cornish girl.

Here we can clearly see the dialogue between amateur and professional film that complicates the argument that amateur film occupies an inherently oppositional space. Similarly, the next sequence focuses on the traditional white headdress or 'gook' worn by women workers in Cornwall, including bal maidens (mining women working at the surface) and flower pickers. The gooks are set on a table before a grand building, handled by an older lady, then demonstrated by a young girl, to the camera, and in colour. 'Serpentine', the local stone of the Lizard peninsula, is demonstrated with shots of pieces of stone and, at Church Cove, a close-up on local flora, stonecrop and sea thrift, is followed by a shot of women walking up from the cove, wearing gooks and posing for the camera outside a rose-covered cottage. Aside from the pan around the harbour at Mevagissey, this is a film of inland views and traditional industries and crafts, with little attention to the coast. At the same time, there is a concern with the picturesque potential of regional specificity and performance to the camera that occupies an ambivalent position: while it is clearly produced *for* recognition by a specific community, brought out of the archive years later it also operates as a display of local curiosity to the onlooker from outside.

The first landscape 'view' in this film is of the towering cliffs at Cligga rising from the sea near St Agnes: a shot pans the coastline, then up to show the height and cragginess of the cliffs, then down again to show waves crashing at their base, followed by a shot of turquoise sea and white foam crashing on rocks. While this sequence of shots is clearly in dialogue with the commercial grammar of region which newsreel and travelogue films show is established by this point in the early 1930s, the sequence that follows distinguishes it as a 'local' film, in its differentiated and intimate relation to place. At the top of the spectacular cliffs there is quarrying of granite by pick axe and blasting and, while a shot of blocks being 'carted away' shows the coastline in background, the landscape is not here as 'view', but in relation to labour and industry. Where one might expect the shot to linger on the view after the horse and cart are out of frame, instead it cuts to a medium shot of horse and driver. Similarly, a shot following the title '"Scat Bals" and ancient mine-workings cover this desolate headland' briefly shows an engine house against the sky, but cuts to the mining waste dumps. The visual exploration of an old mineshaft almost promises a view, but the immersed viewpoint means there is no horizon and barely a glimpse of beach. Gill's film looks to individual workers and a title tells us that 'SARRE who works in the beach is surely of Phoenician ancestry', suggesting Cornwall's ancient international cross-fertilization and trading history. A shot pans down the cliff to watch him working for wolfram on the beach, from a cave, then climbing back up, a sequence which is utterly within the landscape and with no interest in a coastal 'view'—the sea is only visible in background as we see him loading onto a pony at the clifftop.

While it is evident that Gill's films were in dialogue with wider screen imaginings of Cornwall, 'local' images such as these offer a significant point of contrast, for example, with the ubiquitous picturing of heroes and presenters standing at the cliff edge, with the coastal view spread out behind or before them, in a proprietary and neocolonial prospect stance which emblematizes the political and economic reactions of tourism. In contrast, the Gill and Newton Kennedy films present a different relation to place, one not necessarily always in opposition to the tourist view. The views of labour here are not the isolations of weird rituals and myths common to the newsreel and cinemagazine, but rather recordings of regional life. Gill, for example, films the china-clay landscape at Roche, and while there are many panning shots associated with the presentation of a view for the tourist gaze, here the landscape is industrialized and inland, not romanticized and coastal. The pans take us down, into the clay pits, into the landscape to immerse us, but not emotionally. At South Crofty, a long shot of the head-frame, engine house, stack and outbuildings includes two young girls walking towards and past the camera as the wind blows their skirts, then takes us below ground with the miners, beyond any possibility of a romantic gaze at the landscape. Trolleys are filled and hauled, tin is washed and the by-product—arsenic—is highlighted as we see the miners with their faces wrapped in protective cloth. A title notes that streaming for tin is still being carried on much as it was a thousand years ago; while the same discourse of antiquity and tradition is present here as in newsreels of the same period, in Gill's films the 'views' of process are differently inflected because they are not presented within a wider tourist moving image grammar of place. Such images are not about travelling through place on a whistle-stop tour of sights/sites, but about being present in, and experiencing, place.

These amateur films of Cornwall in the 1930s, while clearly in dialogue with mainstream film conventions circulating at the time, hint at the possibility of a slightly different, more embedded view of place, one based in experience and connection. It is striking that writing on the St Ives artist Peter Lanyon, a Cornish Modernist working among incomer artists to St Ives in the 1940s and 1950s, has also been discussed in such terms, and this offers a useful starting point for imagining a critically regionalist moving image aesthetics of Cornwall. Crouch and Toogood have pointed to Lanyon's different perspective on Cornwall, one that directly challenges typical landscape views of the region, and one based in experience of and situatedness in the landscape (1999: 75–77).[11] Lanyon's attitude to the landscape, and picturing of it, is understood to come from an embodied and political experience of it, and a desire to challenge the static view of landscape from a fixed position outside of it by painting from a perspective which emphasized the tactility of landscape beyond its visualizing, drawn from walking and climbing it, cycling and driving through it and gliding over it, though he has also been accused of essentializing and elegizing it (Daniels 1993; Causey 2006). Causey describes Lanyon's work as 'a complex semi-abstract art, imbued with immediate emotion and place-specific allusion' (8), and emphasizes Lanyon's regional yet internationalist outlook on and from Cornwall. He contrasts Lanyon with the other, 'outsider' artists working in Cornwall, from Newlyn and Lamorna to the Modernists at St Ives, noting his politicized understanding of the relations between non-resident mine owners and the miners whose labour they exploited (16). In thinking about the connection between Lanyon's culturally regionalist creative practice and the potential for critically regionalist moving images of Cornwall, the way in which Causey sees his work, post-World War I, as challenging the appropriation of landscape by tourism and for nationalism and making figure and landscape one, where 'possession is synonymous with belonging' (19), is helpful:

> From the first, artists' colonies were a product of evolving tourism and the interaction of urban and rural—of urban demands on the rural—that grew from it. Tourism is about stereotypes, a place of view that conforms to expectations, and in that sense has much in

common with the original theorization of the Picturesque. Lanyon's mature work rejects the single viewpoint, excludes the possibility of landscape as scenic backdrop. His identification with place, unlike the artist colonist's, is deeply embedded, and the means to express this idea of being inseparable from the Cornish landscape was modernist near-abstraction (20).

Lanyon's most frequently cited painting in relation to this is 'St Just', which memorializes the Levant Mine disaster of 1919 as a crucifixion. It is interesting to think about this work in relation to the early newsreel film of it, in which the early romanticization of the mine as a site of tragedy is emergent in the use of three shots: the head-frame, the collapsed mine and the miners' distressed reaction. By contrast, in Lanyon's painting the dark head-frame and mineshaft are within, beneath and part of the landscape, removed from any possible romantic elevation above the landscape. This is a politicized work of immersion and critically regionalist affect, one based in local knowledge and experience of the landscape, one that resists conventional panoramic picturings of the Cornish landscape. Here it becomes clear that this perspective on place is both related to and distinct from the immersive landscape aesthetics discussed in Chapter 3, where a relation to the landscape through the moving image is constructed for dramatic, romantic affect. Lanyon's creative practice has been understood as oppositional to the colonial, appropriating tourist gaze, presenting a different, experiential and embedded view of place. Is it possible to discern such a critically regionalist perspective in moving images of Cornwall, and must this come from 'inside' the region as 'subaltern' speech or, as Wattchow has suggested, is it also possible to develop 'reciprocal relationships' with places, becoming (in Relph's terms) 'empathetic insiders', working between interpretation of landscape and experience of place (2013: 92)?

Cornwall in Contemporary Screen Practice

Kent has called repeatedly for moving images of Cornwall that move away from romantic fiction and towards greater realism and 'gritty' authenticity (1995, 1997, 2003). He values the Cornwall of *Blue Juice* (Prechezer, 1995) for its 'authentic' capturing of the Cornish surfing community (2003: 121), despite its recourse to deeply romanticized constructions of Cornwall. This contradiction precisely articulates the challenge of speaking of Cornwall differently, outside of the established commercial audiovisual grammar of place, in ways that might prompt change by reaching a wider audience beyond the recognition of the local. Kent has also praised surrealist political short films of Cornwall operating outside of mainstream distribution (124), and it is in recent independent and experimental film that some of the most interesting, provocative and progressive screen Cornwalls can be found.

The director Brett Harvey and producer/actor Simon Harvey of the Cornish film and theatre production company o-region have had critical success with their 2016 film *Brown Willy*, described in the *New Statesman* as 'Cornwall's answer to *Withnail and I*' (Gilbey 2016). Brett and Simon initially brought the film to local audiences in village and town halls, much as Gill did in the 1930s, but this happened as a consequence of the ad hoc fundraising process necessary to get a film made, or any other creative endeavour under way, in Cornwall, perceived by the creative community there as radically underfunded compared with other places (Goodman and Moseley 2014). This 'local', 'regional' film did not attract national distribution, though it was screened successfully in Cornish cinemas, and bringing it to Warwick Arts Centre was made possible through a bid for internal 'Research Impact' funding, designed to raise awareness of the issues around regional film production and mainstream place-myth.[12] This demonstrates the difficulties to be faced in reaching audiences beyond the immediate community of interest, whereby change in thought, practice or policy might be prompted. While scholarship on 'local film' emphasizes the importance of recognition and intimacy in relation to place, and discussion with the makers of *Brown Willy* also demonstrated this, the important distinction is that contemporary film work such as this is not only intended for a local audience, but also for a wider one. The potential of its aesthetic challenge to the existing screen grammar of Cornwall is to a large extent dependent upon securing that wider audience.[13]

Brown Willy is a drama following a strict classical unity of time and place, taking place over a couple of days during which Michael (Ben Dyson) and Pete (Simon Harvey), two school friends now in their forties, climb Brown Willy (Cornwall's highest peak, on Bodmin Moor) as a 'stag' event, while their friendship unravels. The film represents a significant challenge to the screen grammar of region elaborated in *Picturing Cornwall*: a contemporary feature film, it is shot entirely inland on the moor, in black and white, and insists relentlessly on place beyond the bright, coastal edge of the region. Indeed, Brett Harvey noted his pride in making a film of Cornwall without a single shot of the sea.[14] Monochrome wide-angle pans of the (seemingly) endless moor are quite different in impact from coastal pans in emerald and turquoise, and emphasize scale, lack of differentiation and the impossibility of navigation, in comparison with the typically gestural, defining pan which traces the coastal edge

Figure 17 Unfamiliar moorscape in *Brown Willy* (Harvey, 2016). By permission of the Malabar Film Unit.

in a romantic drama such as *Poldark*. Indeed, Simon Harvey noted that anyone local would know that, in fact, 'it's practically impossible to get lost on Bodmin Moor', highlighting the film's playful approach to shooting geographical space and alluding to the way in which screen Cornwall is often composite and nonsensical as a 'local view'.[15] Landscape here is not restricted to scene transitions, but is insisted upon throughout with static, long-duration shots of place, a moorscape rarely seen on screen and made more unfamiliar by the use of black and white (Figure 17).

Sound design is critical to the film; its first moments make audible the sounds of wind and birdsong over the title plate, and throughout the film a sense of place beyond the visual is emphasized through both soundscape, on which the wind blusters constantly, and the extremely fine grain of the film, which lends a significant tactility to the image—the textures of granite and lichen, the smoothness and sharpness of thorns, the depth and patterning of the lines, pores and hairs on the men's faces. Often, this produces unsettling effects, for example when a long-duration close-up of a gorse branch in flower against the sky produces an unsettling jolt in its lack of spectacular gold and blue, or when, as in Lanyon's work, figure and ground become one as the depth of focus and fine grain of the film juxtapose skin with stone (Figure 18). There is another challenge here, too, in the romanticizing of a different kind of regional male body in its connection to the landscape, a fleshy, and sometimes ridiculous one which got 'fucked up on Bodmin Moor and climb[ed] Brown Willy with a massive hangover', instead of the dark, chiselled and windswept romantic heroes of mainstream screen Cornwall.

The film plays freely with such familiar conventions; *Brown Willy* bears a clear relation to the 'wilderness' genre discussed in the previous chapter, allowing the characters a slightly tongue-in-cheek moment of spiritual communion with the landscape and a heart-to-heart around the campfire. In general, though, the quest is decidedly undramatic, unspectacular, ridiculous and disgusting by turns, in contrast to the mainstream place-image of mystery and even horror which has attended Bodmin Moor on screen. Cornwall appears as a kind of 'Wild West' when, desperate for water, they fall to their knees on the deserted moor to drink from a stream, in which the bleached skull of a rotting animal is visible to the viewer (leading to extraordinary, comically horrific scenes of bodily purging). The music, by Three Cane Whale, features an Appalachian harp, securing the reference to the American (South) West. Drifter Pete is a familiar character of 'relaxed, alternative lifestyle' Cornwall, and Michael's comment that Pete has 'this habit of leading us off the path' is a brilliant metaphor both for the lack of narrative thrust and clarity which characterizes the film's structure, but also for its extraordinary challenge to the defining journey at the edge, the repeated return to familiar spaces, and the typical narrative thread of moving images of Cornwall. In *Brown Willy*, the lack of a clear itinerary, the emphasis on the unfamiliarity and interminability of the moor (Figure 17), and the extreme expansion of time, which includes time-lapse photography to quite a different effect as Pete drags Michael to the summit, is a direct challenge to the romantic narratives and spectacularized landscape and motifs of conventional screen Cornwall.

The work of the Cornish filmmaker Mark Jenkin offers a radical and politically engaged cinematic picturing of the region across both short, experimental and feature-length narrative films filmed largely on the remote West Penwith peninsula. *The Essential Cornishman* (2016) is shot on Super 8 and is described as 'an audio-visual stream of consciousness … [an] homage to the spontaneous prose of the Beats, from the mythical Cornish West' (Jenkin 2016). The film works simultaneously as a self-aware memorialization of its eponymous hero, ode to the connection between

Figure 18 Skin and rock in *Brown Willy* (Harvey, 2016).
By permission of the Malabar Film Unit.

worker and landscape, and critique of the tourist industry. The breathless 'Beat' narration is an assault of ideas that moves from the 'strong, sure, sacred, essential Cornishman, effortless and aloof, magnetic' to 'the violent pornification of the industrial past', to the honeymooners and the 'stag and hen' tourists attracted to the west and north coasts of the region respectively. The monologue accompanies restlessly moving black-and-white footage of a fisherman hauling in, emptying and rebaiting pots, shot entirely from within his small boat; the film eschews a wide, panoramic view of the coast and sea, remaining close to the subject and only occasionally moving away to draw attention to the graphic qualities of the image, on an urchin posed on the sill of the boat, or a rope running over the edge of a granite step on the quay (Figure 19).

Like much of Jenkin's work, *The Road to Zennor (An Ode to Ektachrome)* (2015),[16] which was shot on a single, unedited roll of Kodak Ektachrome 100D Super 8 Film, draws attention throughout to the process of image-making, with the titles painted directly onto the film stock and the sound

Figure 19 *The Essential Cornishman* (Jenkin, 2016; Super 8 black-and-white reversal film). By kind permission of Mark Jenkin.

of the film running through the gate often dominant in the soundscape in a refusal to allow any relaxation into the views of West Penwith (moorland roads, stone hedges, wind-blown gorse) that the film presents. While the film begins with a shot of a road sign for Zennor and St Just, and ends in approaching the village (the coast and the deep blue sea, finally, visible behind it), it is not a smooth, road movie narrative. Rather, to a viewer unfamiliar with the journey it might appear jumbled and disjointed, a series of unconnected views. The Ektachrome Super 8 stock produces a quality of grain and colour that recalls earlier holiday movies, but any potential nostalgia is challenged by the use of sound and an attention to the graphic potential of the landscape: a rusted corrugated shed fills a held frame, a browned field and a hedge act as a high horizon, denying access to the view beyond. A view across the fading layers of the Penwith landscape, with a golden lens flare diagonal across the frame, recalls the titles of the BBC's first adaptation of *Poldark* (1975) but is accompanied not with a single, high-pitched violin note; rather, the film running loudly through the apparatus draws attention to the process. Beyond the credits, and before the final Independent Film Unit frame, is a brief shot of a standing stone beside a moorland road. It's brick, though—perhaps part of a ruined agricultural building—not ancient granite. There's nary a romantic engine house to be seen on *The Road to Zennor*.

These concerns have carried over into Jenkin's feature films, too. *The Midnight Drives* (2007) is the story of Andy (Colin Holt) who, estranged from his two young children for the past four years following the end of his relationship, takes them on holiday in February, 'out of season', to the West Penwith area where he once enjoyed a family holiday and beat his dad in a race to the centre of a maze. The quietly affective narrative concerns Andy's attempts to repair his relationship with his children through a disastrous holiday, including a Merry Maidens-invoked nightmare, closed attractions, inadvertent dogging, a visit to the inland (clay country) pool where he learned to swim and which is now a suicide spot, a trip to A&E and a broken-down car. Wound through it, though, in the plot and in the film's aesthetics, is a strategic challenge to tourist views of Cornwall and existing screen representations. In *The Midnight Drives*, Cornwall is wet, windy and miserable, in muted tones of grey, brown and green. It takes an age to walk across the deserted beach towards the camera, and the real-time duration, desaturated image and widescreen format accentuate the boredom felt by the children (and, we suspect, by Andy himself, whose nostalgia is thoroughly refused for much of the film). The landscape is bleak and empty, and panoramic shots hug stone hedges and deny a view, or take in closed arcades, the down-at-heel Jubilee Pool on the seafront at Penzance, grey seas and horizontal rain. The remote holiday cottage is grotty, the owner unfriendly, and the television can't be tuned in; the sound of static irritates resoundingly at moments throughout the film, and the wind whistles endlessly. The score is a repetitive, melancholy piano melody, amplifying the bleakness of the diegesis.

The film critiques tourist attitudes to Cornwall in a low-key but discomforting way: as the elderly owner of a guest house struggles to put up a garden sunlounger as an extra bed, Andy tries to make conversation. 'It's beautiful all year round, there's a certain magic about the place, isn't there?' he says. 'Your lives must be one long holiday.' As with so many films set in Cornwall, this film dramatizes a moment of crisis, but here the search for self belongs to an ordinary man. His crisis and epiphany result from a more prosaic situation than previous Cornish 'dramas of the edge', but are no less affective for that. *The Midnight Drives* is the anti-seaside-Cornwall film, and here it is not summer in February. In the end, the specificity of place does not matter at all, for Andy and his children, despite his quest throughout the film to find the site of his victorious race, and the commemorative photograph he keeps tucked inside his outdated guide book. The climactic moment is anticlimactic and unrelated to the film's location in any meaningful way as, for the first time, father and children share the same bed.

Enough to Fill Up an Eggcup (2016), perhaps Jenkin's most political film to date, 'was produced by Golden Tree as part of the project Miss You Already, an artistic exploration of extreme weather and coastal change in Cornwall'. The medium and the filmmaking process are drawn attention to by the constant visibility of the frame edge, its attendant dust and dirt and damage to the surface of the film, and by the inclusion of the sound of a voice recorder being turned on and moved around. The film successfully walks a knowing line between elegy and critique, redeploying some familiar moving imagery of Cornwall's coast through creative sound design, juxtaposition with less conventionally picturesque 'views' of place and objects, and shots of uncomfortable length. A familiar, slow pan from the sea, across the coast and into the cove, for example, is held, and then followed by an unexpected close-up of the face of a man, presumably Richard 'Taffy' Matthews, the Penberth fisherman interviewed on the soundtrack, followed by a shot of the sea from his point of view, and the sound of water over rocks. In subverting our expectation in this way, the film insists that our focus is returned to the connection between 'tourist view' and local labour, and the film carries a significant critique of the impact of tourism on the community. Matthews comments on the way in which visitors from the campsite up the road photograph him bringing in fish, saying he'd be a wealthy man if he had a penny for each picture. 'If Penberth had to depend on the visitors for its living, we should all be starving by now,' he says, as the film cuts to a shot of fish being unloaded, as a visiting couple watch from close by. 'When the last boat stops fishing here, it'll be their playground. A rich people's playground.' From this point onwards in the film, shots of fishing boats and the slip carry a different weight and significance.

In this film, too, Jenkin is concerned with the graphic potential of the Cornish landscape in black and white, and the film often presents held shots in which texture and movement are foregrounded and the tonalities of a flattened image take precedence over any sense of a wider 'view' of landscape (see Figure 20 in which the contrast between the texture and movement of the sea, against the granite cliff, is the primary focus).

The camera is often extremely close to its subject, whether rushing water, stone, gear or flora, offering a different perspective on place. There is a strong continuity between Jenkin's experimental films and the work of Peter Lanyon, not just in their shared attention to the graphic quality of the Cornish landscape, but also in their concern with a politicization of place. Sound plays a significant role in foregrounding this agenda; the score, by Rick Williams, features pipes and accordion and is elegiac but repetitive and insistent. Ambient sound is often inescapably present,

Figure 20 The graphic qualities of the Cornish landscape in *Enough to Fill Up an Eggcup* (Jenkin, 2016; 16mm black-and-white negative). By kind permission of Mark Jenkin.

emphasized through duration and the use of auditory close-up, as when the deafeningly loud sound of wind rushing through bamboo and then trees, over matching pans of the foliage, drowns out a snippet from a radio documentary. Voice-over narration is constructed from extracts of an interview with Matthews about climate change, weather and understanding of the land and sea, with the addition of a sound-bite from a US scientist on thermal expansion and the threat to the coast, in which it is made clear that while the instance in *Enough to Fill Up an Eggcup* is local, the issue is global, insisting on Cornwall in connection, not isolation.

Enough to Fill Up an Eggcup is a film of insistent, immersive aesthetics, at the level of both sound and image. This is a haptic film about being in place, close to the landscape, between rocks and foliage, surrounded by sound and landscape made place. But this is not the narrative immersion of romantic dramas of Cornwall; it is not tied to the progression of story or development of character. Rather, its immersive potential is the means by which the film offers critique, rather than emotional suture. As the film progresses, the tone of the score shifts, becoming discordant and vaguely more threatening, and the image falls slightly out of focus as the sea seems to encroach on and attack the coast. In the narration, Matthews comments on the risk of West Penwith becoming an island as sea levels rise, long after he is gone. The score ends, and the images of the coast are calm again as the film moves into evening and the sound of the shipping forecast is heard over the darkening coast, which fades out and is replaced by the sound of the sea. In *Enough to Fill Up an Eggcup*, 'immersion' is no longer a device of dramatic affect, but becomes sinister, global as well as regional. In this film, the familiar moving image grammar of Cornwall is remobilized, and wielded with political intent.

Jane Darke's documentary about her husband (the Cornish playwright and wrecker Nick Darke) operates in a similar way. An impressionistic film about the interconnectedness of Cornwall, via the Gulf Stream, to other parts of the world, *The Wrecking Season* (BBC, 2004) uses common devices of Cornwall's audiovisual grammar of place, including wide-angle pans, acceleration, time-lapse and the pose in front of the 'view', but these read quite differently in their juxtaposition with Nick's narration of his connection to the place on screen, and with extracts from phone calls with people around the world whose property has washed up on Cornwall's north coast, from fishermen to oceanographers and marine biologists. The emblematic shot of Cornwall, waves crashing onto rocks, is slowed down and placed in counterpoint with a phone call about climate change with an oceanographer on the other side of the world.

Molly Dineen's *The Lie of the Land* (Channel 4, 2007) offers one instance of a critical picturing of Cornwall from outside which might meet Wattchow's call for reciprocity and empathetic insideness, in its avoidance of conventional coastal landscape imagery and focus on a different aspect of rurality from those usually foregrounded in mainstream media. Channel 4's remit to 'innovate, experiment and complement', however, means that its audience is limited and, while a one-off political documentary on a minority channel might reach a small national audience of a certain class and inclination, a BBC comedy series holds significantly greater potential for reach. *Wild West* (BBC, 2002–04) was a satire set in a Cornish fishing village starring the well-known British comedian Dawn French, resident for several years in Cornwall. *Wild West* perfectly demonstrated the difficulty of parody in relation to place-image, and the risk involved in a practice dependent on the very representation it attempts to critique. Romantic drama has been Cornwall's defining fictional mode, in literature as well as in the moving image, but the bucolic potentialities of rural regionality have also been exploited, either within drama in the figure of the comic local (as in *Doc Martin* [ITV, 2004–]) or, as in *Wild West*, with parodic purpose. Kent gives a significant critique of *Wild West* (2003: 135), but this analysis seems to miss the programme's satirical intent. The title immediately draws attention to the longer history of Cornwall on screen explored in this book, and the way in which it has occupied a similar role in relation to the nation as the West, and the South, have in the USA.

The typical use of the Cornish coast is commented on throughout. The title sequence, in which a helicopter shot zooms in to shore over a glittering blue sea, accompanied by a soaring string score, plays out the conventional articulation of the contrast between the epic scale of the coast and the isolation of the tiny fishing village. The first shot of each episode, however, almost always undercuts the drama, as characters peer out through a rainy window at the mist, or sit, bored, behind the counter of the local shop. Scenes randomly take place near the cliff edge or in a tiny boat at sea, for instance when the local police officer is investigating a crime wave. The series' play with aesthetics is endlessly clever, as in the first episode, for instance, where the actress Gilly, whose home the locals occupy in protest, drives to Cornwall with a soundtrack by Aretha Franklin and spectacular, panoramic views of the sunny coast while the disgruntled village locals exist in a wet and misty Cornwall beyond the tourist gaze.

Wild West is also persistently political, taking on local ire over second-home ownership, the boredom of local youth, or a shopkeeper's annoyance at tourists 'shopping at Waitrose' before they travel rather than when they arrive, thereby not putting money into the local economy. *Wild West* thus draws on the tropes of 'West Barbary' and 'Delectable Duchy' identified by Deacon (1997), but in the process it offers both insider and outsider views of place, for instance in the exaggerated use of stock characters (such as alternative lifestyles, pagan separation ceremonies in the woods, and the stupid police officer who does every other job in the village too) as well as 'insider' critiques of tourism and second-home ownership, satirizing both. 'I don't even know his name!' repeats Harry (Richard Mylan), of an incomer resident of the village, to his friends in the pub (which has saloon doors). 'Terry. His name's Terry,' reply his friends. A fisherman in yellow oilskins whittles on the beach, and the melancholy theme from David Lynch's postmodern television serial *Twin Peaks* (1990), itself a satire on place-myth, plays over the scene as a romantic, mysterious score. Something washes up wrapped in plastic, and he rushes to recover not a body but rather a shipment of Tupperware, which becomes a side narrative for the episode in a significant undercutting of romanticized narratives of Cornwall. The series format of the sitcom is particularly useful for such a satire of representations of region; its automatic reset at the beginning of every episode means that issues around cultural and economic peripherality are never resolved, but are repeatedly hammered home in each episode.

o-region's feature film *Weekend Retreat* (Harvey, 2011) takes a similar approach in the story of a couple who come to Cornwall for a romantic weekend getaway. The film is set and shot inland and any sense of a view, beyond the fields surrounding the Victorian Gothic house, is absent. The film descends into horror and the romance of the central couple falls apart as the husband's affair, and the baby he is expecting with another woman, are discovered by his wife, and two locals break into the house, a second home rented out for income, in order to empty the safe. The film plays upon existing screen Cornwalls and, in particular, it is hard not to recall the violent horror of Peckinpah's *Straw Dogs* (1971). In *Weekend Retreat*, however, the landscape is deliberately deromanticized in post-production, creating an unfamiliar grainy, high-contrast image from which the coast is, again, absent. Outsider and insider views of both place and character are juxtaposed, with the 'barbaric' locals revealed not as two-dimensional psychopaths, but as people with a history and an emotional life. The film highlights poverty and crime as aspects of Cornwall as a place, and dramatizes the difference that might be made by genuine emotional encounters between people, in which the root causes of social conditions are revealed (in an instance of what Wattchow might call reciprocity [2013]). The film's resistance to a tidy denouement (we never discover what was inside the safe, and the relationship plot remains unresolved) offers a challenge to conventional romantic narratives of Cornwall. While the film acts against a number of audiovisual conventions of place explored in *Picturing Cornwall*, it also runs the risk of remaining defined by them, as does *Wild West*. While the stereotype of the 'barbaric local' is undercut, those of the 'bumbling bucolic' and strange rurality are reinforced. Kennedy and Kingcome have argued that long-standing myths of Cornwall are reinforced through the pastiche process and public discourse of the heritage and tourism industries, 'making it difficult to challenge the assumptions and produce alternative representations' (1998: 53). How exactly does one successfully market a film set in Cornwall, which eschews the coastal view, beyond its borders?

Two recent challenges to mainstream screen Cornwall have taken existing screen representations and reworked them 'from within'. William Overman's social media meme, based on a widely published still from *Poldark* (BBC, 2015–) in which Aiden Turner as Ross Poldark stands shirtless in a field, scythe in hand, tanned abdominals oiled and glistening, was Photoshopped to substitute a less well-conditioned male body below Turner's neck, and captioned 'Poldark: the pasty and ale years'. The meme brutally deconstructed the association of a particular version of heroic masculinity with the Cornish landscape, to ridicule a key convention of moving image representations of the region, one so commercially successful that it has even colonized Cornwall's self-representation.[17] Tony Goodman's YouTube series *Poldark—the Proper Version* made a similar manoeuvre, overdubbing key scenes from the BBC's 2015 adaptation with Cornish dialect and local humour. The scene from episode two of series one, in which the duel between Captain Blazey and Francis Poldark is refigured as a scrap between a Cornishman and a 'bae' from over the bridge (Devon), counted down in pasty-makers instead of numbers with the point of firing marked with a yelled 'Giiiiiiinsterrrrrrrrrs!!!!', pokes fun not just at the romantic rhetoric of screen image of Cornwall, but also at aspects of the wider place-image, Cornwall as a land of pasties. At the same time, much of the humour here is based upon in-jokes meaningful only to 'insiders'. These direct, deconstructive appropriations of mainstream screen images of Cornwall also, however, risk replacing one stereotype with another through parody (that of the indolent rural labourer in the vein of servants Judd and Prudy, *Poldark*'s comic relief), and herein lies the difficulty of challenging established place-myths, the difficulty of the subaltern's speech. Deacon has commented on ways in which the colonized have appropriated and used imposed identities for empowerment, pointing out that such practices may not break down binaries to 'recapture ... the fragmentary, the subjugated and the local' (2000: 224). How does one speak in a new voice, and still be understood? As Gifford notes, hegemonic views of place can be reproduced from within the margins (1999: 2), but Bhabha's more nuanced emphasis on the ambivalent space between the colonized and the colonizer, and the potential of the liminal boundary at the edge of territory as a place from where the minority and the emergent might speak (1990: 300), offers a starting point from which new screen Cornwalls might continue to be developed, given the necessary economic and cultural support for regional film and television production and, most critically, for distribution beyond the local.

In concluding with a consideration of what might be termed 'critically regionalist aesthetics', we come full circle in response to the question of 'outsider' views of region linked to tourism and economics with which *Picturing Cornwall* began. Cornwall is just one iteration of the ambivalent relationship between landscape, region and the moving image which can produce powerfully affective and delimiting picturings of place. It is my hope that this exploration of the ways in which film and television make and remake place might inspire further work, not just on the question of Cornwall's landscape on screen, but in relation to the audiovisual grammar of other places which have been similarly positioned, analyses which might provide the basis for challenge and change. There are other kinds of work to be done though, in relation to regional screen heritage and, as Norris Nicholson has noted, 'early film may assist communities as they strive to retain and regain cultural identity and recognition and reclaim their past' (1997: 209). This is not just a matter for early film and local communities, but might also highlight the importance of localism and (critical) regionalism in a globalized world, allowing incomers 'to engage even briefly in a social act of belonging and being in place' (Norris Nicholson 2015: 30) beyond affective immersive aesthetics of place which persistently reproduce place-myths. Projects around regional screen histories, then, might encourage us to ask about the impact of chaotic visual pastiches of place on screen. They might even help us to consider how an examination of the longer history of the construction of regionality in the moving image might reveal connections between aesthetics, and the structural and economic conditions of place.

Notes

Introduction

1. Cornish was officially recognized by the UK Government in 2002, under the Council of Europe's Charter for Regional and Minority Languages (Cornwall Council 2017). 'Malcolm Bell, head of Visit Cornwall, said: "The Cornish language is an essential part of the Cornwall brand"' (BBC News 2016); here, the privileging of tourism in the regional economy is clearly demonstrated.
2. ITV News (2016).
3. Philip Payton, in *Cornwall: A History* ([2004] 2017), details the county's complex constitutional status and semi-autonomous relationship to England, Britain and the other Celtic peripheries of the nation in prehistoric and historical times, exploring geography, culture, language and legislation. See also Goodman (2012, 2016) for an account of the industrial, tourist and devolutionary contexts in Cornwall.
4. Goodman (2016) offers a detailed account of the impact of screen and other fictions on tourism in Cornwall. See also Orchard (2015).
5. Chadwick notes that the ancient Brythonic Celtic language survived in Wales, Cornwall and Brittany (1963: 19).
6. See, for example, the Facebook group 'The Cornish are a Nation', and the Mebyon Kernow blog at <http://mebyonkernow.blogspot.co.uk> [accessed 17 March 2018].
7. See also Laviolette (1999), Kennedy and Kingcome (1998).
8. See also Hollander (1991), Ehrlich and Desser (1994), Dalle Vacche (1996), Nead (2007) and Allen and Hubner (2012).

Chapter 1

1. See also Deacon (1997).
2. See Thornton (1997), Thomas (1997), Perry (1999), Kennedy and Kingcome (1998) and Hewlett (2005).
3. See also Dickinson (2008) and Lowerson (1994).

4. See also Hubback (1997), Trezise (1997) and Goodman (2016) on du Maurier's Cornwall as a space of potential, and Goodman (2018) on alternative literary Cornwalls.
5. The exceptions: Kent's survey of films and programmes shot in the region and the challenges facing indigenous production (2003), Moody's analysis of the role of nostalgia in the reception and marketing of Winston Graham's *Poldark* novels and the BBC's popular 1970s adaptation of them (1997), and Moseley (2009, 2013a, 2013b).
6. See also *Cinematic Countrysides* (Fish 2007), which brings together scholars to think specifically about the countryside on screen, by way of addressing a perceived absence of attention to screen ruralities in the face of increasing work on the cinematic city, noting that 'the countryside is outside of, and lost to, modernity' (6).
7. Brunsdon (2007a, 2007b, 2018), Koeck and Roberts (2010) and Davies and Moran (2011).
8. McArthur (1982), Rockett, Gibbons and Hill (1987), McLoone (2000), Petrie (2000), Pettitt (2000), Barton (2004), Barton and O'Brien (2004) and Perrins (2015).
9. Rockett, Gibbons and Hill (1987), McLoone (2000), Pettitt (2000) and Barton (2004).
10. See also Barton (2004) on Ireland and Perrins (2015) on Wales.
11. See also Iordanova (2006) and Iordanova, Martin-Jones and Vidal (2010), and Laviosa (2010) on Apulian film.
12. See Crosby and Kaye (2008) and McKernan (1992, 2002).
13. See Woods (2005) and Pini and Leach (2011).
14. See also Robertson and Richards (2003).
15. See also Wattchow (2013).
16. NUTS (Nomenclature of Territorial Units for Statistics) is the scheme within which the European Commission identified Cornwall and the isles of Scilly as 'less developed' in need of economic support: one of the poorest regions in Europe.
17. Objective 1 funding led, among other things, to the establishment of a Cornish Film Fund in 2000 (Kent 2003: 133).
18. See Urry (1995: 193–210) on the Lake District.
19. See also Vall (2011).
20. See also Söderbaum and Shaw (2003: 6).
21. See also Rhodes (1995) and Breslin, Higgott and Rosamond (2002).

Chapter 2

1. See also Harrison (2014, 2015).
2. The gendered address of the cinemagazine, as in the very clear example of *Eve's Film Review*, which began in 1921, should also be noted, as Jenny Hammerton's work has shown (2002).

3. The British Pathé archive online (http://www.britishpathe.com, accessed between January and June 2016), Screenonline (http://www.screenonline.org.uk) and the BFI Player (https://player.bfi.org.uk), as well as the archivists and Research Viewing Services at the British Film Institute, have been invaluable sources in the writing of this chapter. All newsreel and cinemagazine films cited in the book were accessed via the British Pathé website.
4. See also Schivelbusch (1979), whose concept of 'panoramic perception' has been formative in this field, as well as Kirby (1997), Harrison (2014) and Keiller (2013) on the specific relationship between the moving image, vision and the train.
5. See also Thornton (1993), Deacon and Payton (1993).
6. See Goodman (2016).
7. Kirby notes, via Sontag, the 'colonization' enabled by the conjunction of the railway and photography at an earlier moment in relation to the American West (1997: 37).
8. The clifftop watcher for pilchard shoals.
9. See Feigel and Harris (2009).
10. Though this experience was always presented as available at the larger resort of Newquay.
11. Heath (1911), Mais (1928), Val Baker (1973), Collins ([1851] 1982), Trewin ([1948] 1982), du Maurier ([1967] 1972) and Rawe ([1986] 1996). See Goodman (2018) for a thorough investigation of Cornwall in literary travelogues.
12. The *Great Western Railway Magazine* makes it clear that promotional travelogue films such as *By Cornish Coasts* (1934) had 'been sent to the United States' (February 1934, 64).
13. The BFI Screenonline resource dates *Scenes in the Cornish Riviera* as 1904 (http://www.screenonline.org.uk/film/id/1186024/, accessed 17 March 2018), but given that Burdett Wilson notes that 'The Holiday Line' was a new slogan for GWR in 1908 (1987: 24), it is likely that the Screenonline film is a slightly later print.
14. See also Peterson (2013: 7–18).
15. As Bryony Dixon has argued, early British cinema often portrayed the countryside as 'timeless and idealised. The rural setting was used to highlight the corruptions of progress as presented by urbanization', and she includes 'Cornwall and the South-West' as traditional tourist destinations accentuated in non-fiction films of the early period (2007: 7).
16. Causey notes the renewed attention to Cornish mining in this period (2006: 50).
17. See the Cornish Mining World Heritage Site <http://www.cornish-mining.org.uk> [accessed 17 March 2018] and <http://www.wheal-martyn.com>.
18. See Genaitay and Dixon (2010) and Brown (2009).
19. Cornwall Airport Newquay (2018) records that rules on civil use of the airstrip at RAF St Mawgan, near Newquay, were relaxed in 1959, and regular weekend Stairways flights began during the summer tourist season. In

1960, Stairways services connecting St Mawgan with Exeter, Birmingham, Manchester, Newcastle, Leeds and London began, followed in 1961 with a Mayflower Air service from Newquay to St Mary's in the Scilly Isles. In 1962, a portion of RAF St Mawgan became known as Newquay Airport and a modest civil terminal was built. In 1963 British Eagle International Airlines took over the Stairways routes, including the summer service to Newquay.

20. Flower films of other regions exist, but they are a persistent way of representing Cornwall, and resonant given the centre–periphery hierarchy.
21. Kennedy and Kingcome (1998) note that the eighteenth-century, pre-tourism narrative of Cornwall is also one of modernity and progress.
22. Note the way in which Cornwall and the Isles of Scilly are often cut off maps of the nation, such as those used for television weather forecasts, like other peripheral sites.

Chapter 3

1. Other early British fiction films set in Cornwall included *The Smugglers* (Raymond, 1904), *A Cornish Romance* (Northcote, 1912), *The Fishergirl of Cornwall* (Northcote, 1912), *The Great Anarchist Mystery* (Raymond, 1912), *The Floodtide* (Brabin, 1913), *The Nest on Black Cliff* (Martinek, 1913) and *A Fisherman's Infatuation* (Waller, 1915) (http://www.bfi.org.uk/archive-collections, accessed 17 February 2016). While the only viewing copy remaining is of *A Tragedy of the Cornish Coast* (Northcote, 1912), the titles of these films, in themselves, are indicative of the early establishment of a place-image centred on romance, fishing, mystery, danger and, of course, the edge.
2. The film ends rather abruptly here without resolution; it is possible that the viewing copy is incomplete.
3. The *Radio Times* noted Cornish viewers' mirth at the composite construction of place in *Poldark* (Dowell 2015).
4. The immersive high horizon is also evident in GWR advertising posters of Cornwall.
5. Vernon (1988), Westland (1995, 1997), Moseley (2009, 2013a) and Husk and Williams (2012).
6. I am indebted to Misha Kavka and Flavia Laviosa for their invaluable comments on the notion of 'peninsularity' at the Screen Studies Conference, University of Glasgow, July 2012.
7. See Barr (1986), Landy (1991), Higson (1995), Gledhill (2003) and Laing (2017).
8. As Philip Norman pointed out, during the war all the film had to be pooled and used for propaganda: in the end the newsreels were simply a national public address system and after the war 'The newsreels came to a standstill as journalistic instruments. They were—as they finished up—like home movies' ([1971] 2002: 11).

9. In the television adaptations of popular romantic novels *The Camomile Lawn* (Wesley 1984) and *Coming Home* (Pilcher [1995] 2008), both set during World War II, Cornwall is the site of the family or adopted home to which the central characters inexorably return as a refuge from war, functioning simultaneously as both home and away.
10. Goodman (2016: 178–79) identifies this trope in literary fictions of Cornwall, and particularly in the work of Daphne du Maurier, as well as in the writer's own narrative of escape to Cornwall, a place in which, for instance, the wearing of trousers, unlike in London, was acceptable.
11. Ashby notes the significance of the narrative in *Miranda* (Annakin, 1948) to changing ideas of female sexuality, but does not attend to the Cornish setting (2000: 169–70; see also Harper 2000: 157). Similarly, Landy notes only that Lissa in *Love Story* (Arliss, 1944) 'moves to the country' (1991: 221). The Cornish setting is mentioned only by Laing (2017: 18).
12. The mermaid, that parabolic coastal figure of liminality and uncertain identity, is central to Cornish folklore, with perhaps the most famous story being that of the mermaid of Zennor who, moving with ease between land and sea, takes a young man of the parish as her lover and bears his children. See, for instance, the children's version of this story where the tale is described as taking place on 'the Rugged Cornish coast, where the land meets the sea … in West Penwith, the most mysterious part of all Cornwall' (Causley 2012). Chris Wormell's children's story *The Sea Monster* (2006) also features a monstrous but kindly creature who is sometimes part of the land, sometimes part of the water, moving easily between the two. The sense, alluded to in 'The Mermaid of Zennor', that the Cornish coast is also a space of seduction, sexuality and danger is one pursued below, in relation to Gainsborough's mermaid film *Miranda* and other romantic dramas. Ron James devotes an entire chapter to the mermaid of Zennor and other mermaid stories in his book *The Folklore of Cornwall* (forthcoming 2018).
13. Dame Laura Knight RA (1877–1970), 'In the Open Air', 16 June–8 September 2012, Penlee House Gallery and Museum, Penzance, Cornwall. See Knowles (2012).
14. In her earlier work in Cornwall, Knight had worked on *plein air* paintings of groups of young women, bathing and sun worshipping on the Cornish coast, on the rocks around secluded coastal pools. Unable to secure local girls to pose nude in the open air, Knight's models for these works were brought to Cornwall from London (Fox 1988: 34). The later, clothed paintings I refer to here include 'A Green Sea' (1917), 'On the Cliffs' (1917), 'The Cornish Coast' (1917) and 'The Dark Pool' (1918). See <http://www.damelauraknight.com> [accessed 24 July 2017].
15. See Moseley (2013a) for a fuller discussion of these stylistic distinctions and the relationship of Newlyn School imagery to *Poldark* (BBC, 1975).
16. Deacon (2001) and Hockenhull (2005) also comment on the 'waiting women' of the Newlyn School.

17. The accompanying lyrics would be 'All together in the Floral Dance', and the song as a whole is about being caught up and incorporated in the lively, community whirl of the dance which passes in and out of the houses of Helston. The song was composed in the early twentieth century, during the period of Celtic revivalism.
18. The Minnack Theatre at Porthcurno on the Penwith peninsula.
19. See Donnelly (1997) for a detailed discussion of Bath's composition.
20. Knight also made a number of studies of the china-clay mining region of inland Cornwall, but these works have not had the same kind of impact and ongoing life in the place-myth as her clifftop women.
21. The cliff-edge summer house is also central to the pilot episode of ITV's detective series *Wycliffe*, as the spectacularly located site of adultery and murder in a conflict over coastal property development.
22. With thanks to Gemma Goodman, who alerted me to this practice.
23. The analysis of *Poldark* in this chapter owes much to seminar discussions with the students who took my module 'Television History and Criticism' at the University of Warwick in March 2017; thank you all for your enthusiasm, attention and critical creativity.
24. Bodmin was the location of the psychiatric hospital and the prison.
25. Gibson notes the long-standing connection between Cornwall and the Gothic and horror modes (2013: 145).
26. A circular or semicircular outdoor theatre where cultural gatherings were held in Cornwall. See <https://goldentree.org.uk/portfolios/plen-an-gwari-the-playing-places-of-cornwall/> [accessed 1 June 2018].
27. *Caught in the Net* (Haggarty, 1959), *Four Winds Island* (Villiers, 1961) and *The Mine and the Minotaur* (Gowing, 1980) are other key films made by the Children's Film Foundation and set in Cornwall.
28. Cited in an on-screen extra on the DVD of *Straw Dogs – Ultimate 40th Anniversary Edition* (1971), FreemantleMedia Enterprises, 2011.
29. Goodman also notes the instability of the Cornish edge in her analysis of the writing of Daphne du Maurier (2016: 42).
30. Such as Caughie (1981, 2000), MacMurraugh-Kavanagh (1997, 1999) and Shubik (2000).

Chapter 4

1. For example *Stone Figures* (1955) and *Cornish Pottery*, aka *Mevagissey Pottery* (1955).
2. See Ferrier (2016) for a (slightly) tongue-in-cheek article on Cadgwith fisherman chic.
3. See also Pathé's *St Ives* (1959).
4. The chough is a corvid with red legs and beak, native to Cornwall.
5. The footage appears to be from *China Clay* (1964).

6. Padstow, where Stein established his culinary empire, is known locally as 'Padstein'; further restaurants have opened around Cornwall, and Jamie Oliver now has a 'Fifteen' restaurant in Newquay. Such developments could be understood to tread a fine line between development and colonization.
7. See also *Bamboo* (1950) and *The Starling Menace* (1954).
8. Conversations between Cadgwith residents and the author.

Chapter 5

1. Email correspondence between the author and Sue Coney, 5 December 2016.
2. <http://swfta.co.uk/pages/resources/other-collections/69> [accessed 17 March 2018].
3. In the transfer to DVD for research viewing purposes, the films have necessarily been edited together into a flow which may not be representative of their creator's intended organization of them.
4. It is unclear to me whether the amateur colour footage described in this chapter was hand-tinted or shot in colour, though Kodachrome was available from the mid-1930s.
5. The credits read 'presented by David Kennedy. With acknowledgements to G. W. Railway, Isles of Scilly Steamship Co.[,] Covent Garden Authority and The Flower Farmers'.
6. <http://swfta.co.uk/pages/resources/other-collections/69> [accessed 17 March 2018].
7. The film Gill calls 'The Spirit of Cornwall' in his lecture scripts seems to be titled simply 'Cornwall' on the print.
8. Royal Cornwall Museum, Major Arthur William Gill Collection, TRURI.1990.2.1.
9. A title gives the words to the Hal-an-Tow: 'With Hal-an-Tow, Rumble, O! / For we were up as soon as any day, O! / And for to fetch the Summer home, / The summer and the May, O! / For summer is acome, O! / And winter is agone, O!'
10. Royal Cornwall Museum, Major Arthur William Gill Collection, TRURI.1990.2.1.
11. See also Daniels (1993), Causey (2006) and Howard (2013).
12. The same challenges apply to publishing research on the regional, which is typically perceived as 'too specialized' to be of any wider significance.
13. Public Q&A session with Brett Harvey and Simon Harvey following the Film/Region event and screening of *Brown Willy*, Warwick Arts Centre, 17 June 2017.
14. Ibid.
15. Ibid.
16. Winner, Best Experimental Film, London Short Film Festival 2017.
17. *Poldark* mugs, fridge magnets, postcards and tea towels have become ubiquitous in Cornish gift shops and post offices.

Filmography

Across England in an Aeroplane (UK, 1919–20). Photography: Claude Friese-Greene.
Air Mail New Style (UK, British Pathé, 1959).
All Soul's Day (UK, Pathé, 1910–19).
And They Sang As They Danced Along (UK, British Pathé, 1926, 1929, 1930 and 1933).
Around Britain—Cornwall—Floods (UK, British Pathé, 1948).
Artists' Colony (UK, British Pathé, 1948).
Away to the West! (UK, Williamson Kinematograph Company, 1926). Producer: Harry B. Parkinson.
Bamboo (UK, British Pathé, 1950).
Barbara Hepworth Sculptress (UK, British Pathé, 1960–69).
Battle of St Columb (UK, British Pathé, 1948).
The Beacon! (UK, British Pathé, 1931).
Belles of Cornwall (UK, British Pathé, 1936).
Blue Juice (UK, Skreba/Creon Films, 1995). Writer: Carl Prechezer; Producers: Peter Salmi, Simon Relph. Main cast: Sean Pertwee (J. C.), Catherine Zeta-Jones (Chloe), Steven Mackintosh (Josh Tambini).
Brighter Signs! (UK, British Pathé, 1931), *Eve's Film Review* 534.
Britain's Wild West (UK, British Pathé, 1933), *Eve's Film Review* 652.
Brown Willy (UK, o-region, 2016). Director: Brett Harvey; Producer: Simon Harvey: Photography: Adam Laity; Editor: Brett Harvey; Music: Three Cane Whale. Cast: Michael (Ben Dyson), Pete (Simon Harvey).
By Cornish Coasts (UK, Community Service Ltd for GWR, 1934). Narrator: C. E. Hodges.
Caught by the Camera 28 (UK, British Pathé, 1935).
Caught in the Net (UK, Wallace Productions for the Children's Film Foundation, 1959). Director: John Haggarty; Producer: A. Frank Bundy. Main cast: Jeremy Bulloch (Bob Ketley), Anthony Parker (Peter Ketley), Larry Burns (George Johnson).
China Clay (UK, British Pathé, 1964).
Coast Guards (UK, British Pathé, 1945).
Cornish Fishermen (UK, British Pathé, 1955).
Cornish Gorsedd—Ancient Rites (UK, British Pathé, 1946).

FILMOGRAPHY

Cornish Pottery (aka *Mevagissey Pottery*) (UK, British Pathé, 1955).
A Cornish Romance (UK, British and Colonial Kinematograph Company, 1912). Director: Sidney Northcote; Scenario: Harold Brett. Main cast: J. Wallett Waller (Sir Ralph Chetwynd), Dorothy Foster (Sybilla Chetwynd), O'Neill Farrell (Jules Marx), Ruth Sampson (Miss Baston), Sidney Northcote (Dark Davy).
Cornish Tin Mine Disaster (UK, British Pathé, 1919).
Cornish Tin Mining—Camborne (UK, British Pathé, 1966).
Cornouaille (France, Move Movie/TF1/UGC, Canal+/Cine+/France 2/France Tele, 2012). Director: Anne Le Ny; Producer: Bruno Levy. Main cast: Vanessa Paradis (Odile), Samuel le Bihan (Loïc), Jonathan Zaccaï (Fabrice).
Cornwall—The Western Land (Strand Film Company for GWR, 1938).
Coves and Caves (UK, 1920). Photography: Claude Friese-Greene.
Crab Pots (UK, British Pathé, 1949).
Cross Pilgrimage (UK, British Pathé, 1965).
Daffodils (UK, British Pathé, 1928), *Eve's Film Review* 355.
Devon and Cornwall (UK, British Pathé, 1939), *Stepping Out*.
Enough to Fill Up an Eggcup (Cornwall, Golden Tree/IFU, 2016). Director: Mark Jenkin; Production Manager: Natalia Eernstman; Score: Rick Williams. Main cast: Richard (Taffy) Matthews; interview conducted by Will Coleman.
The Essential Cornishman (Cornwall, Early Day Films/IFU, 2016). Director: Mark Jenkin; Executive Producers: Kate Byers, Inn Waite; Featuring: Stretch.
Eve Helps the Flower Harvest (UK, British Pathé, 1932), *Eve's Film Review* 568.
The Farm of Many Industries (UK, British Pathé, 1935).
Figures in a Landscape (UK, BFI Experimental Film Fund, 1953). Writer/Director/Photography: Dudley Shaw Ashton; Music: Priaulx Rainier; Narrator: Cecil Day Lewis; Words: Jacquetta Hawkes.
The Fishergirl of Cornwall (UK, British and Colonial Kinematograph Company, 1912). Director: Sidney Northcote; Scenario: Harold Brett. Main cast: Dorothy Foster (Mary Trelawney), J. Wallett Waller (Tom Long).
A Fisherman's Infatuation (UK, Cunard, 1915). Director: J. Wallett Waller.
Fishing Village (UK, British Pathé, 1946).
The Floodtide (UK, Edison, 1913). Director: Charles J. Brabin; Scenario: Goring Cholmers. Main cast: Mark McDermott (Sidney Brandon), Miriam Nesbitt (Connie Lee), Frederick Annerley (Joe Muzzey), Alice Mansfield (Mr Lee).
Flower Harvest—in Cornwall (UK, British Pathé, 1927), *Eve's Film Review* 308.
Flowers (UK, British Pathé, 1937).
For Men Must Work: Port Isaac (UK, British Pathé, 1938).
Four Winds Island (UK, Merton Park for Children's Film Foundation, 1961). Director: David Villiers; Producer: Frank A. Hoare. Main cast: Amanda Coxell (Mary), Annette Robertson (Leila), Iain Gregory (George).
Fowey (UK, British Pathé, 1938).
Furry Clock (UK, British Pathé, 1941).
Furry Dance (UK, British Pathé, 1955).

Gallivant (UK, Tall Stories/Arts Council, 1996). Director: Andrew Kötting; Producer: Ben Woolford. Main cast: Gladys Morris, Eden Kötting, Andrew Kötting.
Girl Water Diviner (UK, British Pathé, 1954).
Goat Farm (UK, British Pathé, 1949).
Going Places: Tintagel (UK, British Pathé, 1937).
The Great Anarchist Mystery (UK, British and Colonial Kinematograph Company, 1912). Director: Charles Raymond. Main cast: Percy Moran (Jack Logan), Dorothy Foster (Betty Lyndhurst), Derek Powell (Peter Nickoloff), Charles Seymour (Inspector Keen).
Haunters of the Deep (UK, Longbow Film Company for Children's Film and Television Foundation, 1984). Director: Andrew Bogle; Producer: Gordon L. T. Scott. Main cast: Andrew Keir (Captain Tregellis), Barbara Ewing (Mrs Holman), Bob Sherman (Roche), Gary Simmons (Josh), Amy Taylor (Becky).
Helston's Ancient Furry Dance (UK, British Pathé, 1921).
Horse Sense (UK, British Pathé, 1950).
Jamaica Inn (UK, Mayflower Pictures Corporation, 1939). Director: Alfred Hitchcock; Producer: Erich Pommer. Main cast: Charles Laughton (Sir Humphrey Pengallan), Maureen O'Hara (Mary Yellen), Leslie Banks (Joss Merlyn), Marie Ney (Aunt Patience), Robert Newton (Jem Trehearne).
Johnny Frenchman (UK, Ealing Studios, 1945). Director: Charles Frend; Producer: Michael Balcon. Main cast: Tom Walls (Nat Pomeroy), Françoise Rosay (Florrie Kervarec), Patricia Roc (Sue Pomeroy), Ralph Michael (Bob Tremayne).
Knights of the Round Table (UK/USA, MGM/Loew's Inc., 1953). Director: Richard Thorpe; Producer: Pandro S. Berman. Main cast: Valentine Dyall (Narrator), Robert Taylor (Sir Lancelot), Ava Gardner (Queen Guinevere), Mel Ferrer (King Arthur Pendragon).
Kynance Cove Cornwall (UK, British Pathé, 1957).
Ladies in Lavender (UK, Take Partnerships/Scala Productions, 2004). Director: Charles Dance; Producers: Nicolas Brown, Elizabeth Karlsen, Nik Powell.
Land's End Airport (UK, British Pathé, 1962).
Look Out, Lobsters! (UK, British Pathé, 1965).
Love Story (UK, Gainsborough Pictures, 1944). Director: Leslie Arliss; Producer: Harold Huth; Score: Hubert Bath. Main cast: Margaret Lockwood (Lissa Campbell), Stewart Granger (Kit Firth), Patricia Roc (Judy Martin), Tom Walls (Tom Tanner).
Mad About Men (UK, Group Film Productions, 1954). Director: Ralph Thomas; Producer: Betty E. Box. Main Cast: Glynis Johns (Caroline and Miranda Trewella), Donald Sinden (Jeff Saunders).
Major Gill Amateur Film Collection (South West Film and Television Archive, 1930s).
Malachi's Cove (aka *The Seaweed Children*) (UK, Penrith Productions/Impact Quadrant Films, 1973). Director: Henry Herbert; Producers: Andrew Sinclair,

Kent Walwin. Main cast: Donald Pleasence (Malachi), Veronica Quilligan (Mally), Dai Bradley (Barty).

The Midnight Drives (o-region/Midnight Films, 2007). Director/Writer: Mark Jenkin; Producer: Oliver Berry; Original score: Alcatraz Swim Team. Main cast: Colin Holt (Andy Stafford), Sam Mills (Casey Stafford), Megan Robertson (Gabrielle Stafford).

Millions Like Us (UK, Gainsborough Pictures, 1943). Directors: Frank Launder, Sidney Gilliat; Producer: Edward Black. Main cast: Patricia Roc (Celia Crowson), Gordon Jackson (Fred Blake), Anne Crawford (Jennifer Knowles).

The Mine and the Minotaur (UK, Sailorman Films for Children's Film Foundation, 1980). Director: David Gowing; Producer: Emma Gowing. Main cast: Adam Rhodes (Jake Driscoll), William Booker (Dan Driscoll), Felicity Harrison (Julia Driscoll).

Miranda (UK, Gainsborough Pictures, 1948). Director: Ken Annakin; Producer: Betty E. Box. Main cast: Glynis Johns (Miranda), Googie Withers (Clare Martin), Griffith Jones (Paul Martin), Margaret Rutherford (Nurse Carey).

Mullion Cove (UK, British Pathé, 1946).

The Nest on Black Cliff (UK, Big Ben Films/Union, 1913). Director: H. O. Martinek. Cast: H. O. Martinek (man), Ivy Martinek (girl).

New Surf Boat (UK, British Pathé, 1968).

Newton Kennedy Amateur Film Collection (South West Film and Television Archive, 1930s).

Old Superstitions (UK, British Pathé, 1961).

On with the Furry Dance! (UK, 1925), *Topical Budget* 715-2.

Open Air Theatre (UK, British Pathé, 1955).

The Open Road (UK, 1925). Director/Producer: Claude Friese-Greene.

The Padstow 'Hobby Hoss' (UK, British Pathé, 1932).

People in Camera (UK, British Pathé, 1946).

Pilchard Fishing Industry (UK, British Pathé, 1949).

Pyramids of Cornwall—A West Carnclaze Study (UK, British Pathé, 1929).

Rebecca (USA, Selznick International Pictures, 1940). Director: Alfred Hitchcock; Producer: David O. Selznick. Main cast: Laurence Olivier (Maxim de Winter), Joan Fontaine (Mrs de Winter), George Sanders (Jack Favell), Judith Anderson (Mrs Danvers).

The Road to Zennor (An Ode to Ektachrome) (Cornwall, Early Day Films, 2015). Director: Mark Jenkin; Executive producers: Kate Byers and Linn Waite; Narrator: Mary Woodvine.

RSPCA Rescue (UK, British Pathé, 1952).

Sailor's Return (UK, British Pathé, 1946).

Saving Grace (UK, Fine Line, 2000). Director: Nigel Cole; Producer: Mark Crowdy. Main cast: Brenda Blethyn (Grace), Craig Ferguson (Matthew), Martin Clunes (Dr Bamford), Tchéky Karyo (Jacques).

Scenes in the Cornish Riviera (UK, Charles Urban Trading Company for GWR, 1904).

Scilly Isles (UK, British Pathé, 1963).
Serpentine Rock (UK, British Pathé, 1963).
Sheaf Pitching Record (UK, British Pathé, 1935), *News in a Nutshell*.
The Smugglers (UK, Warwick Trading Company, 1904). Director: Charles Raymond.
So That You Can Live (UK, Cinema Action, 1982). Director/Producer: Cinema Action. Main Cast: Shirley Butts, Roy Butts, Royston Butts, Diane Butts.
St Ives (UK, British Pathé, 1959).
The Starling Menace (UK, British Pathé, 1954).
Stone Figures (UK, British Pathé, 1955).
Straw Dogs (UK/USA, ABC Pictures, 1971). Director: Sam Peckinpah; Producer: Daniel Melnick. Main cast: Dustin Hoffman (David Sumner), Susan George (Amy Sumner), Peter Vaughn (Tom Hedden), T. P. McKenna (Major Scott), Del Henney (Charlie Venner), Jim Norton (Chris Cawsey).
Straw Dogs (USA, Screen Gems, 2011). Director: Rod Lurie; Producer: Daniel Melnick. Main cast: James Marsden (David Sumner), Kate Bosworth (Amy Sumner).
Summer in February (UK/USA, Crossday/Apart Films, 2013). Director: Christopher Menaul; Producers: Jeremy Cowdry, Janette Day, Pippa Cross, Dan Stevens. Main cast: Dominic Cooper (A. J. Munnings), Dan Stevens (Gilbert Evans), Emily Browning (Florence Carter Wood), Hattie Morahan (Laura Knight), Max Deacon (Joey Carter Wood), Mia Austen (Dolly).
Summer is Y Comen In (UK, British Pathé, 1930).
Tamar Bridge (UK, British Pathé, 1962).
They Bring You Fish (UK, British Instructional Films Ltd via British Pathé, 1949).
Tin Mining (UK, British Instructional Films Ltd via British Pathé, 1940–49).
Tinstone—How it is Obtained in a Cornish Mine (UK, British Pathé, 1933), *Eve's Film Review* 643.
A Tragedy of the Cornish Coast (UK, British and Colonial Kinematograph Company, 1912). Director: Sidney Northcote; Scenario: Harold Brett. Main cast: J. Wallett Waller (Tom), Dorothy Foster (Mark Trelawney), O'Neill Farrell (villain), Sidney Northcote (villain).
Treasure Island (UK/USA, RKO-Walt Disney British Productions, 1950). Director: Byron Haskins; Producer: Perce Pearce. Main cast: Bobby Driscoll (Jim Hawkins), Robert Newton (Long John Silver), Basil Sydney (Captain Smollett).
TV from Space (UK, ATV/GPO via British Pathé, 1962).
The Uninvited (USA, Paramount Pictures Corporation, 1944). Director: Lewis Allen; Producer: Charles Brackett. Main cast: Ray Milland (Roderick Fitzgerald), Ruth Hussey (Pamela Fitzgerald), Donald Crisp (Commander Beech), Cornelia Otis Skinner (Miss Holloway), Gail Russell (Stella Meredith).
Veryan (UK, British Pathé, 1938).
Wait for It! Polperro (UK, British Pathé, 1937).
Weekend Retreat (Cornwall, UK, 0-region, 2011). Director/Writer: Brett Harvey; Producer: Simon Harvey. Main cast: Dominic Coleman (Duncan), Laura

Frances-Martin (Chloe), Esther Hall (Karen), Daniel Harvey (Dave), Simon Harvey (Kevin), Dean Nolan (Gary).

West Country Journey (UK, British Transport Films, 1953). Director: Syd Sharples; Producers: Edgar Anstey, Ian Ferguson; Narrators: Victor Platt, Max Brimmell.

Westward Ho! (UK, Associated British Pathé for British Travel and Holidays Association, 1961). Director: Martin Rolfe.

While I Live (UK, Edward Dryhurst Productions, 1948). Director: John Harlow; Producer: Edward Dryhurst; Main cast: Tom Walls (Nehemiah), Clifford Evans (Peter Sloane), Carol Raye (Sally Grant), Sonia Dresdel (Julia Trevelyan).

The Wicker Man (UK, British Lion Film Corporation, 1973). Director: Robin Hardy; Producer: Peter Snell. Main cast: Edward Woodward (Sergeant Neil Howie), Britt Ekland (Willow MacGregor), Diane Cilento (Miss Rose), Ingrid Pitt (librarian), Christopher Lee (Lord Summerisle).

The Wild Bunch (USA, Warner Bros/Seven Arts, 1969). Director: Sam Peckinpah; Producer: Phil Feldman. Main cast: William Holden (Pike Bishop), Ernest Borgnine (Dutch Engstrom), Robert Ryan (Deke Thornton).

Television Programmes

All Roads Lead Home (UK, BBC, 2011). Director: Andrew Fettis. Main cast: Stephen Mangan, Sue Perkins, Alison Steadman.

Amish: The World's Squarest Teenagers (UK, Keo Films for Channel 4, 2010).

The Art of Cornwall (UK, Aenon Ltd and Fresh One Productions Ltd for BBC4, 2010). Director: Spike Geilinger; Producer: Adam Barker; Writer/Presenter: Dr James Fox.

The Camomile Lawn (UK, Zed Productions for Channel 4, 1992). Director: Peter Hall; Producers: Sophie Balthechet, Glenn Wilhide. Main cast: Felicity Kendal (Helena), Paul Edmonton (Richard), Rebecca Hall (Sophy), Jennifer Ehle (Calypso).

Coast (UK, BBC, 2005–). Writer: David Stafford; Producer: Steve Evanson.

Coming Home (UK/Germany, Yorkshire Television/Portman Entertainment Group/Tele München Fernseh Produktionsgesellschaft/Zweites Deutsches Fernsehen, Österreicherischer Rundfunk for ITV, 1998). Director: Giles Foster; Producer: Rikolt van Gagern. Main cast: Joanna Lumley (Diana Carey-Lewis), Peter O'Toole (Edgar Carey-Lewis), Katie Ryder-Richardson (Loveday), Emily Mortimer (Judith).

Cornwall with Caroline Quentin (UK, Two Four Productions for ITV, 2012). Director: Christopher Williams; Producer: Sharon Ryan; Presenter: Caroline Quentin.

Delicious (UK, Sky, 2016). Writer: Dan Sefton; Directors: Clare Kilner, John Hardwick; Producers: Anna Ferguson, Anne Mensah. Main cast: Dawn French (Gina Benelli), Iain Glen (Leo Vincent).

Doc Martin (UK, Buffalo Pictures/Home Run Productions for ITV, 2004–). Creators: Mark Crowdy, Craig Ferguson, Dominic Minghella; Producer: Philippa Braithwaite. Main cast: Martin Clunes (Dr Martin Ellingham), Caroline Catz (Louisa Glasson).

Echo Beach (UK, Channel 4, 2008). Writer: Jane Bodie; Producer: Howard Burch; Director: Stephen Woolfenden. Main cast: Jason Donovan (Daniel Marrack), Martine McCutcheon (Susan Penwarden).

The Fisherman's Apprentice (UK, BBC, 2012). Director/Producer: James Smith; Presenter: Monty Halls.

Hugh's Three Hungry Boys (UK, Keo Films for Channel 4, 2012). Director: Tom Watt-Smith; Producer: Craig Hunt. Main cast: Hugh Fearnley-Whittingstall, Trevor Brinkman, Tim Cresswell, Thom Hunt.

Jamaica Inn (UK, HTV, 1983). Director: Lawrence Gordon Clark; Producer: Peter Graham Scott; Screenplay: Derek Marlowe. Main cast: Jane Seymour (Mary Yellan), Patrick McGoohan (Joss Merlyn), Trevor Eve (Jem Merlyn).

Jamaica Inn (UK, Origin Pictures for BBC, 2014). Director: Philippa Lowthorpe; Producer: David M. Thompson, Dan Winch; Screenplay: Emma Frost. Main cast: Jessica Brown Findlay (Mary Yellan), Matthew McNulty (Jem Merlyn), Sean Harris (Joss Merlyn), Joanne Whalley-Kilmer (Aunt Patience).

Joanna Lumley's Japan (UK, ITV, 2016). Directors: Neil Ferguson, Ewen Thomson; Producers: Joanna Lumey, Clive Tulloh; Presenter: Joanna Lumley.

The Lie of the Land (UK, Molly Dineen/RTO Pictures for Channel 4, 2007). Director/Producer/Narrator: Molly Dineen.

The Lost World of Friese-Greene (UK, BFI/BBC, 2006). Director: Annabel Hobley; Producer: Simon Ford; Presenter: Dan Cruickshank.

Outlander (USA, Tall Ship Productions/Story Mining and Supply Co./Left Bank Productions/Sony Pictures Television for Starz, 2014–). Creator: Ronald D. Moore; Producer: David Brown. Main cast: Caitriona Balfe (Claire Randall), Sam Heughan (Jamie Fraser).

A Picture of Britain: The Mystical West (UK, BBC, 2005). Director/Producer: Jonty Claypole; Presenter: David Dimbleby.

Poldark (UK, BBC, 1975; 1977). Director: Chris Barry; Producer: Morris Barry; Script: Morris Pulman. Main cast: Robin Ellis (Ross Poldark), Angharad Rees (Demelza Poldark).

Poldark (UK, Mammoth Screen for BBC, 2015–). Director: Edward Bazalgette; Producer: Eliza Mellor; Writer: Debbie Horsfield. Main cast: Aidan Turner (Ross Poldark), Eleanor Tomlinson (Demelza).

A Seaside Parish (Tiger Aspect Productions for BBC, 2004). Director: Charles Forman; Producer: Nigel Farrell; Narrator: Dervla Kirwan.

Stocker's Copper (UK, BBC, 1972). Director: Jack Gold; Producer: Graeme McDonald; Screenplay: Tom Clarke; Music: Carl Davis, Treviscoe Male Choir, St Dennis Silver Band. Main Cast: Gareth Thomas (Herbert Griffith), Bryan Marshall (Manuel Stocker), Jane Lapotaire (Alice Stocker).

Summoned by Bells: John Betjeman Remembers his Childhood (UK, BBC, 1976). Director and Producer: Jonathan Stedall. Main Cast: John Betjeman.

Wild West (UK, BBC, 2002–04). Creator: Simon Nye; Director: Jonathan Gershfield, Juliet May; Producer: Jacinta Peel. Main cast: Dawn French (Mary Trewednack), Catherine Tate (Angela Phillips).

The Wrecking Season (UK, Boatshed Films for BBC, 2004). Director: Jane Darke; Producers: Jane Darke, Nick Darke, Mark Jenkin; Presenter/Narrator: Nick Darke.

Wycliffe (UK, Red Rooster/Harlech Television for ITV, 1994–98). Director: Martyn Friend, Alan Wareing; Producer: Michael Bartley. Main cast: Jack Shepherd (Wycliffe), Helen Masters (DI Lane), Jimmy Yuill (DI Kersey).

Bibliography

Adams Sitney, P. (1993) 'Landscape in the Cinema: The Rhythms of the World and the Camera' in S. Kemal and I. Gaskell (eds) *Landscape, Natural Beauty and the Arts* (Cambridge: Cambridge University Press) pp. 103–26.

Adorno, T. (1991) 'Culture Industry Reconsidered' in J. M. Bernstein (ed.) *The Culture Industry: Selected Essays on Mass Culture* (London: Routledge) pp. 85–92.

Allen, S. (2008) 'British Cinema at the Seaside—the Limits of Liminality' *Journal of British Cinema and Television* 5/1 pp. 53–71.

Allen, S., and L. Hubner (eds) (2012) *Framing Film: Cinema and the Visual Arts* (Bristol: Intellect).

Armes, R. (1978) *A Critical History of the British Cinema* (New York: Oxford University Press).

Ashby, J. (2000) 'Betty Box, "The Lady in Charge": Negotiating a Space for a Female Producer in Postwar Cinema' in J. Ashby and A. Higson (eds) *British Cinema, Past and Present* (London: Routledge) pp. 166–78.

Barr, C. (1972) '*Straw Dogs*, *A Clockwork Orange* and the Critics' *Screen* 13/2 pp. 17–31.

—— (1986) *All Our Yesterdays: 90 Years of British Cinema* (London: BFI).

Barton, R. (2004) *Irish National Cinema* (London: Routledge).

Barton, R., and H. O'Brien (eds) (2004) *Keeping it Real: Irish Film and Television* (London and New York: Wallflower).

BBC News (2016) 'Cornish Language Funding Stopped by Government' *BBC News* 21 April <http://www.bbc.co.uk/news/uk-england-cornwall-36104716> [accessed 17 March 2018].

Bell, D., and J. Hollows (2007) 'Mobile Homes' *Space and Culture* 10/1 pp. 22–39.

Bell, I. A. (1995) 'To See Ourselves: Travel Narratives and National Identity in Contemporary Britain' in I. A. Bell (ed.) *Peripheral Visions: Images of Nationhood in Contemporary British Fiction* (Cardiff: University of Wales Press) pp. 6–26.

Berger, J. (1972) *Ways of Seeing* (London: BBC/Penguin).

Betjeman, J. ([1955] 2006) *John Betjeman: Collected Poems* (London: John Murray).

Bhabha, H. K. ([1986] 1994) 'Remembering Fanon: Self, Psyche and the Colonial Condition' in P. Williams and L. Chrisman (eds) *Colonial Discourse and Post-Colonial Theory* (New York: Columbia University Press) pp. 112–23.

—— (1990) 'DisseminNation: Time, Narrative and the Margins of the Modern Nation' in H. K. Bhabha (ed.) *Nation and Narration* (London: Routledge) pp. 291–322.
Bourdieu, P. (1984) *Distinction: A Social Critique of the Judgement of Taste* (Cambridge, MA: Harvard University Press).
Bowring, J. (2013) 'Navigating the Global, the Regional and the Local: Researching Globalization and the Landscape' in P. Howard, I. Thomas and E. Waterton (eds) *The Routledge Companion to Landscape Studies* (London: Routledge) pp. 263–71.
Boym, S. (2011) 'Ruinophilia' <http://monumenttotransformation.org/atlas-of-transformation/html/r/ruinophilia/ruinophilia-appreciation-of-ruins-svetlana-boym.html> [accessed 1 June 2018] .
Brace, C. (1999) 'Finding England Everywhere: Regional Identity and the Construction of National Identity, 1890–1940' *Ecumene* 6/1 pp. 90–109.
Breslin, S., R. Higgott and B. Rosamond (2002) 'Regions in Comparative Perspective' in S. Breslin, C. Hughes, N. Phillips and B. Rosamond (eds) *New Regionalism in the Global Political Economy: Theories and Cases* (London: Routledge) pp. 1–19.
Brown, S. (2009) 'Colouring the Nation: Spectacle, Reality and British Natural Colour in the Silent and Early Sound Era' *Film History* 21/2 pp. 139–49.
Brunsdon, C. (2007a) 'Towards a History of Empty Spaces' *Journal of British Cinema and Television* 4/2 pp. 219–34.
—— (2007b) *London in Cinema: The Cinematic City Since 1945* (London: BFI).
—— (2018) *Television Cities: London, Paris, Baltimore* (Durham, NC: Duke University Press).
Burdett Wilson, R. (1987) *Go Great Western: A History of GWR Publicity* (Newton Abbot: David St John Thomas).
Butler, J. (2011) *Gender Trouble: Feminism and the Subversion of Identity* (London: Routledge).
Campbell, J. ([1949] 2008) *The Hero with a Thousand Faces* Bollingen Series vol. 17 (Novato: New World Library).
Carter, E., J. Donald and J. Squires (eds) (1993) *Space and Place: Theories of Identity and Location* (London: Lawrence & Wishart).
Caughie, J. (1981) 'Rhetoric, Pleasure and "Art Television"—Dreams of Leaving' *Screen* 22/4 pp. 9–31.
—— (2000) *Television Drama: Realism, Modernism, and British Culture* (Oxford: Oxford University Press).
Causey, A. (2006) *Peter Lanyon: Modernism and the Land* (London: Reaktion).
Causley, C. (2012) *The Mermaid of Zennor* (London: Orchard).
Chadwick, N. K. (1963) *Celtic Britain* (London: Thames & Hudson).
Collins, W. ([1851] 1982) *Rambles Beyond Railways: Notes in Cornwall Taken A-Foot* (London: Anthony Mott).
Cook, P. (ed.) (1997) *Gainsborough Pictures* (London: Cassell).
Corbin, A. (1995) *The Lure of the Sea: The Discovery of the Seaside in the Western World 1750–1840* (London: Penguin).

Cornwall Airport Newquay (2018) 'History of Cornwall Airport Newquay' <https://www.cornwallairportnewquay.com/about-us/airport-history> [accessed 17 March 2018].

Cornwall Council (2017) 'Cornish Language Status' *cornwall.gov.uk* 21 February <http://www.magakernow.org.uk/leisure-and-culture/the-cornish-language/cornish-language/cornish-language-office/cornish-language-status/> [accessed 17 March 2018].

Craig, S., and D. Fitzgerald (1999) *Filmed in Cornwall* (Launceston: Bossiney).

Crosby, E. (2008) 'The "Colour Supplement" of the Cinema: The British Cinemagazine, 1918–1938' in E. Crosby and L. Kaye (eds) *Projecting Britain: The Guide to British Cinemagazines* (London: BUFVC) pp. 1–18.

Crosby, E. and L. Kaye (eds) (2008) *Projecting Britain: The Guide to British Cinemagazines* (London: BUFVC).

Crouch, D., and M. Toogood (1999) 'Everyday Abstraction: Geographical Knowledge in the Art of Peter Lanyon' *Ecumene* 6/1 pp. 72–89.

Czach, L. (2014) 'Home Movies and Amateur Film and National Cinema' in L. Rascaroli and G. Young (eds) *Amateur Filmmaking: The Home Movie, The Archive and the Web* (London: Bloomsbury) pp. 27–37.

Dalle Vacche, A. (1996) *Cinema and Painting: How Art is Used in Film* (London: Athlone).

Daniels, S. (1993) *Fields of Vision: Landscape Imagery and National Identity in England and the United States* (Cambridge: Polity).

Davies, E., and A. Moran (2011) 'TV City: Brisbane 1959–1965' *Studies in Australasian Cinema* 5/3 pp. 239–50.

Deacon, B. (1997) '"The Hollow Jarring of the Distant Steam Engines": Images of Cornwall Between West Barbary and Delectable Duchy' in E. Westland (ed.) *Cornwall: The Cultural Construction of Place* (Penzance: Patten Press) pp. 7–24.

—— (2000) 'In Search of the Missing "Turn": The Spatial Dimension and Cornish Studies' in P. Payton (ed.) *Cornish Studies Eight* (Exeter: University of Exeter Press) pp. 213–30.

—— (2001) 'Imagining the Fishing: Artists and Fishermen in Late Nineteenth Century Cornwall' *Rural History* 12/2 pp. 159–78.

—— (2002) 'The New Cornish Studies: New Discipline or Rhetorically Defined Space?' in P. Payton (ed.) *Cornish Studies Ten* (Exeter: University of Exeter Press) pp. 24–43.

Deacon, B., and P. Payton (1993) 'Re-Inventing Cornwall: Culture Change on the European Periphery' in P. Payton (ed.) *Cornish Studies One* (Exeter: University of Exeter Press) pp. 62–79.

DeSilvey, C., and T. Edensor (2012) 'Reckoning with Ruins' *Progress in Human Geography* 37/4 pp. 465–85.

Dickinson, R. (2008) 'Changing Landscapes of Difference: Representations of Cornwall in Travel Writing, 1949–2007' in P. Payton (ed.) *Cornish Studies Sixteen* (Exeter: University of Exeter Press) pp. 167–82.

Dixon, B. (2007) 'Location, Location, Location: The Sixth British Silent Cinema Weekend' in L. Porter and B. Dixon (eds) *Picture Perfect: Landscape, Place and Travel in British Cinema Before 1930* (Exeter: Exeter Press) pp. 5–9.

Doane, M. A. (1987) *The Desire to Desire: The Woman's Film of the 1940s* (Washington, DC: Georgetown University Press).

Donnelly, K. J. (1997) 'Wicked Sounds and Magic Melodies: Music in 1940s Gainsborough Melodrama' in P. Cook (ed.) *Gainsborough Pictures* (London: Cassell) pp. 155–69.

Dowell, B. (2015) 'Why Does Aidan Turner's Ross Like to Ride Beside the Seaside When his Home in Poldark is Inland?' *Radio Times* 17 March <http://www.radiotimes.com/news/2015-03-17/why-does-aidan-turners-ross-like-to-ride-beside-the-seaside-when-his-home-in-poldark-is-inland> [accessed 17 March 2018].

du Maurier, D. ([1967] 1972) *Vanishing Cornwall: The Spirit and History of Cornwall* (Harmondsworth: Penguin).

Dubow, J. (2000) '"From a View on the World to a Point of View in It": Rethinking Sight, Space and the Colonial Subject' *Interventions* 2/1 pp. 87–102.

Dunmore, H., and R. Cobb (2011) *The Islanders* (Saltash: Mabecron).

—— (2012) *The Ferry Birds* (Saltash: Mabecron).

Durgnat, R. (1970) *A Mirror for England: British Movies from Austerity to Affluence* (London: Faber & Faber).

Edensor, T. (2005) *Industrial Ruins: Space, Aesthetics and Materiality* (Oxford: Berg).

Ehrlich, L. C., and D. Desser (1994) *Cinematic Landscapes: Observations on the Visual Arts and Cinema of China and Japan* (Austin: University of Texas Press).

Eisenstein, S. M. (1987) *Nonindifferent Nature* (Cambridge: Cambridge University Press).

Feigel, L., and A. Harris (eds) (2009) *Modernism on Sea: Art and Culture at the British Seaside* (Oxford: Peter Lang).

Ferrier, M. (2016) 'Fisherman Fashion—Making Waves in Menswear' *Guardian* 26 January <https://www.theguardian.com/fashion/2016/jan/26/fisherman-fashion-menswear-workwear-trend> [accessed 17 March 2018].

Fish, R. (2007) 'What Are These Cinematic Countrysides?' in R. Fish (ed.) *Cinematic Countrysides* (Manchester: Manchester University Press) pp. 1–14.

Fox, C. (1988) *Dame Laura Knight* (Oxford: Phaidon).

Franklin, I. (2015) 'Introduction' in I. Franklin, H. Chignall and K. Skoog (eds) *Regional Aesthetics: Mapping UK Media Cultures* (London: Palgrave Macmillan) pp. 1–13

Fullerton, J. (2005) 'Introduction: Local Film' *Film History* 17/1 pp. 3–6.

Fullerton, J., and E. King (2005) 'Local Views, Distant Scenes: Registering Affect in Surviving Mexican Actuality Films of the 1920s' *Film History* 17/1 pp. 66–87.

Gaudreault, A. (2006) 'From "Primitive Cinema" to "Kine-Attractography"' in W. Strauven (ed.) *Cinema of Attractions Reloaded* (Amsterdam: Amsterdam University Press) pp. 85–104.

Genaitay, S., and B. Dixon (2010) 'Early Colour Film Restoration at the BFI National Archive' *Journal of British Cinema and Television* 7/1 pp. 131–46.

Gibson, M. (2013) 'Wicker Men and Straw Dogs: Internal Colonialism in Celtic Novels and Films 1968–1978' *National Identities* 15/2 pp. 139–56.

Gifford, T. (1999) *Pastoral: The New Critical Idiom* (London and New York: Routledge).

Gilbey, R. (2016) '*Brown Willy* is Cornwall's Answer to *Withnail and I*' *The New Statesman* 27 April <https://www.newstatesman.com/culture/film/2016/04/brown-willy-cornwall-s-answer-withnail-i> [accessed 1 June 2018].

Gledhill, C. (2003) *Reframing British Cinema* (London: BFI).

Goodman, G. (2012) 'Rural Geographies: The Figure in the Landscape in Literature of Cornwall', *Cornish Studies Twenty* (Exeter: University of Exeter Press) pp. 148–65.

—— (2014) 'At Work and at Play: Charles Lee's *Cynthia in the West*' in G. Goodman and C. Mathieson (eds) *Gender and Space in Rural Britain, 1840–1920* (London: Pickering & Chatto) pp. 41–54.

—— (2016) 'Women at Sea: Locating and Escaping Gender on the Cornish Coast in Daphne du Maurier's *The Loving Spirit* and *Frenchman's Creek*' in C. Mathieson (ed.) *Sea Narratives: Cultural Responses to the Sea, 1600–Present* (London: Palgrave Macmillan) pp. 171–93.

—— (2018) *Writing Cornwall: Alternative Versions of Place* (Exeter: University of Exeter Press).

Goodman, G., and R. Moseley (2014) 'Investing in Culture in Cornwall: A Report on a Networking Lunch Held at the Royal Cornwall Museum, Truro, 30 June' for The Warwick Commission on the Future of Cultural Value.

—— (2015) 'Why Academics Are Interested in the Male Body in *Poldark* and *Outlander*' *The Conversation* 2 June <https://theconversation.com/why-academics-are-interested-in-the-male-body-in-poldark-and-outlander-42518> [accessed 17 March 2018].

—— (forthcoming 2018) 'Television Costume Drama and the Eroticised, Regionalised Body: *Poldark* and *Outlander*' in J. Leggott and J. Taddeo (eds) *Conflicting Masculinities* (London: I.B.Tauris).

Gopinath, G. (2008) 'Queer Regions: Locating Lesbians in *Sancharram*' in G. E. Haggerty and M. McGarry (eds) *A Companion to Lesbian, Gay, Bisexual, Transgender and Queer Studies* (Oxford: Blackwell) pp. 341–54.

Graham, W. ([1946] 1973). *Ross Poldark: A Novel of Cornwall 1783–1787* (London: Fontana).

Gray, A. (2003) *Research Practice for Cultural Studies* (London: Sage).

Gunning, T. ([1981] 1990) 'The Cinema of Attractions: Early Film, its Spectators and the Avant-Garde' in T. Elsaesser (ed.) *Early Cinema: Space Frame Narrative* (London: BFI) pp. 56–67.

—— (1997) 'Before Documentary: Early Non-Fiction Films and the "View" Aesthetic' in D. Hertogs and N. De Klerk (eds) *Uncharted Territory: Essays on Early Nonfiction Film* (Amsterdam: Stichting Nederlands Filmmuseum) pp. 9–24.

—— (2006) '"The Whole World Within Reach": Travel Images Without Borders' in J. Ruoff (ed.) *Virtual Voyages: Cinema and Travel* (Durham, NC: Duke University Press) pp. 25–41.

Hall, N. (forthcoming 2018) '*The Privileged*: A Case Study of Regional Television Documentary Production in the 1960s' *Historical Journal of Film, Radio and Television*.

Hallam, J., and L. Roberts (eds) (2014) *Locating the Moving Image: New Approaches to Film and Place* (Bloomington: Indiana University Press).

Hammerton, J. (2002) 'Everything That Constitutes Life: Pathé Cinemagazines 1918–1969' in L. McKernan (ed.) *Yesterday's News: The British Cinema Newsreel Reader* (London: BUFVC) pp. 268–80.

Harper, G., and J. Rayner (eds) (2010) *Cinema and Landscape* (Bristol: Intellect).

—— (2013) *Film Landscapes: Cinema, Environment and Visual Culture* (Newcastle: Cambridge Scholars).

Harper, S. (2000) *Women in British Cinema: Mad, Bad and Dangerous to Know* (London: Continuum).

—— (2010) 'The Ownership of Woods and Water: Landscapes in British Cinema 1930–1960' in G. Harper and J. Rayner (eds) *Cinema and Landscape* (Bristol: Intellect) pp. 147–59.

Harrison, R. (2014) 'Inside the Cinema Train: Britain, Empire, and Modernity in the Twentieth Century' *Film History* 26/4 pp. 32–57.

—— (2015) 'Writing History on the Page and Screen: Mediating Conflict Through Britain's First World War Ambulance Trains' *Historical Journal of Film, Radio and Television* 35/4 pp. 559–78.

Hawkins, H. (2013) 'Picturing Landscape' in P. Howard, I. Thompson and E. Waterton (eds) *The Routledge Companion to Landscape Studies* (London: Routledge) pp. 190–98.

Heath, S. (1911) *The Cornish Riviera* (London: Blackie and Son).

Hechter, M. (1975) *Internal Colonialism: The Celtic Fringe in British National Development, 1536–1966* (London: Routledge & Kegan Paul).

—— (1999) *Internal Colonialism: The Celtic Fringe in British National Development* 2nd edn (New Brunswick: Transaction).

Hell, J., and A. Schönle (2010) 'Introduction' in J. Hell and A. Schönle (eds) *Ruins of Modernity* (Durham, NC: Duke University Press) pp. 1–14.

Fowler, C., and G. Helfield (2006) 'Introduction' in C. Fowler and G. Helfield (eds) *Representing the Rural: Space, Place and Identity in Films about the Land* (Detroit: Wayne State University Press) pp. 1–14.

Hettne, B., and F. Söderbaum (2002) 'Theorising the Rise of Regionness' in S. Breslin, C. Hughes, N. Phillips and B. Rosamond (eds) *New Regionalism in the Global Political Economy: Theories and Cases* (London: Routledge) pp. 33–47.

Hewlett, J. (2005) 'Putting the Kitsch in Kernow' in P. Payton (ed.) *Cornish Studies Twelve* (Exeter: University of Exeter Press) pp. 30–60.

Hibbert, A. E. (1914) 'The "Story of the Holiday Line," told by Living Pictures. The Home Grand Tour' *Great Western Railway Magazine* 26 (7 July) pp. 185–86.
Higson, A. (1987) 'The Landscape of Television' *Landscape Research* 12/3 pp. 8–13.
—— (1995) *Waving the Flag* (Oxford: Oxford University Press).
—— (1996) 'Space, Place, Spectacle: Landscape and Townscape in the "Kitchen Sink" Film' in A. Higson (ed.) *Dissolving Views: Key Writings on British Cinema* (London: Cassell) pp. 133–56.
Hill, J. (2006) *Cinema and Northern Ireland: Film, Culture, Politics* (London: BFI).
Hockenhull, S. (2005) 'Romantic Landscapes: Visual Imagery in Three Films of Powell and Pressburger' *Journal of British Cinema and Television* 2 pp. 52–66.
—— (2008) *Neo-Romantic Landscapes: An Aesthetic Approach to the Films of Powell and Pressburger* (Newcastle: Cambridge Scholars).
Hollander, A. (1991) *Moving Pictures* (London: Harvard University Press).
Holt, Y. (2003) *British Artists and the Modernist Landscape* (Aldershot: Ashgate).
Howard, P. (2013) 'Perceptual Lenses' in P. Howard, I. Thompson and E. Waterton (eds) *The Routledge Companion to Landscape Studies* (London: Routledge) pp. 43–53.
Hubback, J. (1997) 'Women, Symbolism and the Coast of Cornwall' in E. Westland (ed.) *Cornwall: The Cultural Construction of Place* (Penzance: Patten Press) pp. 99–106.
Hughes, H. (1997) '"A Silent, Desolate Country": Images of Cornwall in Daphne Du Maurier's *Jamaica Inn*' in E. Westland (ed.) *Cornwall: The Cultural Construction of Place* (Penzance: Patten Press) pp. 68–75.
Husk, K., and M. Williams (2012) 'The Legitimation of Ethnicity: The Case of the Cornish' *Studies in Ethnicity and Nationalism* 12/2 pp. 249–67.
Huyssen, H. (2006) 'Nostalgia for Ruins' *Grey Room* 23 pp. 6–21.
Ingold, T. (2000) *The Perception of the Environment: Essays on Livelihood, Dwelling and Skill* (London: Routledge).
Iordanova, D. (2001) *Cinema of Flames: Balkan Film, Culture and the Media* (London: BFI).
—— (ed.) (2006) *The Cinema of the Balkans* (London: Wallflower).
Iordanova, D., D. Martin-Jones and B. Vidal (eds) (2010) *Cinema at the Periphery* (Detroit: Wayne State University Press).
ITV News (2016) 'Proposals Published for "Devonwall" Constituency' *ITV News* 13 September <http://www.itv.com/news/westcountry/2016-09-13/plans-for-devonwall-constituency-will-go-ahead/> [accessed 17 March 2018].
James, A. M. (2006) 'Enchanted Places, Land and Sea, and Wilderness: Scottish Highland Landscape and Identity in Cinema' in C. Fowler and G. Helfield (eds) *Representing the Rural: Space, Place and Identity in Films about the Land* (Detroit: Wayne State University Press) pp. 185–201.
James, R. M. (forthcoming 2018) *The Folklore of Cornwall: The Oral Tradition of a Celtic Nation* (Exeter: University of Exeter Press).
Jenkin, M. (2016) 'The Essential Cornishman (clip)' *Vimeo* <https://vimeo.com/159601579> [accessed 1 June 2018].

Johnson, M. L. (2010) 'The Places You'll Know: From Self-Recognition to Place Recognition in the Local Film' *The Moving Image* 10/1 pp. 24–50.

Kant, I. (1960) *Observations on the Feeling of the Beautiful and the Sublime* (Berkeley: University of California Press).

Kavka, M. (2008) *Reality Television, Affect and Intimacy: Reality Matters* (London: Palgrave Macmillan).

Keiller, P. (2013) *The View from the Train: Cities and Other Landscapes* (London: Verso).

Kennedy, N., and N. Kingcome (1998) 'Disneyfication of Cornwall—Developing a Poldark Heritage Complex' *International Journal of Heritage Studies* 4/1 pp. 45–59.

Kent, A. (1995) 'Smashing Sandcastles: Realism in Contemporary Cornish Fiction' in I. Bell (ed.) *Peripheral Visions: Images of Nationhood in Contemporary British Fiction* (Cardiff: University of Wales Press) pp. 173–80.

—— (1997) 'The Cornish Alps: Resisting Romance in the Clay Country' in E. Westland (ed.) *Cornwall: The Cultural Construction of Place* (Penzance: Patten Press) pp. 53–67.

—— (2003) '"Screening Kernow": Film and Television 1913–2003' in P. Payton (ed.) *Cornish Studies Eleven* (Exeter: University of Exeter Press) pp. 110–41.

Kerridge, R. (2013) 'New Directions in the Literary Representation of Landscape' in P. Howard, I. Thompson and E. Waterton (eds) *The Routledge Companion to Landscape Studies* (London: Routledge) pp. 220–30.

King, K. (2014) 'Jamaica Inn Was Not Only Mumbly, the Cornish Accents Were Ropey Too' *Guardian* 23 April <https://www.theguardian.com/commentisfree/2014/apr/23/jamaica-inn-bbc-cornish-accents-ropey> [accessed 17 March 2018].

Kirby, L. (1997) *Parallel Tracks: The Railroad and Silent Cinema* (Durham, NC: Duke University Press).

Knight, L. (1965) *The Magic of a Line* (London: William Kimber).

Knowles, L. (2012) *Laura Knight: In the Open Air* (Bristol: Sansom).

Koeck, R., and L. Roberts (eds) (2010) *The City and the Moving Image: Urban Projections* (Basingstoke: Palgrave Macmillan) <http://dx.doi.org/10.1057/9780230299238>.

Korossi, G. (2015) 'Documenting Form on Film: Barbara Hepworth Reimagined' *BFI* 3 December <http://www.bfi.org.uk/news-opinion/news-bfi/features/documenting-form-film-barbara-hepworth-reimagined> [accessed 17 March 2018].

Labbe, J. (1998) *Romantic Visualities: Landscape, Gender and Romanticism* (Basingstoke: Palgrave).

Laing, H. (2017) *The Gendered Score: Music in 1940s Melodrama and the Woman's Film* (London: Routledge).

Landy, M. (1991) *British Genres: Cinema and Society, 1930–1960* (Princeton: Princeton University Press).

Laviolette, P. (1999) 'An Iconography of Landscape Images in Cornish Art and Prose' in P. Payton (ed.) *Cornish Studies Seven* (Exeter: University of Exeter Press) pp. 107–29.

—— (2003) 'Cornwall's Visual Cultures in Perspective' in P. Payton (ed.) *Cornish Studies Eleven* (Exeter: University of Exeter Press) pp. 142–67.

Laviosa, F. (2010) 'Apulia and its Filmmakers After 1989: A Mediterranean Frontier' *California Italian Studies* 1/1 pp. 1–9.

Lefaivre, L., and A. Tzonis (2003) *Critical Regionalism: Architecture and Identity in a Globalised World* (Munich: Prestel).

Lefebvre, M. (2006a) 'Between Setting and Landscape in the Cinema' in M. Lefebvre (ed.) *Landscape and Film* (London: Routledge) pp. 19–59.

Lefebvre, M. (2006b) 'Introduction' in M. Lefebvre (ed.) *Landscape and Film* (London: Routledge) pp. xi-xxxi.

Lenman, R. (2003) 'British Photographers and Tourism in the Nineteenth Century' in D. Crouch and N. Lübbren (eds) *Visual Culture and Tourism* (London: Berg) pp. 91–108.

Little, J. (2002) *Gender and Rural Geography: Identity, Sexuality and Power in the Countryside* (Harlow: Pearson Education).

Loshitzky, Y. (1996) 'Travelling Culture/travelling Television' *Screen* 37/4 pp. 323–35.

Lowerson, J. (1994) 'Celtic Tourism—some Recent Magnets' in P. Payton (ed.) *Cornish Studies Two* (Exeter: University of Exeter Press) pp. 128–37.

Lukinbeal, C. (2005) 'Cinematic Landscapes' *Journal of Cultural Geography* 23/1 pp. 3–22.

Macardle, D. ([1942] 2015) *The Uninvited* (Tramp Press).

MacMurraugh-Kavanagh, M. (1997) 'The BBC and the Birth of "The Wednesday Play", 1962–66: Institutional Containment Versus "Agitational Contemporaneity"' *Historical Journal of Film, Radio and Television* 17/3 pp. 367–81.

—— (1999) 'Boys on Top: Gender and Authorship on the BBC Wednesday Play, 1964–70' *Media, Culture & Society* 21/3 pp. 409–25.

Mais, S. P. B. (1928) *The Cornish Riviera* (London: Great Western Railway Company Ltd).

Massey, D. (1994) *Space, Place and Gender* (London: Polity Press).

—— (1995) 'The Conceptualization of Place' in D. Massey and P. Jess (eds) *A Place in the World? Places, Cultures and Globalization* (Oxford: Oxford University Press) pp. 45–85.

McArthur, C. (1982) *Scotch Reels: Scotland in Cinema and Television* (London: BFI).

McKernan, L. (1992) *Topical Budget: The Great British News Film* (London: BFI).

—— (ed.) (2002) *Yesterday's News: The British Cinema Newsreel Reader* (London: BUFVC).

—— (2008) 'Introduction—Cinemagazines: The Lost Genre' in E. Crosby and L. Kaye (eds) *Projecting Britain: The Guide to British Cinemagazines* (London: BUFVC) pp. vii-xii.

McLoone, M. (2000) *Irish Film: The Emergence of a Contemporary Cinema* (London: BFI).
Melbye, D. (2010) *Landscape Allegory in Cinema: From Wilderness to Wasteland* (London: Palgrave Macmillan).
Middleton, K. (2011) '*Poldark*'s Image of Cornwall is Research Topic', *West Briton* 29 September.
Moody, N. (1997) 'Poldark Country and National Culture' in E. Westland (ed.) *Cornwall: The Cultural Construction of Place* (Penzance: Patten Press) pp. 129–36.
Moseley, R. (2001) '"Real Lads Do Cook ... But Some Things Are Still Hard to Talk About": The Gendering of 8–9' *European Journal of Cultural Studies* 4/1 pp. 32–39.
—— (2009) 'A Landscape of Desire: Cornwall as Romantic Setting in *Love Story* and *Ladies in Lavender*' in M. Bell and M. Williams (eds) *British Women's Cinema* (London: Routledge) pp. 77–93.
—— (2013a) '"It's a Wild Country. Wild ... Passionate ... Strange": *Poldark* and the Place-Image of Cornwall' *Visual Culture in Britain* 14/2 pp. 218–37.
—— (2013b) 'Women at the Edge: Encounters with the Cornish Coast in British Film and Television' *Continuum* 27/5 pp. 644–62.
Murphy, R. (ed.) (2009) *The British Cinema Book* (London: BFI).
Musser, C. (1990) 'The Travel Genre in 1903–4: Moving Towards Fictional Narrative' in T. Elsaesser (ed.) *Early Cinema: Space Frame Narrative* (London: BFI) pp. 123–32.
Nead, L. (2007) *The Haunted Gallery: Painting, Photography, Film c.1900* (New Haven: Yale University Press).
Norman, P. ([1971] 2002) 'The Newsreel Boys' in L. McKernan (ed.) *Yesterday's News: The British Cinema Newsreel Reader* (London: BUFVC) pp. 1–11.
Norris Nicholson, H. (1997) 'Framing Time and Space in Home Movies' *History Workshop Journal* 43 pp. 198–212.
—— (2008) '"As If by Magic": Authority, Aesthetics and Visions of the Workplace in Home Movies, Circa 1931–1949' in K. Ishizuka and P. Zimmerman (eds) *Mining the Home Movie: Excavations in Histories and Memories* (Berkeley: University of California Press) pp. 214–30.
—— (2009) 'Framing the View: Holiday Recording and Britain's Amateur Film Movement, 1925–1950' in I. Craven (ed.) *Movies on Home Ground: Explorations in Amateur Cinema* (Newcastle: Cambridge Scholars) pp. 93–127.
—— (2015) 'Living on Location: Amateur Creativity and Negotiating a Sense of Place in Yorkshire' in I. Franklin, H. Chignall and K. Skoog (eds) *Regional Aesthetics: Mapping UK Media Cultures* (London: Palgrave Macmillan) pp. 17–34.
Orange, H. (2008) 'Industrial Archaeology: Its Place Within the Academic Discipline, the Public Realm and the Heritage Industry' *Industrial Archaeology Review* 30/2 pp. 83–95.
Orchard, B. (2015) '"Writing the Heritage": How Can Literature Contribute to Heritage Places in Cornwall?' (MA dissertation, University of York).

Ordish, H. G. (1967) *Cornish Engine-Houses: A Pictorial Survey* (Truro: D. Bradford Barton).
—— (1968) *Cornish Engine-Houses: A Second Pictorial Survey* (Truro: D. Bradford Barton).
Pantenburg, V. (2012) 'Panoramique: Panning Over Landscapes' in C. Girot and F. Turinger (eds) *Landscript 1: Landscape Vision Motion* (Berlin: Jovis) pp. 121–37.
Payton, P. (1992) *The Making of Modern Cornwall: Historical Experience and the Persistence of 'Difference'* (Redruth: Dyllansow Truran).
—— ([2004] 2017) *Cornwall: A History* (Exeter: University of Exeter Press).
—— ([2005] 2015) *The Cornish Overseas: A History of Cornwall's Great Emigration* (Exeter: University of Exeter Press).
—— (2007) *Making Moonta: The Invention of 'Australia's Little Cornwall'* (Exeter: University of Exeter Press).
Perrins, D. (2015) 'Arcadia in Absentia: Cinema, the Great Depression and the Problem of Industrial Wales' in I. Franklin, H. Chignall and K. Skoog (eds) *Regional Aesthetics: Mapping UK Media Cultures* (London: Palgrave Macmillan) pp. 35–54.
Perry, R. (1999) 'The Changing Face of Celtic Tourism in Cornwall, 1875–1975' in P. Payton (ed.) *Cornish Studies Seven* (Exeter: University of Exeter Press) pp. 94–106.
Peterson, J. L. (2006) '"The Nation's First Playground": Travel Films and the American West, 1895–1920' in J. Ruoff (ed.) *Virtual Voyages: Cinema and Travel* (Durham, NC: Duke University Press) pp. 79–98.
—— (2013) *Education in the School of Dreams: Travelogues and Early Nonfiction Film* (Durham, NC: Duke University Press).
Petrie, D. (2000) *Screening Scotland* (London: BFI).
Pettitt, L. (2000) *Screening Ireland: Film and Television Representation* (Manchester: Manchester University Press).
Phillips, A. (2011) 'Fractured Landscapes: Detection, Location and History in Uchida Tomu's *Kiga kaikyo/A Fugitive from the Past*' *Screen* 52/2 pp. 213–32.
Pilcher, R. ([1995] 2008) *Coming Home* (London: Hodder & Stoughton).
Pini, B., and B. Leach (2011) 'Transformations of Class and Gender in the Globalised Countryside: An Introduction' in B. Pini and B. Leach (eds) *Reshaping Gender and Class in Rural Spaces* (Farnham: Ashgate) pp. 1–23.
Rawe, D. ([1986] 1996) *A Prospect of Cornwall* (Wadebridge: Lodenek Press).
Relph, E. (1976) *Place and Placelessness* (London: Pion).
Rhodes, J. D., and E. Garfinkel (2011) *Taking Place: Location and the Moving Image* (Minneapolis: University of Minnesota Press).
Rhodes, M. (ed.) (1995) *The Regions and the New Europe: Patterns in Core and Periphery Development* (Manchester: Manchester University Press).
Robertson, I. J., and P. Richards (eds) (2003) *Studying Cultural Landscapes* (London: Arnold).
Rockett, K., L. Gibbons and J. Hill (1987) *Cinema and Ireland* (London: Croom Helm).

Roden, A. (2010) *Great Western Railway: A History* (London: Aurum Press).
Rose, G. (1995) 'Place and Identity: A Sense of Place' in D. Massey and P. Jess (eds) *A Place in the World? Places, Cultures and Globalization* (Oxford: Oxford University Press) pp. 87–132.
Routh, F. ([1972] 2018) 'Priaulx Rainier' *Classical Music on the Web* <http://www.musicweb-international.com/rainier/> [accessed 17 March 2018].
Ruoff, J. (2006a) 'Introduction: The Filmic Fourth Dimension: Cinema as Audiovisual Vehicle' in J. Ruoff (ed.) *Virtual Voyages: Cinema and Travel* (Durham, NC: Duke University Press) pp. 1–22.
—— (2006b) 'Show and Tell: The 16mm Travel Lecture Film' in J. Ruoff (ed.) *Virtual Voyages: Cinema and Travel* (Durham, NC: Duke University Press), pp. 217–37.
Russell, D. (2004) *Looking North: Northern England and the National Imagination* (Manchester: Manchester University Press).
Schama, S. (1995) *Landscape and Memory* (London: HarperCollins).
Schivelbusch, W. (1979) *The Railway Journey: Trains and Travel in the 19th Century*, trans. Anselm Hollo (New York: Urizen).
Schoonover, K. (2016) 'Cinema's Land Expropriation.' Paper given at World Picture Conference. University of Cambridge, 13 December 2016, also forthcoming in I. Girinia and A. Floris (eds) *Local Cinema: Sardinia and European Periphery* ([n.p.]: Mimesis International).
Shand, R. (2008) 'Theorizing Amateur Cinema: Limitations and Possibilities' *The Moving Image* 8/2 pp. 36–60.
—— (2009) 'Amateur Cinema Re-Located: Localism in Fact and Fiction' in I. Craven (ed.) *Movies on Home Ground: Explorations in Amateur Cinema* (Newcastle: Cambridge Scholars) pp. 156–81.
Shields, R. (1991) *Places on the Margin: Alternative Geographies of Modernity* (London: Routledge).
Shubik, I. (2000) *Play for Today: The Evolution of Television Drama* (Manchester: Manchester University Press).
Simkin, S. (2016) *Straw Dogs* (London: Palgrave Macmillan).
Söderbaum, F., and T. M. Shaw (eds) (2003) *Theories of New Regionalism: A Palgrave Reader* (London: Palgrave Macmillan).
Spigel, L. (1988) 'Installing the Television Set: Popular Discourses on Television and Domestic Space, 1948–1955' *Camera Obscura* 16 pp. 9–46.
Sragow, M. (2012) 'From *The Siege of Trencher's Farm* to *Straw Dogs*: The Narrative Brilliance of Sam Peckinpah' in M. Bliss (ed.) *Peckinpah Today* (Carbondale: Southern Illinois University Press) pp. 69–81.
Steimatsky, N. (2008) *Italian Landscapes: Reinhabiting the Past in Postwar Cinema* (Minneapolis: University of Minnesota Press).
Stevenson, R. L. ([1883] 1995) *Treasure Island* (Cambridge: Cambridge University Press).
Stone, M., and D. Streible (2003) 'Small-Gauge and Amateur Film' *Film History* 15/2 pp. 123–25.

Strange, N. (1998) 'Perform, Educate, Entertain: Ingredients of the Cookery Genre' in C. Gerghty and D. Lusted (eds) *The Television Studies Book* (London: Arnold) pp. 301–14.

Thomas, A. (1994) 'Cornwall's Territorial Dilemma: European Region or "Westcountry" Sub-Region?' in P. Payton (ed.) *Cornish Studies Two* (Exeter: University of Exeter Press) pp. 138–50.

Thomas, C. (1997) 'See Your Own Country First: The Geography of a Railway Landscape' in E. Westland (ed.) *Cornwall: The Cultural Construction of Place* (Penzance: Patten Press) pp. 107–28.

Thompson, F. (2010a) 'Is There a Geography Genre on British Television? Explorations of the Hinterland from *Coast* to *Countryfile*' *Critical Studies in Television* 5/1 pp. 57–68.

—— (2010b) '*Coast* and *Spooks*: On the Permeable National Boundaries of British Television' *Continuum* 24/3 pp. 429–38.

Thornton, P. (1993) 'Cornwall and Changes in the Tourist Gaze' in P. Payton (ed.) *Cornish Studies One* (Exeter: University of Exeter Press) pp. 80–96.

—— (1997) 'Coastal Tourism in Cornwall Since 1900' in S. Fisher (ed.) *Recreation and the Sea* (Exeter: University of Exeter Press) pp. 57–83.

Trewin, J. C. ([1948] 1982) *Up from the Lizard* (London: Anthony Mott).

Trezise, S. (1997) 'Places Only Dreamers Know: The Significance of North Cornwall in the Lives of Thomas, Emma and Florence Hardy' in E. Westland (ed.) *Cornwall: The Cultural Construction of Place* (Penzance: Patten Press) pp. 76–87.

—— (2000) *The West Country as a Literary Invention: Putting Fiction in its Place* (Exeter: University of Exeter Press).

Tzonis, A. (2003) 'Introducing an Architecture of the Present. Critical Regionalism and the Design of Identity' in L. Lefaivre and A. Tzonis (eds) *Critical Regionalism: Architecture and Identity in a Globalised World* (Munich: Prestel) pp. 10–21.

Urry, J. (1995) *Consuming Places* (London: Routledge).

—— (2002) *The Tourist Gaze* 2nd edn (Los Angeles: Sage).

Urry, J., and J. Larsen (2011) *The Tourist Gaze 3.0* (London: Sage).

Val Baker, D. (1973) *The Timeless Land: The Creative Spirit in Cornwall* (Bath: Adams and Dart).

Vall, N. (2011) *Cultural Region: North East England 1945–2000* (Manchester: Manchester University Press).

Vernon, J. (1988) 'Border Crossings: Cornwall and the English (Imagi)nation' in G. Cubitt (ed.) *Imagining Nations* (Manchester, Manchester University Press) pp. 153–72.

Walton, J. K. (2000) *The British Seaside: Holidays and Resorts in the Twentieth Century* (Manchester: Manchester University Press).

—— (2012) 'Foreword' in P. Williams (2012) *The English Seaside* (Swindon: English Heritage), pp. 6-15.

Wattchow, B. (2013) 'Landscape and a Sense of Place: A Creative Tension' in P. Howard, I. Thompson and E. Waterton (eds) *The Routledge Companion to Landscape Studies* (London: Routledge) pp. 87–96.

Wesley, M. (1984) *The Camomile Lawn* (London: Macmillan).

Westland, E. (1995) 'The Passionate Periphery: Cornwall and Romantic Fiction' in I. Bell (ed.) *Peripheral Visions: Images of Nationhood in Contemporary British Fiction* (Cardiff: University of Wales Press) pp. 153–72.

—— (1997) *Cornwall: The Cultural Construction of Place* (Penzance: Patten Press).

Wheatley, H. (2006) *Gothic Television* (Manchester: Manchester University Press).

—— (2011) 'Beautiful Images in Spectacular Clarity: Spectacular Television, Landscape Programming and the Question of (Tele) Visual Pleasure' *Screen* 52/2 pp. 233–48.

—— (2013) 'At Home on Safari: Colonial Spectacle, Domestic Space and 1950s Television' *Journal of British Cinema and Television* 10/2 pp. 257–75.

—— (2016) *Spectacular Television: Exploring Televisual Pleasure* (London: I.B.Tauris).

Willemen, P. (1994) 'Through the Glass Darkly: Cinephilia Reconsidered' in *Looks and Frictions: Essays in Cultural Studies and Film Theory* (London: BFI) pp. 223–57.

Williams, G. M. (1969) *The Siege of Trencher's Farm* (London: Secker & Warburg).

Williams, L. (1991) 'Body Genres' *Film Quarterly* 44/4 pp. 2–13.

Williams, P. (2012) *The English Seaside* (Swindon: English Heritage).

Williams, R. (1985) *The Country and the City* (London: Chatto & Windus).

Woods, M. (2005) *Contesting Rurality: Politics in the British Countryside* (Aldershot: Ashgate).

Wormell, C. (2006) *The Sea Monster* (London: Red Fox).

Zimmerman, P. (2008a) 'The Home Movie Movement: Excavations, Artefacts, Minings' in K. Ishizuka and P. Zimmerman (eds) *Mining the Home Movie: Excavations in Histories and Memories* (Berkeley: University of California Press) pp. 1–28.

—— (2008b) 'Morphing History Into Histories: From Amateur Film to the Archive of the Future' in K. Ishizuka and P. Zimmerman (eds) *Mining the Home Movie: Excavations in Histories and Memories* (Berkeley: University of California Press) pp. 275–88.

Index

A30 1, 34
Absolutely Fabulous 180
Across England in an Aeroplane 64
address 105
    feminine 55
    tourist 66
Adorno, Theodore 5
Aequora Lunae 135
aerial shot 14, 16, 18, 30, 38, 63–64, 106, 125–26, 132, 133, 144, 146, 148–49, 152–54, 156–57, 162
aesthetics
    immersive 48, 52, 60, 74, 76–77, 81, 88–89, 91, 95, 101, 104, 107–08, 111–12, 115, 119, 130, 138, 142, 146, 148–49, 172, 174, 193, 201, 206
        landscape 94
        political 178, 192, 196, 200
        postcard 175, 187
        regional 21–22, 205
affect 6–8, 19, 37, 70, 73, 74, 75, 76–78, 89, 91, 94, 95, 96, 99, 102, 105, 110, 112, 116, 120, 121, 124–26, 130, 132, 140, 172, 178, 205–06
agriculture 48, 52, 159–60, 177
Air Mail New Style 68
All Roads Lead Home 151–58, 173
All Soul's Day 117
Allan Valley 59
Allen, Steven 33
alternative lifestyles 16, 181, 203

Amish: The World's Squarest Teenagers 159
ancientness 46, 49, 54, 58, 118, 142, 152, 154, 159, 160, 161–63
And They Sang As They Danced Along 117
angle
    high 95, 96, 112, 125–26, 139, 169, 172, 175, 176
    low 81, 82, 94, 101, 115, 124–26, 129
    wide 141, 142, 165, 175, 194, 202
anxiety 79, 81–91, 94, 96, 97, 99, 104, 126
archaicism 59, 61, 128, 145, 156, 164, 172, 179
Around Britain—Cornwall—Floods 145
art 34, 38, 53, 63, 69, 76, 86, 93, 96–98, 105, 133–40, 144, 170
Art of Cornwall, The 141, 143
Arthur, King 37, 53, 69, 73, 141
artists 75, 97–104, 121, 134–44, 146, 161, 192
    women 86, 91–99, 134
Artists' Colony 134, 142
Ashton, Shaw 28, 135
Austen, Mia 97
authenticity 153, 159, 169–77
Away to the West! 61–62

bal maidens 190
Balfe, Catriona 115
Balkan Cinema 20

INDEX

Ballykissangel 163
Barbara Hepworth Sculptress 140
Bargaining Stone 95
Barr, Charles 123, 124–25
Bath, Hubert 82, 92–93, 160
Battle of St Columb 117
BBC 140, 202
'Beach, The' (Knight) 87
Beacon!, The 145
Bell, Ian 11
Belles of Cornwall 37
Berger, John 22, 77
Betjeman, John 140–41
Bhabha, Homi K. 79, 186, 205
Birds, The 142
Birch, Lamorna 63, 88
Blue Juice 16, 193
Blyton, Enid 115
Bodmin Moor 36, 53, 111–15, 138, 152–54, 194–96
body 100
  female 14, 101, 105
  male 56, 101
  regional 106–07, 196
Boscastle 34, 70, 163
Boscawen 154
Bossiney 34, 137
Botallack 76
Bourdieu, Pierre 36
Bowring, Jacky 25
Boym, Svetlana 110
Brace, Catherine 24
Bradley, Dai 119
Bramley, Frank 140
Branwells 184
Brexit 26
Brighter Signs! 134
Britain's Wild West 61
British Film Institute 135, 209
British New Wave Cinema 17
British Travel Association 68
Britishness 73, 104, 117
Brittany 3, 12, 24, 26, 53, 79, 148, 207 n.5
Brown Willy 137, 194

Brown Willy 194, 213 n.12
Browning, Emily 97
Brühl, Daniel 91
Brunel, Isambard Kingdom 34, 43, 146, 153
Brunsdon, Charlotte 21, 133
Burdett Wilson, Roger 43
Burke, Patricia 96
Burne-Jones, Edward 141
Butler, Judith 93
By Cornish Coasts 62, 209 n.12

Cadgwith 34, 53, 76, 168–77, 186, 189
Camborne 3, 118
Camel, River 59
Camomile Lawn, The (novel) 79
Camomile Lawn, The (TV) 79, 90, 102, 211 n.9
Cape Cornwall 152–53, 156–57
capitalism 25
Carbis Bay 143
Carlyon Bay 148
Caughie, John 6, 112, 128
Caught by the Camera 28 118
Causey, Andrew 192
Celtic Revival 2, 12, 189, 212 n.17
Celticity 20, 34, 49, 57, 107, 111, 117, 123, 148, 156, 167
centre–periphery relationship 16, 21, 25, 32, 67, 78, 85–86, 93, 104, 118, 121, 130, 132, 140, 143–44, 181, 182
CGI 106, 109–11, 148
Channel 4 18, 202
Chapel Porth 73
Charlestown 56
Cheesewring 153
Children's Film and Television Foundation 118, 212 n.27
China Clay 56, 129
China clay industry 2, 13, 48, 55, 109, 130, 148, 191
chough 148, 212 n.4
Christianity 114, 117, 125, 137, 141, 163, 167
Church Cove 190

237

'Cinema of Attractions' 39–40
cinemagazines 22, 27, 37, 39, 55, 66, 81, 116, 133, 161–63, 188
Clarke, Tom 128
class 24, 34, 36–37, 49, 58, 67, 90, 110, 140, 141, 144, 161, 202
clay country 55, 109, 116, 128–30, 191, 199
Clifford, Hubert 50
cliffs 16, 38, 75, 87, 88–90, 93, 94–95, 97, 106, 141, 144
Cligga 190
close-up 39, 78, 97, 133, 134, 153, 156, 158, 175
auditory 52, 72, 201
Clovelly 61
coast 42, 47, 52, 56, 62, 74, 75, 78, 79, 80, 81, 82, 89, 128, 129, 145, 152, 177, 203, 204
Coast 59, 145–50
Coast Guards 81, 82
colonialism 19, 20, 23, 41–42, 62, 76, 77, 129, 137, 143–44, 146, 149, 180–81, 183, 188
colour 63, 64, 67, 72, 86, 87, 90, 99, 102, 113, 125, 126, 129, 144, 148, 149, 153, 154, 183, 187–90, 194, 195–200
comedy 79, 85–86, 117, 122, 127–28, 154, 202
Coming Home (novel) 79
Coming Home (TV) 79, 90, 102, 211 n.9
commodification 24, 181
Coney, Sue 184
Constable, John 106
consumption 24, 25, 31, 59, 66–67, 69, 132–33, 134, 140, 161, 183
Corbin, Alan 79
Cornish Alps 55–56, 129, 138, 148
Cornish Crafts and Industries 190
Cornish Fishermen 160
Cornish Gorsedd—Ancient Rites 117
Cornish Guardian 105
Cornish language 2, 3, 115, 155
Cornish National Minority 2

'Cornish Rhapsody' 82, 92–93, 94, 160
'Cornish Riviera' 30, 32
Cornish Riviera, The (Broadley) 43
Cornish Riviera, The (Mais) 37
Cornish Riviera Express 29, 43, 49, 50, 64, 118
Cornish Studies 12
Institute of 12
Cornish Tea 104
Cornish Tin Mine Disaster 55, 192
Cornish Tin Mining—Camborne 55
Cornouaille 79
Cornwall
at risk 161–66
inland/interior 9–10, 16, 32, 48, 54, 56, 74, 75, 77, 83, 92, 107, 111–16, 122–31, 136, 148, 151, 177, 183, 191, 194, 199, 204
post-industrial 30, 104, 181
'Cornwall in Childhood' 140
Cornwall—The Western Land 48–50, 54, 56
Cornwall with Caroline Quentin 179
Covent Garden 66
Coves and Caves 59–61, 85
Crab Pots 160
Crosby, Emily 27
and Linda Kaye 27
Cross Pilgrimage 117
Cruickshank, Dan 63
Crying the Neck 189
Cury 177

Daffodils 66
danger 36, 42, 45, 49, 55, 74, 76, 79, 80, 145, 160, 172
Daniels, Ben 114
Daniels, Stephen 40
Darke, Jane 202
Darke, Nick 202
Day Lewis, Cecil 135, 138
Deacon, Bernard 5, 12, 14, 31, 124, 203
and Philip Payton 29, 129
Deacon, Max 97

INDEX

'Deep South' 41, 113, 124, 151, 203
de-industrialization 18, 29, 41, 47, 138
Delabole 190
'Delectable Duchy' 14, 124, 203
Delicious 15–16
Dench, Judi 91
desire 91, 95
devolution 13, 20, 25–26, 106
Devon 1, 2, 11, 23, 26, 34, 43, 49, 51, 61, 62, 63, 68, 70, 121, 123, 158
Devon and Cornwall (Stepping Out) 145
'Devonwall' 3, 23, 26
diaspora, Cornish 2, 24, 26
difference 49–50, 89, 134, 146, 153
Dimbleby, David 141–43
Dineen, Molly 102, 177–79, 202
dissolve shot 63
distillation 75
distinction 36
diversity 11
Doc Martin 16, 31, 64, 109, 127, 169, 202
dolly shot 137, 150
dramatic look 113, 128, 130
'Dream of Olwen, The' 95
Dresden, Sonia 95
drone shot 40
Du Maurier, Daphne 14, 102, 104, 114–15, 142
Dubow, Jessica 42
Dyson, Ben 194

Echo Beach 15–16
eco-criticism 17
economy 3, 4, 159, 162, 168, 172, 178, 206
  tourist 27, 31, 173, 174, 180, 191
Edensor, Tim 110
edge 9, 33, 58, 74, 75, 77, 79, 80, 81, 86, 93–94, 97, 106, 121–22, 134, 136, 138, 140, 144, 148, 150–51, 156, 159, 183, 199
  women at the 38, 46, 84, 86–101, 133, 145, 153, 157, 163–67, 182

Eisenstein, Sergei 15
'Eleventh Hour' (Channel 4) 18
Ellis, Robin 105
emigration 2, 119
emplacement 99, 103, 112, 121, 125–26, 138, 187–88
employment 3
engine houses 2, 16, 54, 104, 108–11, 138, 150, 191, 198
England 2–4, 11–13, 65, 77, 78, 80, 84, 102, 118, 154, 180
Enough to Fill Up an Eggcup 200–02
epiphany 16, 38, 156, 182, 199
escape 11, 132, 153, 156, 179
Escape to the Country 132
Essential Cornishman, The 196
establishing shot 15, 187
Europe 4
European Union (EU) 4
Eve Helps the Flower Harvest 66
Eve's Film Review 55, 60, 66, 134, 208

Falmouth 43, 44, 78, 147, 148, 154
Falmouth Packet, The 148
Famous Five 115
fantasy 86, 103, 120, 143, 169
Farm of Many Industries, The 160
Fascism 149
Fearnley-Whittingstall, Hugh 158
Ferry Birds, The 116
Figures in a Landscape 28, 135–40
Fildes, Audrey 95
film
  amateur 12, 20, 21, 22, 27, 66, 183
  children's 116–18
  civic 185
  Cornish 12, 21, 183
  early 27, 39–48, 75–76, 98, 109, 188, 206
  experimental 194, 196
  heritage 84
  independent 22
  local 185–87, 194
  national 185
  women's 84

Fisherman's Apprentice, The 19, 167–77, 180, 186
fishermen 134, 160, 161, 162–63, 167–77
fishing 2, 26, 53, 69, 146, 147, 159, 168, 179–80
fishing boats 139, 142, 152, 160, 172, 175
Fishing Village 81, 160
flag, Cornish 2
flower film 66–67, 87, 140, 187, 189, 210 n.20
Flower Harvest—in Cornwall 66
Flowers from the Scilly Isles 187
Floyd, Keith 158
Floyd on Fish 132
'Flying a Kite' 87
Food Glorious Food 180
'For men must work, and women must weep …' (Langley) 61
For Men Must Work: Port Isaac 162, 176
Forbes, Stanhope 88
foreignness 13–14, 33, 34, 42, 49, 52, 53, 62, 65–66, 79, 80, 85–86, 89, 91, 102, 122, 146, 149, 156, 162
Fowey 56, 162
Fowey 162
Fowler, Catherine, and Gillian Helfield 20
Fox, James 143
framing 137
Franklin, Ieuan 21
freedom 89, 94, 156, 158
French, Dawn 202
Friedrich, Caspar David 89
Friese-Greene, Claude 59–61, 62
Friese-Greene, William 59
frontier 76, 124, 131, 146, 151, 159
Frost, Terry 144
Fullerton, John, and Elaine King 187
Furry Clock 117
Furry Dance 117
Furry Dance/Floral Dance 57, 68, 70, 93, 117, 154, 189, 212 n.17

Gabo, Naum 143, 144
Gainsborough, Thomas 76
Gainsborough Studios 75, 80, 82, 84
Gallivant 38, 71–74, 136
Galloping Gourmet 158
Gaudreault, André 41
gaze 86
   collective 30–31, 36
   colonizing 47
   documentary 113, 128, 130
   female 90, 96, 101
   male 100
   possessive 150
   Romantic 31, 93, 140, 191
   tourist 5, 12, 18, 21, 29–33, 44, 57, 60, 61, 66, 77, 82, 93, 103, 104, 107, 109–13, 117, 128–31, 132, 139, 142, 147, 148, 161, 168, 170, 171, 179, 181, 183, 186, 188, 200, 203
Genaitay, Sonia, and Bryony Dixon 59
gender 21, 23, 85, 91, 93, 163–66
General Election 2017 26
Gibson, Marion 123
Gifford, Terry 11
Girl Water Diviner 118
glance, tourist 29
Glastonbury 141
globalization 25, 182, 206
Goat Farm 83
Going Places: Tintagel 37
Gold, Jack 128
Golden Tree 200
Goodman, Gemma 2, 14, 101, 106, 109, 111, 207 nn.3–4, 208 n.4, 211 n.10, 212 n.22
Goodman, Tony 205
Google Earth 148, 151, 171
gook 190
Goonhilly Down 68, 73, 177
Gopinath, Gayatri 21, 79
Gorsedd 117
Gothic tropes 113–14, 121, 149, 204, 212 n.25
Graham, Winston 92, 104, 110

grammar of place, audio-visual 1, 6, 16, 19, 28, 38, 40–42, 47, 61, 64, 67, 69, 70, 77–78, 80, 81, 87, 89, 95, 102–03, 120, 125, 129–30, 133, 136, 141, 150–52, 154, 156, 157, 161, 162, 172, 174, 182, 183, 185, 192, 193, 194, 202, 205
Granger, Stewart 92
Gray, Ann 7
Great Western Railway/GWR 29–30, 37, 42, 44–46, 66, 97, 104, 129, 209 nn.12–13
Gunning, Tom 39
Gunwalloe 76, 102

Hal-an-Tow 189, 213 n.8
Hall, Nick 9
Hallam, Julia, and Les Roberts 20
Halls, Monty 168
hapticity 188, 201
Harper, Sue 7, 18
Harris, Sean 112
Harvey, Brett 194
Harvey, Simon 194–95
Haunters of the Deep 118–19
Hawkes, Jacquetta 135
Hawkins, Harriet 22
Hayle 78
HD. *See* high definition
Hechter, Michael 4, 71, 106, 123, 186
helicopter shot 40, 145–50, 153, 157, 164, 166, 170, 171, 172, 173–74, 176, 203
Helston 43, 117, 189
Helston's Ancient Furry Dance 117
Henney, Del 126
Hepworth, Barbara 134–40, 143, 144
heritage, industrial 29, 138
heritage industry 12, 204
hero, romantic male 14, 105, 196, 204
Heron, Patrick 143
hesitation 133, 150, 180
Hess, Nigel 91
Hettne, Björn, and Fredrik Söderbaum 25

Hibbert, A. E. 32
high definition 18–19, 133
Higson, Andrew 6, 17, 18
Hill, John 20
history 184
Hitchcock, Alfred 121, 142, 150
Hockenhull, Stella 7, 89
Hodges, C. E. 62
Hoffman, Dustin 123
holes 118, 137–38
Holt, Colin 199
Holt, Ysanne 88, 90–91
Holywell Bay 76
home 80, 146, 152
home movies 72
'Hopeless Dawn, A' 140
horizon 60, 76–77, 81, 87, 91, 95, 101, 103, 112, 120, 130–31, 152, 168, 187, 191, 198, 210 n.4
horror 42, 75, 79, 80, 96, 97, 102–04, 111, 113, 114–16, 120, 121–28, 133, 149, 165
Horse Sense 118
horticulture 66
Howard, Peter 23
Hugh Town 66
Hughes, Helen 14
Hugh's Three Hungry Boys 158
Hullah, John 162
hurling 189
Hussey, Ruth 120
Hutchinson, Ken 126

identity 79, 89, 170
  dramas of 86, 128
  gender 83, 84, 85, 167
  national 80, 84, 155, 160, 167, 181
  regional 79, 80, 92
  sexual 83, 85–86, 89, 99–100, 115, 122
immersion 19, 23, 32, 48, 52, 53, 60, 74, 75, 76, 77, 79, 80, 81, 88–89, 94, 95, 97, 101, 103–04, 105, 107–08, 111, 119, 130, 138, 142, 144, 146, 146, 149, 172, 174, 182, 187, 191, 193, 202

imperialism   13, 32, 42, 62, 149
inbreeding   14
incomer   42, 76, 102, 121, 129, 134
independence, Cornish   2, 20, 144
industrialization   12
industry   3–4, 13, 66, 159, 161, 172, 177, 191
Ingold, Tim   17
Inshaw, David   141
interdisciplinarity   22
intermediality   87, 98–99, 166
Internal Colonialism   4
internal colony   4–5, 25, 31, 32, 41–42, 46, 61, 62, 67, 71, 77, 78, 85, 106, 113, 118, 123, 130–31, 133, 140, 149, 169, 180–82, 183
Iordanova, Dina   20
Ireland   4, 20, 156, 163
iris in/out   145
island   78, 144, 145
Islanders, The   116
Isles of Scilly   64, 76, 145, 149, 184, 210 n.22

Jamaica Inn   70
Jamaica Inn (novel)   14, 104, 111
Jamaica Inn (1939)   111
Jamaica Inn (1983)   102, 111
Jamaica Inn (2014)   75, 102, 124, 125–26
Japanese film   21
Jenkin, Mark   196–202
Joanna Lumley's Japan   180
Johnny Frenchman   80
Johns, Glynis   85–86
Jones, Griffith   85
journey   34–74, 77, 92, 156, 158–59, 170, 198

Kant, Immanuel   133
Kennedy, Neil, and Nigel Kingcome   13, 204
Kent, Alan   56, 76, 124, 193, 202, 208 n.5
Kerala   21
Kernow King   112

Kerridge, Richard   17
kinaesthesia   40, 96, 99, 143, 147, 150, 172, 174, 182
Kingsley, Charles   61, 162
Kipling, Rudyard   53, 70
Kirby, Lynne   32
Kirwan, Dervla   163
Knight, Harold   88, 99
Knight, Dame Laura   46, 63, 87–91, 97, 99, 101, 211 nn.13–14, 212 n.20
Knights of the Round Table   116
Kynance Cove   34, 159
Kynance Cove Cornwall   38

labour   67, 69–70, 82, 97, 129, 132, 134, 142, 158, 160, 180, 191, 200
Ladies in Lavender   76, 91, 186
Lamorna   62, 69, 87–88, 97, 123, 134, 143, 192
Land's End   45, 51, 52, 54, 62, 64, 68, 69, 73, 136, 137, 158–59
Land's End Airport   64–65
landscape
  composite   76, 103
  documentary   27, 64, 131, 132–82
  film   14–18, 175
  impure   15, 17, 168
  industrial   129
  narrative   15, 27, 168, 182, 187
  orphan   184
  political   19, 23, 26, 27, 41, 133, 178
  porn   106–11
  post-industrial   2, 11, 18, 55, 104, 109
  regional   23, 74, 91, 127, 133, 154
  R/romantic   14, 105, 111, 121, 150
  setting   16–17
  spectacular   15–19, 27, 37, 56, 105, 129, 133, 144, 145, 148, 150, 168, 187, 196
  television   15–18, 133
Langley, Walter   61, 88, 162
Lanyon, Peter   30, 140, 143–44, 192, 200
Lapotaire, Jane   129
Laviolette, Patrick   77

Lefaivre, Liane, and Alexander Tzonis 25
Lefebvre, Martin 14, 16–17, 19, 21, 27, 105, 144
leisure 43, 44, 49, 51, 52, 58, 66, 82, 134, 180
Lenman, Robin 30
Levant Mine 55, 144, 193
liberation 83, 84
Lie of the Land, The 102, 177–79, 202
lighthouses 45, 68, 139, 145
liminality 33, 78, 80, 86, 89, 128, 148, 168, 205
literary adaptation 75
literature 71, 141, 162, 175
    travel 71
Little, Jo 22
Lizard, the 34, 43, 44, 45, 66, 68, 72, 145, 148, 158, 161, 168, 176, 177, 190
local 25, 155
Location, Location, Location 132
Lockwood, Margaret 91
London 29, 43, 51, 58, 62, 64, 66, 68, 74, 77, 84, 85–86, 87, 90, 91, 93, 117, 121, 140, 142, 143, 187, 189
long shot 15
Looe 34, 44, 117, 147
Look Out, Lobsters! 160
Lost World of Friese-Green, The 63
Lostwithiel 69
Love, Damien 123
Love Story 38, 75, 76, 79, 82, 88, 91–96, 98, 121, 160, 169, 211 n.11
Lowerson, John 29
Lumière Brothers 41
Lynch, David 203

M5 34
Macardle, Dorothy 120
Mad About Men 85–86
magic 36, 51, 52, 62, 85, 115, 116, 118, 144, 154
Mahoney, Michael 97
Major Gill Collection (SWFTA) 183–84, 188–92, 194

Malachi's Cove 119, 126
Manacles, the 45, 146, 148
Mangan, Stephen 151–54, 156, 157
Marazion 45, 69
Marconi, Guglielmo 68, 147
Marshall, Bryan 128
masculinity 94, 135, 158–77, 204
Massey, Doreen 23–24, 90
mastery 146, 149, 182
McArthur, Colin 20
Mebyon Kernow 2, 207 n.6
melodrama 15, 75, 91
memes 204
memory 72–73, 80, 94, 140–41, 153, 170
Men-an-Tol 53, 137, 138, 189
'Mermaid of Zennor, The' 85, 116, 211 n.12
mermaids 60, 85–86, 89, 211 n.12
Merry Maidens 53, 95, 152, 199
methodology 7–9
Mevagissey 80, 134, 160, 190
Mexico 26
Midlands, English 24, 34, 71
Midnight Drives, The 199
Milland, Ray 120
Millions Like Us 80
mine engineering 2, 4
Mini 69, 70, 71
mining 2, 11, 12, 26, 48, 54–55, 92, 95, 108–09, 118, 177, 191, 192
'Mining and Methodism' 12, 14, 129
Minnack Theatre 38, 93–94, 212 n.18
Miranda 85–86, 211 n.11
modernism 28, 34, 134–40, 142–43, 163, 192, 200
modernity 18, 26, 29, 32, 37, 45, 46, 47, 59, 60–61, 64–65, 68–69, 71, 72, 82, 85–87, 89–90, 96, 97, 98, 110–11, 132–33, 147, 160, 163, 164, 166, 176, 178, 179
montage 15, 133
    spectacular 147, 150
moor 16, 52, 75, 92, 111–15, 126, 152–54, 194–95
Morahan, Hattie 97

Morvah 123
Moseley, Rachel 8, 45, 46, 77, 79, 91, 102, 105, 106, 211 n.15
Mousehole 69, 152, 155
'Mr and Mrs Andrews' (Gainsborough) 77
Mullion 82
Mullion Cove 81, 94
Munnings, A. J. 88, 97
music 16, 38, 49, 51, 52–53, 54, 56, 57, 62, 68, 69, 70, 81, 82, 92–96, 98, 105, 107, 113, 121–22, 124, 127, 128–30, 135–40, 141–42, 144, 146, 148, 154, 160, 161, 164, 170, 171, 172, 175, 196, 199, 200–01, 203
Musser, Charles 41, 42
Mylan, Richard 203
mystery 52–53, 60–61, 70, 74, 75, 79, 96, 102, 104, 115–16, 118, 121–22, 128, 142, 145, 203
mysticism 16, 29, 62, 68, 69, 73, 116, 118, 137, 141, 144, 146, 152, 154=155
myth 46, 61, 72, 85, 116, 119, 148, 152, 170, 206

Naked Civil Servant, The 128
Nampara 69
narrative 66, 196, 204
 grand 184
nation 18–21, 23–26, 29, 59, 78, 79, 81, 82, 85–86, 117, 145, 151, 152, 155, 166
National Trust 82
nationalism, Cornish 124, 192
Native Americans 76
Nead, Linda 28, 58
New Surf Boat 117
Newlyn 45, 81, 88, 134, 140
Newlyn School 13, 30, 41, 76, 88, 143, 162, 192, 211 n.16
Newquay 44, 57, 61, 64, 72, 209 n.10
newsreels 20, 22, 27, 37–38, 48, 55, 59, 64, 80–84, 101, 116–18, 130, 132–33, 140, 144–45, 156, 160, 161–63, 185, 188, 190, 192, 210 n.8

Newton Kennedy Collection (SWFTA) 183–88
Nicholson, Ben 135, 140, 142–44
Norris Nicholson, Heather 184–85, 206
North, the 24
Northcote, Sidney 75
Norton, Jim 127
nostalgia 29, 60, 63, 110–11, 141, 198, 199
nudes 88, 98
Nyman, Michael 150, 164

o-region 194, 204
'Obby 'Oss 117, 154, 189
Objective One Funding 13, 23
Old Cornwall Society 12, 189
Old Superstitions 118
Oliver, Jamie 158
On with the Furry Dance! 117
Open Air Theatre 38
Open Road, The 59, 62, 63
opening sequences 16, 97, 107, 113, 128, 135–37, 164, 168–70, 203
Orange, Hilary 75, 109
Ordish, H. G. 104
otherness 49, 56, 78, 79, 104, 116
Outlander 101, 106, 115, 169
outsider 28, 76, 130, 163, 168–81
Overman, William 203

pace 19, 70, 73, 92, 133, 149–50, 155, 164
Padstow 59, 116, 154, 189
Padstow 'Hobby Hoss', The 117
Paganism 114, 116, 117, 125, 127–28, 137, 154–55, 163, 203
painting 14, 17, 41, 63, 71, 77, 87, 108, 140–41, 170, 175, 183
 and film 8, 15, 41, 140
panning shot 37, 40, 42, 43, 44–45, 50, 56, 63, 70, 78, 81, 97, 103, 106, 108, 121, 129, 132, 134, 136, 142, 150, 157, 162, 165, 166, 190, 191, 200
panorama 14, 16, 38, 78, 98, 103, 106, 112, 121, 136, 148, 156, 157, 161, 175, 186–87, 197, 199, 203, 209 n.4

INDEX

Pantenburg, Volker 40
participant observer 7
pasties 25, 49, 107, 173, 205
pastness 11, 20, 29, 59, 61, 65, 98, 110–11, 171, 178
pastoral 11, 22
Pathé, British 68, 80–84, 117, 185, 209
Pathé Pictorial 145
pathetic fallacy 15, 37, 91
Paul (village) 155
Payton, Philip 2, 12, 29, 207 n.3
Peckinpah, Sam 75, 116, 123
peninsula 2, 21, 78, 79, 177
  Balkan 21
  Penwith 38, 54, 92, 119, 123, 136, 144, 152
Pentreath, Dolly 155
Penzance 38, 45, 66, 118, 184, 188, 199
People in Camera 117
periphery 1, 3, 8, 9, 11, 14, 16, 22, 52, 62, 68–69, 70, 77, 78, 83, 84, 96, 127, 139, 145, 147, 163, 164, 177
  Celtic 20, 78, 115, 121, 130, 158, 179
Perkins, Sue 151–57
Perranporth 117
Perrins, Daryl 21
Perry, Ronald 29
Peterson, Jennifer Lynn 41–42, 46, 59, 60, 65, 71, 109, 117
Petrie, Duncan 20, 78
phantom ride 40, 43, 45, 49, 92, 153
Phillips, Alastair 21
photography 14, 30, 41, 140, 149, 183, 184
  holiday 87, 153, 200
Picture of Britain: The Mystical West, A 59, 102, 141–43
picturesque 29, 37, 42, 44, 47, 66, 77, 78, 111, 132, 139, 144, 178, 182, 193, 200
Pilchard Fishing Industry 160
piracy 76, 115, 116, 118
place 18, 23, 24
  in the moving image 19–23, 77, 206

place-image 8, 17, 32, 47, 50, 53, 68, 72, 129, 133, 134, 138, 147, 173, 176
place-myth 8, 15, 18, 27, 30, 37, 48, 71, 74, 75, 79, 80, 84, 86, 89, 92, 97, 104, 105, 107, 115, 118, 121, 140, 141, 145, 146–47, 150–53, 165, 179, 182, 189, 205
Play for Today 128
Pleasence, Donald 119
Plen an Gwari 117
Plymouth 34, 43, 145
poetry 140–41
point of audition 94, 143, 157
point of view 15, 17, 22, 38, 40, 57, 93, 95, 96, 98, 113, 120, 129, 141, 152, 157, 200
Poldark (1975; 1977) 15, 31, 54, 104–11, 120, 125–26, 136, 138, 146, 198
Poldark (2015–) 15, 19, 30, 31, 54, 75, 86, 101, 104–11, 119, 125, 138, 146, 195, 204, 212 n.23, 213 n.16
Poldark, Demelza 105, 106, 115
Poldark, Ross 105–06, 204
Poldark-ization 55
Poldark—the Proper Version 205
Poldhu 178
Polperro 34, 44, 69, 161
Polson Bridge 3
Port Isaac 31, 34, 162
Port Quin 145
Porth 59
Porthcurno 38, 76, 147
Porthleven 140, 190
possibility 79, 89, 96, 97, 102, 104, 128, 157, 180
post-colonialism 13–14, 76, 186
post-war period 79–82, 96, 101, 117
pots
  crab 76, 119, 160, 161, 172, 187
  lobster 70, 82, 172, 173
poverty 3, 9, 26, 110, 204
power 24, 26, 77
precariousness 38, 46, 79, 87, 89, 90, 97, 104, 128, 164
Prideaux Place 59

245

Pridmouth Beach 142
Proctor, Dod and Ernest 88
Prussia Cove 76
Pyramids of Cornwall—A West Carnclaze Study 56

Quentin, Caroline 179–80
Quilligan, Veronica 119

Rainier, Priaulx 135
Raye, Carol 95
realism 193
Rebecca 114, 142
Rebecca (novel) 121
Rees, Angharad 105
Referendum on Scottish Independence 26
region 14, 18, 21, 25
regionalism 25
   critical 17, 25–26, 192–93, 205–06
regionality, Romantic 25, 75
Relocation, Relocation 132, 179
Relph, Edward 5, 31, 76, 143, 186
repetition 16–17, 71, 107, 152, 162, 179, 199, 200
retreat 11–12, 179
Rhodes, John David, and Elena Garfinkel 22
Rick Stein's Taste of the Sea 132
RNAS Culdrose 84
road movie 159, 198
Road to Zennor (An Ode to Ektachrome), The 197–98
Roc, Patricia 93
Roche 191
Roden, Andrew 43
romance 80, 82, 83, 94, 95–97, 104, 105, 116, 120–21, 128, 153, 160, 162, 172, 204
Romanticism 30, 89–90, 105, 106, 140, 143, 175
romanticization 13–14, 24, 29, 33, 44, 55, 70, 104, 109–11, 120, 138, 145, 176, 178, 193, 196
Rose, Jacqueline 23

Ross Poldark (novel) 92
Rough Tor 137
Royal Cornwall Museum (RCM) 184
RSPCA Rescue 55
ruin porn 110
ruins
   post-industrial 110–11
   romantic 2, 37, 42, 54, 55, 75, 104, 108–11, 138, 144
Ruoff, Jeffrey 27, 32, 41, 48, 58
rurality 11–12, 18, 20, 22, 29, 46, 54, 62, 79, 80, 113, 116, 118, 122–27, 154, 177–80, 202, 209 n.15
Russell, Dave 24
Russell, Gail 120
Rutherford, Margaret 85

Sailor's Return 82–83
Saltash 43–44, 145, 152
sandcastles 25, 33
Sardinia 21
Saving Grace 16
Scenes in the Cornish Riviera 43–48, 134, 138, 147, 153, 161, 209 n.13
Schama, Simon 22
Schoonover, Karl 21
science fiction 116
Scilly Isles 64–67, 180
Scotland 4, 20, 21, 78, 101, 123
sculpture 134–41, 144
Sea Monster, The 116, 211 n.12
seaside 33, 36, 44, 58, 72, 134, 140, 199
Seaside Parish, A 145, 163–68
second homes 3, 26, 132, 148, 168, 176
self 153, 157, 158, 163, 167, 169
Sennen Cove 159
seriality 16, 59, 105, 107, 163–68
series 203
Serpentine Rock 160
sexuality 21
Sheaf Pitching Record (News in a Nutshell) 118
Shields, Rob 8

shipwrecks   49, 61, 115, 144, 146, 148, 175
shot. *See* aerial shot; dissolve shot; dolly shot; drone shot; establishing shot; helicopter shot; long shot; panning shot; transition shot; travelling shot
Siege of Trencher's Farm, The   123
Sitney, P. Adams   14
slow motion   91, 108, 113, 121, 164
'Smuggler's Song, A'   53, 70
smuggling   25, 33, 38, 53, 76, 81, 82, 111, 115, 116, 118, 155, 161, 162, 180
So That You Can Live   18
sound   77, 99, 113, 115, 119, 120, 125–26, 128, 130, 160, 195, 197, 200–01
South Crofty   191
South West   9, 11, 23, 61, 121, 183
South West Film and Television Archive (SWFTA)   183, 186
spatial turn   20
spatialization   8
Spigel, Lynn   59
Spirit of Cornwall, The   188
spirituality   149, 163–68, 196
Spotlight News   9
Spriggens   119
Sragow, Michael   124–25
St Agnes   73, 116, 190
St Austell   56, 78
St Buryan   123, 154
St Columb   189
St Enedoc   141
St Ives   34, 41, 45–47, 62, 76, 133, 134–35, 139, 142–44, 146, 163, 192
St Just   55, 64, 140, 157, 198
'St Just' (Lanyon)   144, 193
St Martin   187
St Mary's   66
St Michael's Mount   45, 53, 62, 116
St Piran   2, 152
stacks, mine   2, 104, 108–11, 138
standing stones   49, 53, 58, 110, 116, 118, 144, 152, 198
stasis   26, 54, 61, 71, 127, 161, 162, 175

Steadicam   40, 113
Steadman, Alison   152–53, 157
Steimatsky, Noa   149
Stein, Rick   147, 158
stereotypes   127, 204, 205
Stevens, Dan   97
Stocker's Copper   128–30
Stoke Climsland   160
stone circles   49, 138, 152, 154
Straw Dogs (1971)   75, 116–17, 122–24, 154, 204
Straw Dogs (2011)   124
subaltern   193, 205
sublime   38, 42, 44, 47, 77, 105, 115, 133, 144–58, 163–64, 174, 182
Summer in February   76, 81, 88, 97–104, 120, 138, 186
Summer is Y Comen In   117
Summoned by Bells: John Betjeman Remembers his Childhood   140
surfing   72, 193
SWFTA. *See* South West Film and Television Archive
syntax   133, 136, 139
Syria   26

Tamar
  Bridge   1, 42–44, 52, 153
  River   2, 3, 43–44, 49, 52, 78, 145, 152–53
Tamar Bridge   68
tartan, Cornish   2
taskscape   17
Tate Gallery, London   140
Tate Gallery, St Ives   34, 134, 139, 143
telephoto lens   124–27, 129
television   14, 16–19, 105, 128, 133, 168, 182, 202
  cookery programmes   132, 147, 158–59
  holiday programmes   179
  sitcom   203
Television South West   183
Telstar   68, 147–48
They Bring You Fish   160

Thomas, Chris 23
Thomas, Gareth 128
Thompson, Felix 145, 181
Thomsett, Sally 126
Thornton, Paul 29
Three Can Whale 196
'Three Fishers, The' 162
time lapse 16, 73, 108, 113, 115, 133, 152, 157, 162, 164, 166, 169, 174–75, 196, 202
timelessness 53, 71, 175–76
Tin Mining 55
Tinstone—How it is Obtained in a Cornish Mine 55
Tintagel 34, 37, 69
Tomlinson, David 85
Tomlinson, Eleanor 105
Tor Noon 123
tors, granite 52, 71, 112–14, 126, 137, 144, 149, 154
tourism 2, 3, 13, 24, 26, 27, 28, 29, 32, 89, 109, 133, 143, 162, 170, 178, 182, 192, 197, 204
tradition 26, 29, 46, 53, 61, 68, 79, 116, 118, 160, 161, 163, 179, 183
tragedy 61, 92, 102, 145, 162, 175
Tragedy of the Cornish Coast, A 75, 124, 210 n.1
transition shot 15, 175
travel 28, 30, 36, 77, 182
   air 28, 58, 63–68
   car 1, 34–37, 58–61, 68
   rail 3, 32, 36–37, 42–49, 59, 140, 148, 152, 177
travelling shot 40, 133, 136, 161, 174
travelogue 6, 20, 28, 32–74, 82, 132, 141, 150, 158, 160, 161, 179, 190
Treasure Island 116
Tregothnan 153
Tresco 65
Trezise, Simon 14
Trollope, Anthony 119
Trump, Donald 26
Truro 43, 44, 188
Turner, Aidan 106, 204

Turner, J. M. W. 106, 134
TV from Space 68
Twin Peaks 203
Tyrha Tavas 12, 189

Ukraine 26
Uncle Peter 62
Uninvited, The 120
Urry, John 5, 24–25, 36, 77
   and Jonas Larsen 28, 30

Vernon, James 13
Veryan 118
view 28, 38, 63, 66, 82, 129, 137, 191, 199
   insider 5–7, 12, 14, 23, 47, 56, 63, 76–77, 102, 112, 113, 121, 142–43, 146, 149, 150, 168, 172, 174, 182, 189, 203, 204
   landscape 100
   local 187, 195
   outsider 5–7, 14, 23, 31–32, 36, 41, 44, 48, 56, 63, 76, 128, 130, 143, 150, 168, 182, 183, 190, 203, 204
   prospect 16, 45, 71, 77, 86, 93, 129, 131, 144, 150, 154, 179–82, 191, 202
'view aesthetic' 39, 41, 45, 56, 126
'view film' 39, 44, 47, 56, 66, 78, 103, 117, 140, 154, 161, 172–73
'view programme' 109
vignette 61, 66, 98, 152, 157
villages 149, 171
   fishing 49, 76, 161, 162, 164, 176, 180, 203
violence 122–23
visibility 9–10
visual arts 7–8, 98
Volkswagen 72, 159

Wadebridge 59
Wait for It! Polperro 161
Wales 4, 20–21, 73, 117, 130, 141, 207 n.5
'Walk along the Quay' 144
Wallis, Alfred 140–43

Walls, Tom   92, 95
Walton, John   33, 34, 36–37
'Wanderer Above the Sea of Fog'   89
war   78–104
Warner, David   126
Wattchow, Brian   23
waves   44, 49, 54, 61, 80, 82, 97, 121, 135–37, 141, 142, 144, 145, 157, 164, 168, 175
Wednesday Play   128
Weekend Retreat   204
West, the   14, 46, 60, 61, 65, 68, 141, 151, 159, 196, 203, 209 n.7
West Barbary   14, 105, 116, 124, 203–04
West Briton   105
West Country   53
West Country Journey   48, 50–54, 62, 138
West Penwith   31, 34, 69, 123, 157, 196–202
Western, the   15, 75, 113–14, 116, 123–24, 146, 148, 159, 172
Westland, Ella   14
Westward Ho!   68, 159
Westward Television   183
Wheatley, Helen   18, 19, 105, 106, 133, 145, 147, 150, 160, 171, 179, 180, 187
While I Live   79, 88, 95–97, 121
whiteness   11
Wicker Man, The   123
widescreen   199
Wild Bunch, The   123
Wild West   41, 76, 113, 124, 146, 151, 157, 196

Wild West   116, 127, 146, 151, 180, 202, 204
wilderness   47, 65, 71, 113–15, 131, 133, 146, 151–52, 156, 158, 172, 177, 196
Willemen, Paul   59
Williams, Gordon M.   123
Williams, Peter   33, 44
Williams, Raymond   18, 22
Williams, Richard   200
Wilson, Richard   141
'window on the world'   59
witchcraft   33, 154, 165
Witchcraft Museum, Boscastle   116, 165
Withers, Googie   85
Wolseley   68, 70
women   38, 47, 60, 66, 81, 82, 85–104, 190
Wood, Christopher   143
Woolf, Virginia   100
World Heritage Site   109, 209 n.17
World War I   87–88, 97, 140, 211 n.9
World War II   37, 44, 54, 75, 78, 80, 91–92, 128, 143, 147
wrecking   33, 53, 111, 114, 145
Wrecking Season, The   202
wrestling, Cornish   56, 117–18, 189
Wycliffe   16, 76, 116–17, 127, 212 n.21

YouTube   205

Zennor   198
Zimmerman, Patricia   184
zoom   15, 150

Lightning Source UK Ltd.
Milton Keynes UK
UKHW02f1412200918
329222UK00002B/23/P